Sports Development:
Policy, Process and Practice

edited by
Kevin Hylton, Peter Bramham,
David Jackson and Mark Nesti

London and New York

First published 2001
by Routledge, an imprint of Taylor & Francis
11 New Fetter Lane, London EC4P 4EE

Simultaneously published in the USA and Canada
by Routledge
29 West 35th Street, New York, NY 10001

Reprinted 2002

Routledge is an imprint of the Taylor & Francis Group

Typeset in Garamond by
Florence Production Ltd, Stoodleigh, Devon EX16 9PN
Printed and bound in Great Britain by
TJ International Ltd, Padstow, Cornwall

British Library Cataloguing in Publication Data
A catalogue record for this book is available
from the British Library

Library of Congress Cataloging in Publication Data
A catalog record for this book has been requested

ISBN 0–419–26010–2

Contents

Figures

Tables

Contributors

Peter Bramham is currently based in the School of Leisure and Sports Studies as Senior Lecturer in Leisure at Leeds Metropolitan University, teaching leisure policy and leisure theory, and supervising research into policy communities, race and ethnicity in sport. His recent publications include collaborative writing in *Understanding Leisure* (Stanley Thornes, 1995), *Sociology of Leisure* (E & F Spon, 1995) and *Leisure Research in Europe: Methods and Traditions* (CAB International, 1996), *Policy and Publics* (LSA Publications, 1999)

Hazel Hartley is a Principal Lecturer in law and philosophy applied to sport, recreation and leisure, in the School of Leisure and Sports Studies at Leeds Metropolitan University, where she has worked for twenty years. Her teaching focuses on negligence, criminal assault in a broader socio-legal context, disciplinaries in sport and recreation, and disasters in leisure and sport applied to event management and legal policy. She also teaches on the MA and BA in Sport and Recreation Development, she has recently completed PhD research, through the University of Lancaster, into the legal processes arising out of the 1989 Hillsborough and *Marchioness* disasters, at the Centre for Studies in Crime and Social Justice in Lancashire. Hazel has fifteen years of sport management involved work in British and European Gymnastics in event management, policy development, committee work, coaching and advising on legal and ethical matters in sports policy.

Kevin Hylton is a Senior Lecturer in sport and recreation development in the School of Leisure and Sports Studies at Leeds Metropolitan University. Kevin has been involved in sports development in different contexts. He was involved in setting up and mainstreaming Action Sport in Leeds and has been involved in working with marginalised groups ever since. Kevin has conducted research in 'race' and ethnicity, in particular racism in sport and equal opportunities in local government. Kevin teaches on the MA and BA in Sport and Recreation Development. A founder member of the Black and ethnic minority sports forum (BEMSPORT) in Yorkshire

Kevin sits on the Regional Ethnicity Working Group for Sport England – Yorkshire and ILAM's Ethnicity Working Group.

David Jackson started working in sport in Leeds in 1974. The twenty-one years up to 1995 were spent in facility management including leading Leeds City Council's Sports Division through the experience of Compulsory Competitive Tendering in the early 1990s. With responsibility for one of the largest sports development units in the country, Dave spent five years as Principal Sports Officer. He then left to take up a Senior Lectureship in Leisure and Sports Management at Leeds Metropolitan University. Dave currently leads the undergraduate Sport and Recreation Development degree programme. He is also a staff tutor on the courses provided for industry through the Carnegie National Sports Development Centre at the university.

Mark Nesti is currently Head of the MSc in Sport and Exercise Science and Senior Lecturer in the School of Leisure and Sports Studies at Leeds Metropolitan University. He is a BASES and British Olympic Association registered sports psychologist and has recently completed a PhD in Psychology at the University of Hull, looking at anxiety in sport from an existential psychology perspective. Mark worked in local authority sports development and was a Regional Officer in the Sports Council prior to coming to the university. Mark also teaches on the sport and recreation development degrees and professional courses in Leeds.

Stephen Robson is a Senior Lecturer in sport and recreation development and management in the School of Leisure and Sports Studies at Leeds Metropolitan University. Stephen has previously worked as a Sports Development Officer for Middlesbrough Council. During almost ten years in the field, he developed a particular interest in partnerships with local health authorities, and was instrumental in establishing a number of successful joint initiatives. Stephen is the leader of the Managing and Developing Sport course for sports development professionals and he continues to focus his research work around strategic partnerships in sports development.

Mick Totten is a Senior Lecturer in Community Leisure and Recreation in the School of Leisure and Sports Studies at Leeds Metropolitan University. He mainly teaches Community Sport and Leisure, Sociology, and Recreation Leadership. He is part of a team running the School's Sport and Recreation Development degrees. Prior to higher education, he worked in further education teaching on sport, leisure and drama courses. Mick has a background in community sports and arts, in youth-work, and social services. He has completed postgraduate work in community sports and community arts and consultancy in community leisure.

Foreword

Derrick Anderson

The sports development profession, in the form we know it today, is relatively young. To date, the debates about its historical development and its theoretical and philosophical underpinning have been largely confined to a range of *ad hoc* papers and documents. This book represents, therefore, a watershed in the history of the sector in that it brings together the work of a group of senior lecturers from Leeds Metropolitan University and provides an important single point of reference for the subject.

The editorial board of *Sports Development* can be described as a team of 'poachers turned game keepers'. Many of the writers were there at the start of the sports development movement in the early 1980s. They bring to the debate a vast amount of experience and insight spanning areas as diverse as leisure and sports policy, community sports and recreation, equalities, law and health education. The span of the subjects covered makes it invaluable to those involved in both academic work and those engaged in front-line activities in either a paid or voluntary capacity.

The book presents its arguments using a combination of case studies and optional exercises. The subject matter has been carefully thought through so as to present what are complex issues in an accessible manner. It is a difficult task for a book of this nature to draw out the quintessential nature of the practice. The authors of *Sports Development* have certainly risen to the challenge. They have produced a piece of work that has very pointedly focused on the philosophies and processes which are fundamental to the practice.

I commend this book to you as a good read and great value in its contents, analysis and observations.

Derrick Anderson is the Chief Executive of Wolverhampton Metropolitan Borough Council. He has an academic background in Psychology, PE and Social Work. His professional life has spanned the fields of the arts, sports and local government at practitioner, strategic and policy-making levels. He was Deputy Director of the original Action Sports Programme in the West Midlands between 1982 and 1985. He is currently a member of the thirteen-strong Arts Council of England; a member of the Ministry of Sports – Sports Implementation Strategy Group; an independent member of the West Midlands Cultural Consortium, and sits on a host of other national bodies associated with local government and culture in the broadest sense.

Acknowledgements

The editorial team would like to thank the School of Leisure and Sports Studies at Leeds Metropolitan University for their support in the writing of this book; in particular John Dart, Richard Gillen, Fiona Stoddart and Rachel Clark for their research and administrative efforts.

Chapter 1

Introduction

Peter Bramham, Kevin Hylton,
David Jackson and Mark Nesti

Whilst it is still quite common to hear the view expressed that sport and recreation development is the responsibility of Sports Development Officers (SDOs), this is not the approach taken here. Sports development, it is argued, is more accurately a term used to describe processes, policies and practices that form an integral feature of the work involved in providing sporting opportunities. Such a process-oriented perspective leads to the challenging, radical (and uncomfortable for some) conclusion that PE staff, teachers, coaches, facility managers, community outreach workers, youth workers, health specialists, policy makers and many others, including SDOs, are all engaged in sports development work. Within this occupational matrix, a mixed economy exists of volunteers, paid professionals, policy makers, academics and practitioners. The babble of voices has created a dynamic and ever-changing environment within which this work takes place. However, considerable tensions exist between the different actors due to the dissonance and conflict arising partly as a result of competing discourses, policies and practices.

Sports Development then is a contested term. The use, and some would argue misuse of the term, can be appreciated by a closer examination of what each word is describing. *Sports* have at times been narrowly defined in terms of competitive, rule-governed games, involving some degree of physical activity. *Development* conjures up notions of maturation, education and consolidation of competencies, skills, and knowledge. Consequently, to develop something suggests a new and improved outcome is possible. But put two strange words together, like sports and development, and what do you get? – a new hierarchy or range of meanings could emerge. What if there is an unequal emphasis on both parts ... as in *SPORTS development* or conversely ... *Sports DEVELOPMENT*, or are we dealing with a new hybrid word of equal halves as in *SPORTS DEVELOPMENT*?

Philosophers, linguists and others have warned against the mistaken belief that we can define a word so precisely and so accurately as to distil the essence of the meaning of the word. The definition acts as a sieve to include or catch its essential characteristics, whilst excluding all non-essential elements or meanings. So we have a word that catches sport or sportiness and beyond lies non-sportiness. This is an example of just one language game where words are direct mirrors of reality. There are other language games which focus on how people use words, i.e. meaning is use. The meaning of a particular word becomes a 'form of life'; it depends on how people use the word in their everyday lives. The word 'sports' itself has been remarkably broad and flexible: walking briskly, camping and step aerobics have all been included as sports activities, and have received support from a range of organisations involved in *sports development.* Ultimately it may be easier (and more helpful) to hold fluid and non-dogmatic views on what do or do not constitute sports, given the ever-changing landscape within the world of sport, recreation and leisure.

Those engaging in sports development must be in the business of devising better and more effective ways of promoting interest, participation or performance in sport. This apparently neat account of sports development nevertheless obscures the arguably more important issues of who has the responsibility for this activity, and questions around where, how, why and ultimately what should be done.

These issues are apparent when studying the introduction of Sport England's Active Sports Programme in 1999. Whilst Active Sport Co-ordinators and their colleagues have championed the programme as a tool for sports development to play a more complete role in government policies of social inclusion, some sports development officers and others are critical of what they define as further initiative overload.

Although heated debate and disagreements between policy makers and deliverers afflict all sectors, sports development is particularly affected due to a number of quite unique factors. These are related to the special nature of sport. In simple terms, there are some who believe that sports development should be used to meet broader social, political, economic and cultural aims; the contemporary cross-cutting agenda. Meanwhile others contend that 'sport for sport's sake' is the only legitimate battle cry, whilst another group would see sport equally capable of defending itself on both fronts. There are clearly different intrinsic and extrinsic rationales for sports policies and provision. Sports development is an area where passions can run high and parochial and self-interested views are frequently found. Again, contrary to the general view, politics at both macro (central government) and more micro (local authority, governing bodies) levels play a major part in policy formulation in sports development. Recent high profile examples are the United Kingdom Sports Institute (UKSI), the National Lottery and, at a more local level, the Millennium Games and the establishing of specialist sports colleges.

A further important and contentious area facing sports development has been the need to work at both grassroots levels and in elite sport. Disagreements as to where the focus should be, and disputes about the importance of each, have bedevilled this area. The Sports Council, and more recently Sport England and many others have attempted to provide some means of identifying the different roles and responsibilities for those involved in sports development, from the lowest to the highest levels of achievement. The first, and some argue clearest, sports development continuum locates development on a hierarchical basis from foundation, participation, performance and excellence (see Figure 1.1). The sports development continuum model has been used by diverse organisations to provide a logical coherence to their plans, policies and strategies for sport.

This simple and powerful model of sports development has been further modified and refined by sports agencies as a response to and articulation of new policy agendas and initiatives. (See Figures 1.2 and 1.3.)

These issues and themes are addressed throughout the chapters in the text. Chapter 2 defines the key stages in public policy analysis and the politics of decision-making: policy formulation, implementation and policy evaluation. Here the major political traditions of conservatism, social reformism and of the New Right are introduced and their implications are explored for sports policy and state provision. The second part of this chapter provides an overview of current policy debates in relation to sport and concludes with a case study of youth sports policy to illustrate how political traditions provide both continuity and change in the policy process.

Chapter 3 considers how the introduction of Best Value represents the most recent manifestation of central government's interest in the resourcing of public sector sports development provision. This chapter examines the roles of the public, voluntary and commercial sectors in a context of greater financial accountability, customer service and performance awareness. Economic, political and social dimensions and their impact on the world

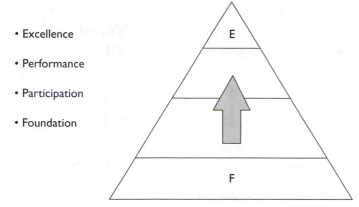

- Excellence

- Performance

- Participation

- Foundation

Figure 1.1 The traditional sports development continuum.

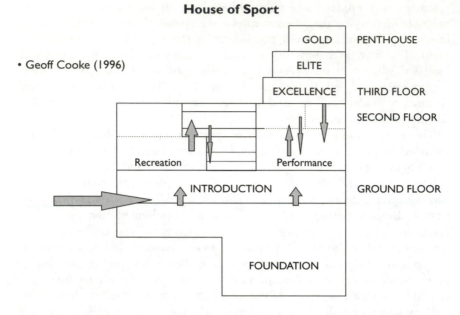

Figure 1.2 The house of sport.

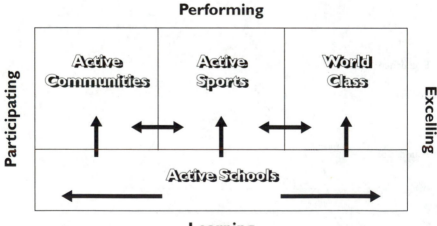

Figure 1.3 The active framework: Sport England.

of sports development are considered here. A particular focus falls on the changing face of local government provision with its increasing emphasis on partnerships across sectors.

Chapter 4 focuses on 'Sport for All?' and particularly equality in sport which, as in wider society, is not yet a reality. This chapter outlines some of the discussions concerning key terms of reference, before focusing upon recent case studies. This work investigates policy and practice in the area and offers 'active sociology' as a tool for the critical sports professional.

Chapter 5 illustrates the wider current and historical context that makes up the work of community sports development. Community sports development as community development and as performance development are two key dimensions that are clarified here. The diversity of rationales and working practices of this community sports continuum are explored, drawing upon case study material and 'good practice' in the UK. The second half of this chapter examines different theoretical perspectives that help sports professionals clarify community sports policy and practice.

Chapter 6 contextualises the growing importance of partnership working in sports development. National and local agendas are shifting so that, where partnership working was once a discretionary activity, it is now *de rigueur*. This chapter briefly reviews different dimensions of partnerships and integrates a case study of sports development work in relation to Middlesbrough Metropolitan Council's Get Active On Prescription (GAP) scheme. The range of benefits accruing from working together is documented. Equally, whilst problems of some form are inescapable, trusting partners can both plan for them and overcome them. The final section highlights the possibilities for those with a scholarly interest in organisational analysis to develop new areas of study around partnerships. The chapter concludes with a detailed case study of the Derbyshire and Peak Park Sport and Recreation Forum.

Chapter 7 considers how health promotion specialists throughout the UK are becoming increasingly sympathetic towards the notion of physical activity as a positive health intervention. It is now generally accepted that physical inactivity is an independent risk factor for coronary heart disease. This represents a major challenge for healthcare providers and the promoters of healthy living. The chapter focuses upon how sports managers can use the provision of fun and informal physical activity opportunities as a means of introducing people to the world of sport. Practical examples of successful collaborations between sport and healthcare are presented.

Chapter 8 discusses how the emergence of the National Lottery has dramatically altered the funding of sports provision. This has produced an impact that has been felt from village teams to world champions. This chapter also considers how providers of sporting opportunities have attempted to maximise the potential of past and current funding environments.

Chapter 9 seeks to provide a general guide to legal principles, disciplinary cases and incidents that illustrate issues and good practice in managing disciplinaries and education programmes in organisational contexts. Judged cases, contemporary incidents and hypothetical scenarios are used to illustrate the challenges of putting 'natural justice' into practice. The second part of the chapter applies a critical lens to organisational and masculine subcultures, power relations and their impact on the implementation of codes and rules.

Chapter 10 highlights career development opportunities for sports professionals and how they can be achieved through a comprehensive analysis of the history of sports development work. It does this by focusing on skills, competencies, values and attitudes. The second half of the chapter considers career and personal development from a socio-psychological perspective by interrogating the demands and pressures facing sports professionals.

Finally, whilst this area of work is relatively youthful and is often dynamic, vibrant and high profile, it is viewed by some as *ad hoc* in approach, weak in focus and pragmatic. Established professionals in sport, health, education and leisure services may often view sports development as idealistic, unconventional and beyond the mainstream (i.e. as outsiders), but clearly the chapters in this book argue that sports development lies at the heart of public policy. As the boundaries between the private, public and voluntary sectors dissolve rapidly in these new times, spaces appear for new policy discourses, new professional partnerships and innovatory sports practice. The conventional wisdom about the intrinsic and extrinsic rationales of sport become far less convincing in the face of growing individualism, more flexible lifestyles and, not least, sports globalisation. Sports development therefore faces an ever more volatile and uncertain environment in which it must continually make its own case as an essential and significant factor in the lives of individuals, local communities and the nation as a whole. This book provides interesting and compelling perspectives on the ever-evolving debates across sports policy and practice.

Chapter 2

Sports policy

Peter Bramham

This chapter provides a general introduction to understanding the policy process and then focuses on sports policy in the UK. It starts with a simple outline of the key stages in public policy as depicted in mainstream policy texts. It then explains the nature of major political ideological traditions that have shaped both government policy and policy institutions in the post-war years in the UK. The final section concludes with a case study of youth sports policy to illustrate how political traditions provide both continuity and change in the policy process.

Understanding the policy process

The starting point for most policy analysts is a descriptive model of discrete stages in the overall policy process. Jones, B. *et al.* (1994) trace three main stages in the policy journey: *initiation, formulation* and *implementation*. Others often further subdivide this threefold division to provide a more precise account.[1] One detailed model which has dominated policy literature has been provided by Hogwood and Gunn (1984: 4).

Stages in the policy process

- Deciding to decide (issue search or agenda-setting)
- Deciding how to decide (or issue filtration)
- Issue definition
- Forecasting
- Setting objectives and priorities
- Options analysis
- Policy implementation, monitoring and control
- Evaluation and review
- Policy maintenance, succession or termination.

But even this more sophisticated model of stages in the policy process is not without problems. Some are openly acknowledged by the authors themselves.

Viewing the policy process in terms of stages may seem to suggest that any policy episode is more or less self-contained and comprises a neat cycle of initial, intermediate and culminating events. In practice, of course policy is often a seamless web involving a bewildering mesh of interactions and ramifications.

(Hogwood and Gunn, 1984: 24)

The above model therefore provides a heuristic device or ideal type for rational decision-making: policy makers define policy problems, plan policy strategies, implement best policies and evaluate policy outcomes. The cycle then starts up again in the light of the policy outcomes from the original policy. Policy makers therefore do appeal directly to elements of such a model to legitimate their own choice of policy and its subsequent implementation. Policy can then be presented as rational process, as simply a technical discourse with clear stages of decision-making, informed by objective professional advice and agreed processes of implementation and policy evaluation.

In practice, policy can also appear to be irrational, pragmatic and incremental, often driven forward by powerful vested interests. When it comes to cities competing to host international sporting mega-events, conventional rationality, realistic timescales, forecasting and accurate data collection disappear. Decisions to locate the summer or winter Olympic Games for example, are also clearly shaped by the internal politics of international sports federations, transnational agencies, media sponsorship, as well as by the legitimate lobbying by officials and representatives.

Roche's (1994) case study of Sheffield City Council's decision to host the World Student Games in the 1990s has documented that policy decisions were taken with limited economic forecasting, crucial financial information was suppressed from public debate and democratic partisan processes bypassed. Both the short-term and long-term costs and benefits are still being studied and assessed.

Such marked deviations from the rational model of decision-making have led writers such as Lindblom to describe policy makers as having 'bounded rationality', informed by partial knowledge and with limited room for manoeuvre as they seek quick, satisfactory, rather than perfect solutions to pressing policy issues. Policy makers rarely solve policy problems but quickly move on to other problems as they appear on the political agenda. They seldom wait to judge and evaluate earlier decisions. Success and failure in policy terms have little to do with rational decision-making in order to solve long-term problems but rather have more to do with political short-term gains to appease interested parties, to secure re-election and to maintain control over the policy process.

A distinction can be drawn between people directly involved in the policy process who are committed advocates of particular policies and of discrete

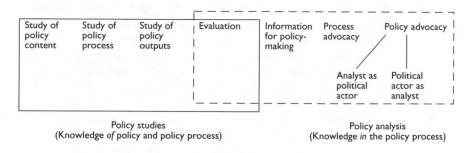

Figure 2.1 Types of study of public policy making.
Source: Hogwood and Gunn (1984), cited in Ham and Hill (1993: 8).

professional lines of implementation and those who lay claim to a more detached and holistic approach. The latter tend to have knowledge of policies and policy process, often social science academics interested in politics, society and organisational analysis (see Figure 2.1).

Ideologies

If one wants to understand the policy process, it is essential to start at the policy studies end of the continuum by examining the broad ideological assumptions that not only direct policy but also underpin the very institutions that shape and deliver policy. Consequently, before spelling out three major ideologies of *conservatism, liberalism* and *social reformism*, it is worthwhile attempting to clarify some points about how ideologies work in general.

Political ideologies are best described as reflections *of* the world and reflections *on* the world. They offer a prescription of how the world ought to be and subsequently a guide or mandate for political policies and action. One of the major functions of political ideology is to provide a particular perspective on the world and to highlight the key issues, debates and problems that need to be tackled. Ideologies therefore provide understanding of how the world works as well as mapping out mission statements as to how the world needs to change and be managed.

In the 'restricted' view, ideology refers to different political ideas debated and contested between and within political parties and party activists. In the more 'relaxed' or broader view, ideologies permeate aspects of economic, social and cultural life. Coherent frameworks of interpretation shape social practices in the family, at work, in the media, in education, and in local communities. Common-sense ideas about what is natural, about men, about women, social class, race, ethnicity and so on are embedded in institutions, in relationships and in language.

In the conventional account of policy analysis and rational decision-making, political ideologies provide the value positions, the ideals and prescriptions for action, whereas policy sciences can provide the technical knowledge and advice to administer policies rationally, neutrally and efficiently. Politics provides the valued ends, with policy and administration providing the means to achieve political ends. This division between political values and the facts of policy administration is one of the cornerstones of Weber's view of social science. Politics and political debates are inevitably based in different values and beliefs about how the world ought to be – differences of opinion are inevitable and irreconcilable. Politics is a battlefield, fought by warring gods with different values. In sharp contrast Weber argues that social science must be value free. It must produce knowledge about the world as it is. Social research must be objective, neutral and unbiased and not subjective, partisan and or committed to some form of politics. As individual citizens we can voice and act upon personal beliefs and idiosyncratic prejudices, but as social scientists and researchers we must exercise value freedom and neutrality.

This boundary between facts and values, between science and ideology has been fiercely contested throughout the history of the social sciences. More recent developments in post-modern analysis argue that many of the claims of scientific method to provide objective detached knowledge are bogus. Like any other stock of knowledge, science does have its own coherent ontology, epistemology, and its own distinctive logical techniques for generating and testing data. But it can no longer claim to provide a universal objective truth about the world, as there are other discourses to listen to . . . non-Western, non-scientific and so on. Science does have its own coherent discourse but this is just one approach amongst many. Other voices can provide distinctive and different narratives about the world, how it works and who and what is important. One only needs to think of the criticisms of mainstream science and technology from the radical politics of Marxism and feminism, and the 'green' politics of environmentalism. Within these counter-traditions themselves there are many internal debates. Scientific knowledge itself is directly challenged by religion, most powerfully from fundamentalists reasserting in Christian, Islamic or Buddhist traditions.

Post-modern times offer a variety of discourses. In the past, in modernity, it was felt that scientific knowledge alone could provide universal laws to explain natural and social worlds. Politics and policy makers would be knowledgeable and could legislate to impose a single scientific order on the world. It was as if the natural and social worlds were gardens that could be carefully cultivated and improved by knowledgeable policy makers or horticulturists. With post-modern thinking, the ideal of an orderly garden gives way to diversity and disorder. Neat horticulture is not an option as relativism thrives, like weeds and wilderness. Moreover, there is a babble of competing voices of different sorts of gardeners, different experts each providing conflicting advice. It is hard to choose or know who to trust. In post-modern times, risk and uncertainty seem to be inherent features of decision-making.[2]

Political ideologies: conservatism

One strategy of dealing with uncertainty and change is to turn to the past and rely upon tradition. Conservatism has deep historical roots and emerged as a coherent political ideology of the aristocracy to resist the 1789 political revolution in France which demanded democracy, political representation and citizenship. Conservative ideas then sought to legitimate the status quo and protect it from democratic demands for equality. For conservatism, existing inequalities were natural, pre-ordained and inevitable; people should accept their position in the world and perform their defined roles within tried and tested institutions. The status quo was a moral order, ordained by religion, by the monarchy, and ingrained in custom and practice.

The three core values of the French Revolution 'Liberté, Equalité and Fraternité' still divide modern political ideologies. For conservative thinkers, fraternity is not possible under the conditions of equality and liberty – they simply produce chaos and anarchy. Conservatism as a political tradition is clearly anti-individualistic, as individuals are not citizens with political rights but are subjects who must be loyal to the state. In conservative ideology, the state is seen as a powerful organism that has the will to destroy external and internal enemies that threaten its life blood. All people therefore intuitively, intimately and emotionally belong to the state – they are born into it, they constitute its tribe – with a shared language, with shared institutions, shared heritage, history and landscape. For an updated exposition of conservative political ideology, Scruton (1980) *The Meaning of Conservatism* maps out the key values of tradition, allegiance and authority. Linked with a fear of democracy, such values carry shades of totalitarianism. However, these tendencies are tempered by the conservative affinity with pragmatism and intuition which permit conservative political ideologies to slowly absorb incremental changes rather than be blindly committed to defending the past. Conservatism aims to be a living museum rather than a mausoleum.

Liberalism

If the origins of conservatism lay with the French aristocracy straining to protect privilege in turbulent revolutionary times, liberalism was the political creed of emerging middle classes, the bourgeoisie, made up of industrialists, financiers and intellectuals. Liberalism demanded individual freedom in thought and deed from control by tradition and privilege, embedded in the institutions of church and monarchy. Liberalism as a political ideology stresses both individualism and democracy: individuals should be free from governance, free to exercise rights to property, free speech and political suffrage. A contract is struck between the individual and the state: the individual is free to maximise his/her self-interest but s/he must abide by legislation to guarantee order. Individual citizen rights can be written down as constitutional guarantees protected by the courts against state encroachment and any misuse of authority and power.

The main function of the liberal or minimalist state is to provide law and order, a secure context within which individuals are free to maximise their own self-interests. Unlike conservative ideology, liberalism demands a clear divide between private and public spheres, as the state has no justi-fication for penetrating the boundary between its own public domain and civil society. The institutions of the family, education, work, and the mass media are private matters; they must be free from state intervention. Market forces, the equation of supply and demand through price mechanisms, are the lifeblood of liberalism and of consumer choice. The invisible hand of the market is seen as the most efficient and, more importantly, most just means to maximise individual self-interest and to distribute scarce resources. Governmental bureaucracy and state regulation serve only to distort market forces, to weaken work discipline, and to discourage profit-maximisation and capital accumulation. These themes and others have recently been devel-oped and promoted by Hayek and Friedman. Both have been strong advocates of monetarism which demands a minimal state whose major func-tion is to control the money supply and inflation.

In the world of politics, democracy enables individuals to choose their own rulers through representational democracy, and even more direct forms of democracy may be possible at a local or community level. In the same democratic vein, individuals are free to organise themselves into pressure groups to protect their collective interests and influence political parties in both shaping and implementing policies. Such pluralism denies the concen-tration of power into a strong state and encourages governments to seek consent to legitimate and secure their policies.

Social reformism

If the political ideology of conservatism developed in the pre-industrial eighteenth century, and liberalism blossomed in the industrialist capitalism of the nineteenth century, social reformism is very much the product of the twentieth century. It grew out of a range of working-class movements which sought government intervention to mitigate the intended and unin-tended consequences of market forces. Confronted with capitalist economics that spawned gross inequalities of income, capital and property, social reformists stressed the need for equality, for the state to redistribute resources in order to protect wage labourers and the poor, particularly those groups who were unable to sell their labour power through force of circumstance – the sick, mentally ill, the unemployed, and the elderly.

In the early part of the twentieth century, radical sections of the working class looked towards Marxist ideologies and revolutionary struggle to destroy class inequalities as well as political dominance of the state by the ruling class. In sharp contrast, social reformists were disenchanted with socialism and Marxism, feeling that gradual change or reform was both possible and desirable. Rather than overthrowing capitalism by civil war and establishing a communist state, social reformism argued that equality in capitalism could be achieved by political intervention in the form of a welfare state. Governments had a major role to play: they should own and plan sectors of the economy, guarantee minimum wages and income support for all by redistributing wealth from the rich to the poor through direct taxation. The welfare state must abolish poverty and deprivation by providing health care, social services, education and adequate housing. It would be funded out of taxation, social insurance paid by the working population and by a growing economy. It would also witness the growth of a powerful public sector bureaucracy, staffed by professionals and semi-professionals who would set standards of care and define appropriate levels of social need and provision.

For social reformism, individual freedom could not be realised under the conditions and constraints of inequality, so substantial central and local government intervention would have to be targeted at disadvantaged groups. For example, children could not be expected to develop their full potential if they were trapped in poverty, living in inadequate overcrowded housing, learning at underachieving schools and playing out in damaged communities. Consumer choice was no real option for the working classes unless the state intervened to manage capitalism and its social consequences. In social reformist ideology, government had to deal with market failure, with negative externalities in markets and had to control monopolistic and oligopolistic practices which generated surplus profits for business and commerce. Many of the key ideas of social reformism have been articulated by Titmuss (1963) in *Essays on the Welfare State*. He has argued that one of the key values that should inform welfare is altruism, which is closely linked to fraternity. Citizens should seek to generate collective welfare for the good of others rather than pursuing their own self-interest, often at the expense of others. To illustrate his position, he contrasts the gift relationship of blood donorship in the UK with market relationship of blood sales in the USA. In the UK, healthy donors provide good blood for nothing, whereas in the USA, many disadvantaged groups sell their own blood, possibly contaminated by drugs and problems of ill health, to supplement their meagre incomes.

New Right

New Right ideas were developed in the UK through a variety of think tanks and pressure groups, including notably the Institute of Economic Affairs, the Adam Smith Institute and many others. They were dissatisfied with the institutional legacy of the welfare state, underpinned by social reformism, arguing that state intervention was inefficient, ineffective and led to dependency on the state rather than encouraging self-responsibility and self-reliance. No part of institutional structure of welfarism was exempt from criticism – politicians promised to increase public expenditure and services to secure re-election; bureaucrats maximised their own budgets and departmental power, whilst professionals denied choice to the individual. These criticisms in academic circles led to the elucidation of *public choice* theory which demanded a restructuring of the state and introduction of market forces. Voters must be made to pay more directly for the public services received which must be shaped by the tested disciplines of the private sector – profitability, entrepreneurship, income generation, customer care, quality audits and performance-related pay.

Although New Right ideas were the clear restatement of liberalism in the face of an established social reformist welfare state, it was more than that. The startling contradiction or paradox in the heart of New Right thinking was the fusion of market liberalism with elements of its arch ideological enemy, conservatism. The New Right was a mixture of the two – a strong nation-state and a strong deregulated market. In the persona of Margaret Thatcher, the Conservative Party was driven forward to restructure the welfare state and change its relationship with local government. Throughout the last two decades, central government introduced a series of fiscal and legislative measures to control local government expenditure as well as open up local professionals to New Right thinking, enshrined in such initiatives as the Community Charge, Standardised Spending Assessments, the Local Management of Schools and Compulsory Competitive Tendering. Quangos and agencies were created to implement policy and the Audit Commission could assess the performance of central and local government departments against market ideals expressed in performance indicators about cost, efficiency and customer care.

New Labour

It has been suggested that elections are lost by governments rather than won by the opposition. Indeed, it was the failure of conservative supporters to turn out on election day, tactical voting in marginal seats and general disenchantment with Tory sleaze that resulted in a landslide majority for the Labour Party in 1997. Having modernised the party by distancing itself from its trade union and socialist roots, the Blair government accepted New Right economic policies of the previous Major administration as the parameters to guide the first two years of the new government. So there were substantial continuities in policy. If New Right ideology draws on liberalism and conservatism, New Labour is driven by another hybrid ideology which draws selectively from the roots of liberalism and social reformism. Under the guidance of new think tanks and not least Anthony Giddens, Director of LSE, Labour prefers to present itself as offering a 'third way'. New Labour argues that neither the 'first way' of liberal capitalism nor the 'second way' of state socialism are viable any longer. Both free unfettered markets and planned socialist states are anachronisms. Indeed, the forces of conservatism (of both left and right) were targeted by Blair in his millennium speech, as major opponents to progressive politics. Nation-states must embark on policy strategies which open themselves up more to global processes, new technologies and render themselves more democratic.

Political traditions, quangos and sports policy

Major political ideologies of conservatism, liberalism and social reformism clearly offer different prescriptions for public policy; they define the preferred relationship between nation-state, civil society and market. Several writers have spelt out what sports policies would look like if driven directly by political ideology (see Whannel, 1983; Bramham and Henry, 1985; Wilson, 1988; Bramham and Henry, 1991; Henry, 1993).[3] There is also a wealth of cross-national literature on socialist ideology which has historically shaped sports policies in communist nation-states (see Riordan, 1978).

Political traditions provide general direction to public policy as well as the domain ideological assumptions which map out key institutions and define and empower stake holders in the policy process. In the post-war UK period, public policy has been shaped by social reformism, and in the domain of culture, leisure and sport, governments have established quangos as the institutional means to shape and implement policy. Governments provide subsidy and appoint quango personnel but are not directly accountable in Parliament for policy decisions and outcomes. This 'arm's length' approach to sports policy has been both politically and ideologically expedient by providing institutional continuity, despite changes in governments. This is in no way to suggest that sports policy is an ideologically battle-free zone.

Detailed histories of the development of the Sports Council are already well established. Accounts have been provided by its own personnel (Coughlan, 1990; Pickup, 1996); by academics writing textbooks (Houlihan, 1991; Henry, 1993; Haywood et al., 1995) as well as a range of detailed studies evaluating various policy initiatives, e.g. for the unemployed (Glyptis, 1989), for community sport (Lentell, 1994), for women (Talbot, 1979; MacDonald, 1995; Haywood, 1994). The establishment of the Sports Council was in part a response by a conservative government to provide sport and recreation for disaffected British youth. National culture had to be preserved within the next generation as the 1960s witnessed growing moral panic about the corrosive impact of American media and consumer culture. The 'expressive' revolution of sex, drugs and rock n' roll diluted the traditional authority of the family, school and community. Equally black youth were scapegoated as the cause of inner-city problems rather than victims as the news media amplified 'mugging' into a symptom of a violent racially divided society (Hall *et al.*, 1976; Chibnall, 1977). Youth work and sport were therefore seen as crucial ingredients to divert youth, particularly those unemployed and living in inner-city working-class neighbourhoods away from crime and delinquency and into sport and active lifestyles (Carrington and Leaman, 1982). Youth sport, whether organised by youth development workers, sports animateurs or the police, was a crucial site to re-establish moral values and healthy lifestyles and to rebuild fragmenting communities.

Conservatism defined the performance of national teams in international sport as the important indicator of a successful sports policy. Conservatism valued traditional male 'English' team games, such as cricket, rugby and football. Failures in World and Olympic Games were read as significant historical indicators of the decline in UK culture and competitiveness. Consequently, the tension between elite national performance and local community participation, albeit often focused in targeted populations, has been the persistent hallmark of post-war UK sports policy. The conflicting priorities in sports policy were concealed in the Sports Council's own sporting pyramid, a continuum from foundation, to participation, performance and on to elite excellence. A broad base of mass participation was perceived as a *sine qua non* of national excellence.

If the conservative government was attracted to sport because of extrinsic benefits, during the 1970s a social reformist Labour government was keen to promote sporting opportunities as an integrated part of a comprehensive welfare state. Such an inclusive approach was heralded in the 'Sport for All?' campaign. One important physical expression of this policy appeared in the planning, management and development of sports facilities. Local authorities, encouraged by Regional Sports Councils, invested heavily in both large-scale and community-based facilities. As with other aspects of state welfare provision, there developed a growing professionalism within the public sector around the marketing and delivery of leisure services. At the same time, there was a growing dissatisfaction with social reformism, mounted by New Right ideas around public choice. Sports policy had been dominated by the public sector and the nature of sports provision was seen to be inefficient, ineffective and unnecessary.

New Right ideologies argued that government subsidy in sport was inappropriate. Individuals should be free to meet their sporting wants through the commercial or voluntary sectors rather than having their sporting needs defined by distant quangos or central or local government. Elites and national governing bodies should look to business sponsorship for support rather than rely on welfare subsidies from a 'nanny state'. However, faced by inner-city riots, the New Right Thatcherite government was not completely deaf to the extrinsic benefits of sports provision for troublesome youth. During the 1980s, unemployed and black minorities were drawn into a variety of community-based sports leadership schemes, financed by urban aid programmes. This was the emergence of what came to be seen as the new profession of sports development through the 'Active Sport' programme.

Another paradox of New Right policies at this time was the growth of diverse government quangos to bypass the power of local authorities and to weaken the collective professional base and trade union rights of public sector producers. The Thatcher hegemonic New Right project vaunted a minimalist state yet simultaneously presided over the expansion of a wide range of government agencies and quangos. Traditional government bureaucracies and civil servants were viewed by the New Right as self-serving inefficient bureaucrats and the Sports Council itself was subjected to numerous reviews which raised severe doubts about its future policy direction and possible organisation.

During the mid-1990s the Major government pragmatically breathed new life into the Sports Council through National Lottery Funding and with its commitment to the UK Sports Institute to secure excellence. The government reasserted the intrinsic benefits of team sports and introduced a raft of policy initiatives in *Raising the Game* to strengthen sporting opportunities within the PE curriculum and within extra-curricular activities. The emergence of the Youth Sports Trust provided new pathways for youth sport through TOP initiatives in combination with the National Coaching Foundation's Champion Coaching scheme. Some commentators argued that media panic about loss of school playing fields and sports opportunities has overstated the crisis in youth sport (Roberts, 1995).

Notes

1 See for example a fivefold division by Forman (1991) policy germination, policy formulation, decision making, policy execution and policy fulfilment.
2 See Beck (1992) *The Risk Society* for a full discussion of how the development of scientific knowledge and technological intervention seems to mean that no one knows and worse still no one is in control.
3 See Yule (1992) 'Gender and Leisure Policy', *Leisure Studies* 11(2) for a discussion on how a political counter ideology such as feminism, would shape sport and leisure policy.

References

Beck, U. (1992) *The Risk Society: towards a new modernity*, London: Sage.
Bramham, P. and Henry, I. P. (1985) 'Political ideology and leisure policy', *Leisure Studies*, 4(1): 1–19.

Bramham, P. and Henry, I. P. (1991) 'Explanations of the Organisation of Sport in British Society', *International Review for the Sociology of Sport*, 26, 139–50.

Carrington, B. and Leaman, O. (1982) 'Work for Some, Sport for All?', *Youth and Policy*, 1(3): 10–15.

Chibnall, S. (1977) *Law and Order News*, London: Tavistock.

Coughlan, J. (1990) *Sport and British Politics since 1960*, London: Falmer Press.

Department of National Heritage (DNH) (1995) *Sport: Raising the Game*, London: HMSO.

Forman, F. (1991) *Mastering British Politics*, London: Macmillan.

Glyptis, S. (1989) *Leisure and Unemployment*, Milton Keynes: Open University Press.

Hall, S., Critcher, C., Jefferson, T., Clarke, J. and Roberts, B. (1976) *Policing the Crisis*, London: Hutchinson.

Ham, C. and Hill, M. (1993) *The Policy Process in the Modern Capitalist State*, London: Harvester Wheatsheaf.

Haywood, L. (ed.) (1994) *Community Leisure: Theory and Practice*, Oxford: Butterworth-Heinemann.

Haywood, L., Kew, F., Bramham, P., Spink, J., Capenerhurst, J. and Henry, I. (1995) *Understanding Leisure*, Cheltenham: Stanley Thornes.

Henry, I. P. (1993) *The Politics of Leisure Policy*, London: Macmillan.

Hogwood, B. and Gunn, L. (1984) *Policy Analysis for the Real World*, Oxford: Oxford University Press.

Houlihan, B. (1991) *Government and the Politics of Sport*, London: Routledge.

Houlihan, B. (1997) *Sport, Policy and Politics: a comparative analysis*, London: Routledge.

Jones, B., Gray, A., Kavanagh, D., Moran, M., Norton, P. and Seldon, A. (1994) *Politics UK*, London: Harvester Press.

Lentell, Bob (1994) 'Sports Development: Goodbye to Community Recreation?', in C. Brackenridge (ed.), *Body Matters: Leisure Images and Lifestyles* (LSA Publications No. 47). Eastbourne: Leisure Studies Association.

MacDonald, I. (1995) 'Sport for All – 'RIP' in S. Fleming, M. Talbot, and A. Tomlinson (eds), *Policy and Politics in Sport, Physical Education and Leisure* (LSA Publications No. 55). Eastbourne: Leisure Studies Association.

Pickup, D. (1996) *Not Another Messiah: an account of the Sports Council 1988–93*, Edinburgh: Pentland Press.

Riordan, J. (ed.) (1978) *Sport under Communism*, London: C. Hurst.

Roberts, K. (1995) 'Young people, schools, sport and government policies', *Sport, Education and Society*, 1(1): 47–57.

Roche, M. (1994) 'Mega-events and urban policy', *Annals of Tourism Research*, 21(1): 1–19.

Scruton, R. (1980) *The Meaning of Conservatism*, Harmondsworth: Penguin.

Talbot, M. (1979) *Women and Leisure*, London: SSRC/SC.

Titmuss, R. (1963) *Essays on 'The Welfare State'*, 2nd edn, University Books.

Whannel, G. (1983) *Blowing the Whistle*, London: Pluto Press.

Wilson, J. (1988) *Politics and Leisure*, London: Allen & Unwin.

Yule, J. (1992) 'Gender and Leisure Policy', *Leisure Studies*, 11(2): 157–73.

Chapter 3

Sports practice

David Jackson and Mark Nesti

Introduction

This chapter sets out to provide a brief resume of the developments in sports provision from a historical perspective, linking key moments to changes in different sectors. Debates around contemporary policy issues are related to the political, social and economic contexts of the times. A number of important themes have emerged; in particular the value of volunteers and partnerships have frequently been highlighted. In addition, financial and market-led pressures have become more prevalent alongside expanding economic and cultural values. Finally, at the highest levels of government, political enthusiasm for sport has fluctuated. Nevertheless, a significant level of interest in sport and recreation has always been evident.

A close examination of the history of sports development in the UK reveals a reality of irregular evolution, although claims have been periodically made that major revolutions were taking place. Arguably the most recent high profile example of this is the current government's commitment to Best Value. This has been conceived in an attempt to improve service delivery across local government, and the delivery of public sector sports services is as much a part of this new vision as are other traditional local government services. The clear intention is to shift the philosophy to joined-up thinking across voluntary and commercial sectors as well as the range of public services. There has been a long history of fragmented approaches by different agencies and services in sports development although there has been greater success in partnership working in recent years. Undoubtedly Best Value will impact as much on the voluntary sector and to a lesser extent on the commercial sector, as the powerful arguments in favour of an integrated approach are fully felt.

Best Value has itself evolved from the drive towards improved value for money and greater accountability in public services which gathered momentum during the 1980s and 1990s. This was led by a philosophy which gave dominance to the principles of market forces and was experienced throughout many of the economies of the developed world. The major policy manifestation of the Conservative administration from 1979 onwards that impacted on sport was the introduction of Compulsory Competitive Tendering (CCT) established by the Local Government Act 1988. This legislation was targeted at a wide range of local government services including the management of sports and leisure facilities, with the aim of introducing greater awareness in local authority provision. The legislation sought to encourage commercial sector involvement in the running of public sector sports and leisure facilities. That only a very small number of contracts were won by commercial operators in the initial rounds of contract bidding revealed, for a variety of reasons, that this latter aim was largely unfulfilled.

The implementation of Compulsory Competitive Tendering highlighted a major tension between the financially driven contracted services and the broader cultural and social aims associated with traditional sports development, both within leisure departments and schools.

Although many in the industry have emphasised the destructive elements imposed by the rigidity of CCT, it seems unlikely that the progression to Best Value would have ever been achieved without this policy initiative. History may well reveal that Best Value, despite claims made on its behalf, is not in itself revolutionary but merely a continuation of the ever evolving development of improved sporting opportunities. This all seems some distance when viewed from the earliest stages of government involvement in sport and recreation. Analysis of the history of the development of sport clearly reveals a halting progress in public, voluntary and commercial activity. These changes were frequently accompanied by legislation or were shaped by various cultural influences such as demographic or socio-economic changes. The balance between these has changed over history.

The early days

At the end of the decade in which England won the football World Cup, the 'swinging sixties' took off and the Beatles were the most famous pop group on earth, there were only a handful of sports centres across the UK. Terms and concepts such as sports development, performance indicators, customer care and quality management were more than a decade away. According to Torkildsen (1999) the sport and recreation sector was overwhelmingly about voluntary sport with clubs, governing bodies and local associations delivering activity on the ground. The rapid and massive public investment in specially designed sport and leisure facilities and the recruitment of a professional and skilled workforce would take place throughout the 1970s and the early years of the 1980s. Driven in the main by local authorities, the emphasis was on increasing opportunities to participate in sport by providing state-of-the-art indoor swimming pools and sprung-floor three and four badminton court size sports halls, often on the same site. A shocked and excited public were generally very enthusiastic recipients of these facilities, and at this juncture few dissenting voices were heard irrespective of political colour. However, this was not the first time that local government had played a key role in the expansion of sport and recreation facilities.

Concerns over public health, disease and hygiene especially in the overcrowded and cramped conditions of the large industrial cities, began to impact on both local and national government. Although the late-Victorian era to the period before World War I (1914–18) saw an increase in legislation and provisions relating to education, health and safety at work and the representation of workers, for the most part little mention was made of sport and recreation. Nevertheless, as McIntosh (1984) has pointed out, public authorities were increasingly aware of the need to ensure that the working classes had access to health and physical recreation opportunities. Public baths for both swimming and personal hygiene became a feature of many cities and larger towns. Parks and open spaces were increasingly planned for. The accent clearly was on sustaining the physical fitness and mental health of the huge numbers of people working in often dangerous, dirty and morale-sapping conditions. The rationale for this type of physical recreation provision cannot be denied, given that these areas and facilities were most usually located on the edge of the inner city where the working population lived and worked. This utilitarian and functional view of sport and recreation has recently been promoted by the New Labour government and Sport England through their policy document The Value of Sport (Sport England, 1999a). This justifies sports development expenditure in terms of an unambiguous utilitarian argument that sport is good for health both at an individual and community level and in terms of social order. These approaches echo much earlier times where according to McIntosh (1984) games, chariot races and 'bread and circuses' were provided by the Roman emperors to keep the populace in their place.

During the inter-war years, the UK was largely preoccupied with managing the decline of an empire, surviving the world economic recession of the 1930s and worrying about the rise of Nazi Germany. Partly to prepare the population for the eventuality of war, the government enacted the Physical Training and Recreation Act (1937). However, beyond the development of new flagship specialist facilities such as Wembley Stadium for football, White City for athletics, and within physical education Carnegie College and Loughborough, little real change was evident. Again, sport and recreation development in the years post-Second World War was largely non-existent as the country faced more fundamental problems of rebuilding shattered infrastructure and sustaining a badly damaged economy. As competitive sport at international levels began to take place more frequently in the late 1940s and early 1950s it became clear that British sportsmen and sportswomen could no longer be relied upon to achieve easy victories. Indeed, in some sports, notable high-profile failures shook national self-confidence and searching questions were asked in political circles and within sports governing bodies. These experiences contributed to the increase in coach education and the appointment of national coaches in sports such as football and athletics. During the next forty years, this cycle of media- and politician-led inquests into the apparent demise of British sport on international playing fields would be repeated many times. Again, the usual answer would involve much hand-wringing and what has been described as *ad hoc*, inadequate and ill-conceived responses.

The post-war period

It can be argued that the 1960s did witness major events, which had a significant and long-lasting impact on sports development in the UK. The formation (1965) and activities of the Central Council for Sport and Recreation (CCPR) represented a key moment in the decade as far as governing bodies of sport were concerned. The CCPR provided a unified voice for a disparate group of sports and encouraged a more planned and strategic approach from all involved in the provision of sporting opportunities. Through its ever-growing band of technical officers and development staff, the CCPR was successful in helping to improve the quality of facilities, coaches and coach educators. In addition, and arguably of greater importance, this organisation was highly effective in attracting media interest and political support for its various campaigns and policies. So effective was the CCPR in this respect that when the Sports Council was established in 1972 by Royal Charter, ostensibly to replace the CCPR and further develop its work, high-level political support resulted in the continuation of this body albeit in a much more emaciated form. The CCPR transferred most of its resources and staff over to the newly created Sports Councils, but continued to represent the governing bodies of sport and maintained a high profile in British sport.

Much of the tension and outright animosity that appeared subsequently between the CCPR and the Sports Council reflected wider developments taking place. Within many areas of the economy and the service sector in particular, differences in terms of funding, operational climate and political influence were increasingly evident between voluntary organisations and other providers. The residual resentment that accompanied this tension would arguably make an already complex and unsystematic sports development industry even more difficult to guide strategically. This would seriously undermine the effectiveness of those organisations such as the Sports Council, charged with bringing efficiency and order into a loose and at times chaotic area of operation. This greater desire to bring some level of direction and control (through planning and strategic approaches) increased during the decade which was associated elsewhere with strident efforts to challenge the prevailing establishment with its traditional, conservative mores. Psychologists such as Fromm (1994) looking back on this period of dramatic change have described it in terms of a transition where freedom from external constraints occurred for many. However, he warned that the positive aspect of this 'setting free' represented only one side of the equation, in that consensus around *what* these freedoms should serve ultimately was rarely considered. Nevertheless, organisations such as the CCPR hung on tenaciously and, given considerable attempts made by other agencies to remove them from the sport policy landscape, they clearly did not appear to be operating in a value-free, post-modern era but rather in one where the most powerful (i.e. government sanctioned) organisations, attempted to remove their voice from the arena.

A further important juncture during the 1960s was the finding reported by the Wolfenden Committee (1960) in terms of sport development for children and young people. The so-called Wolfenden Gap identified that a major reason for declining sport participation levels in young people was due to the weak and often non-existent links between school sport and local clubs. In simple terms, huge numbers of committed young sports participants were being failed by the system upon leaving school at either fourteen or fifteen years old. The sporting life of those going on to university generally continued whilst for the rest, the ages (14–18) at which they joined the workforce often coincided with the end of their careers in sport. Wolfenden raised the political temperature and had a major impact on the formation of the sports councils, and contributed to the increased roles for local authorities in the provision of sporting opportunities. Local authorities began a massive programme of facility provision during the 1970s. Torkildsen (1999) has pointed out that sport and leisure centres were provided by local authorities in both rural and urban areas and across the political divide as a mood of optimism spread to all areas of public services. A powerful agenda of social welfare and quality of life, coupled with an increasingly hedonistic and leisure-orientated environment offered the optimal conditions for investment in sport. Local authority provision of sport and leisure centres had escalated from four in 1970 to over one thousand by the end of the decade.

By directing funding to encourage local authorities to invest in increased provision Sports Council grant-aid policies fuelled this development apace. The CCPR as representatives of a large voluntary sector in sport, and individual sports governing bodies, did manage on occasion to highlight other concerns, particularly after failures in the international sport arena. However, in general the pattern was set and local authorities flagship facility provision was the most important and visible expression of the collective drive to achieve sport for all. In this climate, little time was allocated to identifying how successful this mass facility approach was in terms of increasing sports participation. Focus was on provision and, consistent with the approach across other business and commercial environments, it was felt that if products were good success would follow. Marketing, targeting and sophisticated differential pricing policies were generally overlooked.

As this huge capital programme of facility development expanded, ever greater pressure began to build up especially in the larger urban areas for local authorities to overtake their neighbouring authorities by providing the best facilities for their residents. Internally, politicians representing housing, leisure (sport and arts) and education put intense pressure on authorities' budgets to gain more funds for major building and construction works. Finally, given that these sport and other facilities in education and housing represented an important source of civic pride, local political groupings vied with each other and promised increased provision should the voters bring them to power. Given these issues, and that the Sports Councils were at last beginning to ask serious questions about how effective this 'build, build, build' policy had been, it seemed inevitable that time was running out.

The bubble burst officially in 1979 when the new Conservative government swept into power on the back of a radical agenda to combine market economics with traditional one-nation Conservatism. That this marriage would seem ill-conceived at times during the next decade and eventually would result in the emergence of New Labour in the 1990s is difficult to deny. Indeed, New Labour according to some and in common with our more self-centred and individualistic times, does not so much represent a marriage but rather the cohabitation of two irreconcilable positions, market economic liberalism on the one hand and the collectivism of social reformism on the other. In terms of sport development little major change occurred during the 1980s as the government devoted its energies to more pressing economic and macro-structural concerns beyond sport.

A subtle yet important change took place in the immediate aftermath of the inner-city riots in 1981. Questions were asked about how successful local authorities had been in attracting traditionally low participant groups to use sport and leisure facilities. Collins and Kennett (1999) have revealed that in many cases those closest to facilities used them least and that this situation was most pronounced within the inner-city areas of large urban conurbations. Partly to address this issue the Sports Council set up the Action Sport initiative in an effort to bring sporting opportunities closer to local communities. However, whilst McIntosh and Charlton (1985) had many positive things to say about both the theory and the practice of Action Sport programmes, others such as Haywood (1992) criticised agencies for paying lip service to genuine community development and for continuing to utilise top-down approaches to managing sports development. This theme is explored further in Chapter 5.

Towards the end of the 1980s attention was re-diverted to considering sporting success at the highest level. The National Coaching Foundation took on a major role in enhancing coach education, and the Sports Council began to divert a more significant proportion of resources to the performance and excellence levels of the sports development continuum. At the end of the decade a major change in funding and managing sport would return facility based sport development to the top of the agenda.

Compulsory Competitive Tendering (CCT)

Following the massive developments which resulted from local government reorganisation in 1974 after the Bains Report, there was a period of relative prosperity in national and local government finances. This allowed councils to carry on the building bonanza sparked by many outgoing authorities and was a clear example of the power of politician and officer alliances in new professionalised departments. It was also an affirmation of the arrival of leisure and sport as significant and legitimate areas for policy intervention. Whilst central government was delivering a consultation paper on the future of sport and recreation and establishing through the Sports Council an agency for developing and disseminating policy, finance was released to a local government system with relative autonomy to spend as it pleased. The recognition of sport as a major factor in the lives of both individuals and communities and people's increasing awareness of the benefits of well-being put pressure on local authorities to make more provision. They were more than happy to oblige in many cases as this was a political 'win-win' situation.

> The publication, in 1975, of the White Paper, *Sport and Recreation*, confirmed the place of sport and recreation services as a legitimate element of the welfare state and also reiterated a conventional rationale for intervention, namely a concern with social order, international prestige, and individual well-being.
>
> (Department of the Environment, 1975)

The marketisation of sport

By 1979 things were about to change. The government led by Margaret Thatcher began a journey of policy intervention at national and local levels that was not directly aimed at sport but which had a major impact on the delivery of sporting opportunities. At national level it may be said that there was some indifference to sporting issues and that policy was reactive and uncoordinated; indeed, there did not appear to be any substantial thought applied to the area. However, the government's agenda for local authorities was to have a significant effect on both sport and recreation.

The major themes of New Right philosophy associated with the Thatcher years revolved around the freedom of the individual and the primacy of free markets and is discussed in Chapter 2. The resultant policy developments from these ideas were logically aimed at a reduction in the role of the state at both national and local levels and the introduction of market forces to the provision of public services. As applied to local government these policies were introduced in a limited way in the Planning and Land Act (1980) where an enforced tendering regime was imposed for contracts relating to building and highways construction and maintenance. However, in the Local Government Act (1988) under the banner of Compulsory Competitive Tendering, a range of services previously provided by local government workforces were exposed to free competition in the marketplace. This was an enforced system of marketisation that covered refuse collection, catering and school meals, street cleansing and lighting, vehicle maintenance and grounds maintenance. After a consultation exercise, the management of sports and leisure facilities was added to the list. This had a major impact on the way that local authorities defined their role as both a direct provider of sporting opportunities and as a facilitator for other deliverers in the sporting matrix.

Much of the government's policy deliberations which resulted in the CCT legislation revolved around notions of value for money in public services and around the premise that no matter how good services appeared to be, local government could not prove that they were providing value for money unless they were tested against private sector entrepreneurs in fair and open competition. Indeed, according to the New Right mantra, exposure to competition was the only way that this proof could be produced. To support this forceful argument in relation to the specific management function of sport and leisure management, the Audit Commission produced two documents that set out the case for changing the status quo and adopting a more positive stance in favour of the marketisation of services. The first of these, *Sport for Whom? Clarifying the Local Authority Role in Sport and Recreation* (1988) sought to establish some general issues about provision that needed more serious consideration than had been previously given. These rested on a view that there was a lack of strategic planning, policy direction and financial accountability in provision. In other words a great deal of public money was being spent and possibly wasted without sufficient application to the philosophy and practical implications of what was being done.

> But whatever their social aims, local authorities also need financial objectives if they are to manage their facilities properly. Local authorities have found it hard to strike the right balance between social and financial objectives.
>
> *Sport for Whom? Clarifying the Local Authority Role in Sport and Recreation* (Audit Commission, 1988)

In summary there were a number of issues:

- Investment decisions to provide facilities were often poorly thought through in relation to other organisations who might make provision if assisted.

- The ongoing revenue costs of facilities were not considered over a sufficient lifespan and therefore left a burden on future budgets for upgrading and renovation to meet future customers' expectations.
- Blanket pricing subsidies that were perceived as achieving social objectives of opening opportunities to the disadvantaged often only supported the new leisure lifestyles of mainly males from professional and management backgrounds.
- A lack of any demonstrable monitoring of the true costs and effectiveness of services being provided meant that these burgeoning activities that were constantly being added to were insufficiently accountable.

In effect there was an indictment that local government was not clear about what it was doing or why it was doing it and that there was a rampant lack of accountabilty right across the country.

In order that authorities be better able to prepare for the rigours of CCT they were advised to:

- Make strategic plans that encompassed the whole of their geographical areas (whilst also bearing in mind issues of local competition with neighbouring authorities).
- Consider the widest range of options for the providers of services, especially the voluntary sector.
- Take a long hard look at pricing, admissions and programming policies so that they might improve their record on targeting special and disadvantaged groups.
- Start to set some performance measurement parameters.

To help them through this process the Audit Commission produced the second of its documents, *Local Authority Support for Sport. A Management Handbook* (1989) and whereas *Sport for Whom?* (1988) had been aimed at the policy and strategic management tiers of senior politicians and chief officers, this new advice was about 'hands-on' process issues and became a working bible for many officers charged with setting up their organisation to comply with legislation.

It was at this point unfortunately that many but not all authorities became embroiled in strategies for dealing with CCT that involved embracing the letter of the law if not necessarily the spirit. They failed to come to terms with planning best-value services for the widest community but rather became engaged in trench warfare that revolved around internal reorganisation and the erection of artificial barriers that gave the appearance of even-handed compliance with the legislation.

As the rolling programme of CCT contract tranches was completed there emerged a number of factors that left a legacy to be tackled eventually through the legislative programme of the new Labour government elected in May 1997. Partly due to political hostility to its rigid regime and the difficulties, real or imagined, in incorporating issues of quality in contract documentation, the reality of the situation was that once service specifications had been set by authorities, contracts were awarded and monitored on a mainly financial basis.

The vast majority of contracts were won by in-house workforces (Direct Service Organisations – DSOs) that were the reconstituted operational arms of the local authority departments; but despite their often long-standing commitment to sport, previously valued services that were not as commercially viable in this new culture were often put to the sword in the name of financial efficiency – or indeed survival. There is some anecdotal evidence to suggest that often the situation appeared where ailing in-house contracting arms were given more leeway in varying the detail of the specifications to enhance their income potential than might have been afforded to an external private sector contractor.

The bias against quality social and welfare services may have been more manifest in the management of sport and leisure facilities as this was the only management function to be subjected to the tendering regime and was quite different to, for example, refuse collection or street lighting. These latter services are to a greater extent finite and measurable; it is possible to count how many dustbins need emptying each week and where they all are. Moreover, customers have their dustbins emptied every week and their street lights maintained whether they like it or not. They have no choice in the matter and are charged for the service whether used or not. It became very clear to many operators of sports facilities that customers had to be attracted, retained and nurtured with innovation and quality services or serious consequences would follow.

The recession that hit the economy in the early 1990s alongside a range of other factors including changes in competing sport and leisure activities, in demographic profiles, education policy and increasing pressure on local government budgets, forced financial imperatives increasingly to the fore. The social and sporting aspirations of a wide range of sporting communities came under pressure. Many did not survive and attempts to implement strategies of equity and equality often received only lip-service at a time when there was an increasing awareness of the importance that sport had for the nation, for local communities and for individuals. The emerging sports development arena whose main function was to reach these unreachable sporting communities was a clear casualty of this focus on bottom-line financial calculations,

> . . . there is also evidence that the policy (CCT) has resulted in a reduction in sports development activity and a preference for activities that generate a more rapid return on investment.
>
> (Sports Council, 1993: 5)

Having seen that the rigidity of the CCT regime across many services resulted in an over-emphasis on quantity in financial terms at the expense of quality as seen as welfare or social services, the Labour government set out after 1997 to redress this imbalance by setting out the principles of Best Value.

BEST VALUE

> In short CCT has provided a poor deal for employees, employers and local people. CCT will therefore be abolished.
>
> *Modernising Local Government. Improving Local Services Through Best Value* (DETR, 1998: 6)

The duty of Best Value is an integral part of the New Labour government's ambitious modernising agenda for local government which includes democratic renewal, community leadership, a new ethical framework, reformed local government finance and Best Value in service delivery. The duty of Best Value as laid down for local authorities is, '. . . to secure continuous improvement in the way in which functions are exercised, having regard to a combination of economy, efficiency and effectiveness' (Local Government Bill 1998 in Sanderson, 1999).

In an unpublished presentation forming part of the National Evaluation of Best Value Pilot Programme, Professor Ian Sanderson of Leeds Metropolitan University describes the overall philosophy of Best Value as having its foundations in the principles of:

- Systematic review of all services as the basis for identifying and addressing weaknesses in performance.
- Setting clear standards and improvement targets for both cost and quality of all services.
- Putting the interests of local people first and giving them a greater say in setting service standards and assessing performance.
- Responsibility to central government for meeting national standards for designated services.
- Enhanced community leadership and partnership working to address cross-cutting issues facing local citizens and communities.
- Commitment to ensuring the most effective, efficient and economic means of service delivery using competitive processes where appropriate.
- Improved reporting and accountability for performance to local people as taxpayers, customers and citizens.
- Rigorous audit and inspection processes to provide an external check on information, processes and performance.
- Intervention by central government where authorities 'fail to remedy clear performance failure'.

In the application of this new policy process to sport there are a number of issues that require examination. If local authorities are to rise to the challenge and opportunities of Best Value they have to seek ways of, '. . . continually improving the quality and cost of local services delivered to local people'. *Delivering Best Value Through Sport* (Sport England, 1999b: 2).

As the major features of Best Value revolve around fundamental performance review and the comparison of performance between authorities there has been an alliance of lead agencies of Sport England and the Local Government Association to provide guidance, support and advocacy for the importance of sport. This has manifested itself in the production of *The Value of Sport – Best Value Through Sport* (Sport England, 1999a).

As sport is still a discretionary service and there is continuing pressure on resources there is a clear need to establish the importance of sport to the whole community in a way that protects and projects services as essential components of national and local policy. To this end the value of sport is clearly promoted under the banner of contemporary policy issues. These are:

- The International Value of Sport as part of a growing worldwide cultural phenomenon.
- The Social Value of Sport as portrayed by the diversity of participation across boundaries of age, ethnicity, gender, disability and social class. This is enhanced by the role of sport in valuing volunteers; promoting community safety and health; providing positive influences for young people and supporting community regeneration.
- The Economic Value of Sport as typified by the generation of 1.6 per cent of Gross Domestic Product by sport related activity, as well as accounting for 1.61 per cent of total employment.   *The Value of Sport – Best Value Through Sport* (Sport England, 1999a: 27).
- The Environmental Value of Sport as a formal and informal resource in a range of urban and rural settings, promoting enjoyment and success in outdoor sport and recreation, access to the countryside and awareness and improvement of the natural environment.

The cross-cutting agenda

There is a subtle but clear shift in the way in which sports policy has moved to respond to the promotion of the concept of Best Value. Sport is now clearly seen as having value as an agent for the promotion of policies relating to a wide range of cross-cutting issues but is seldom promoted as sport *per se*. This is understandable as what is happening is a recognition of the multi-faceted roles that sport plays in the life of the nation, local communities and individuals. Here is real definition of the *true* value of sport and perhaps the clearest campaign for advocating that value in the political and social arena.

This has been made possible and indeed essential in the change from the rigid CCT regime to the more quality-sensitive approach of Best Value. There was considerable comment in the early days of Best Value about the lack of definition of the policy and what this would mean for individual local authorities. However, over a relatively short period of time, some major features have been laid down. What have come to be known as the Four C's of Challenge, Consult, Compare and Compete form the basis of an integrated system of service development that is applicable not just in a sporting setting but right across local government services.

In addition to this broad-based drive for Best Value in all aspects of local government, the Department of Culture Media and Sport with the publication of a new government sports strategy *A Sporting Future for All* (DCMS, April 2000) has added weight and clarity to the interpretations of this evolving legislation for sporting communities at all levels.

> Best Value reviews must consider the wider value and benefits of the sports provision and sports development services to the community. This strategy provides the context for local authorities to link the value of sport to the wider benefits of health, social inclusion, regeneration, educational opportunities and crime prevention.
>
> *A Sporting Future for All* (DCMS, 2000: 39)

The implementation of both Best Value and the strategy espoused in *A Sporting Future for All* are essentially and demonstrably linked to the government's agenda on 'joined up government' which also flows into local tiers of administration.

> In the past there has been a failure to make links between the different parts of government whose policies and activities have an impact on sport. We will put this right. For the first time, we will ensure cross-departmental working at both national and local levels.
>
> *A Sporting Future for All* (DCMS, 2000: 51)

Practical implications of Best Value

The interpretation of the Four C's now provides a significantly clearer focus for those entrusted with developing national and local strategies for sport. These may be summarised as follows.

- *Challenging*

    Fundamental performance review requires that current policies are thoroughly examined and criticised providing a more sophisticated attempt at ensuring that local authorities question why and how they deliver sport to local people. The importance of connecting with authority-wide policies on health, education, social inclusion, economy, environment and community safety and regeneration is an essential part of 'joined-up thinking' at national and local government levels. The connection with the Audit Commission's attempts at promoting self analysis in *Sport for Whom?* (Audit Commission, 1988) are clear.

- ### Consulting

This stress on creating strategies that consider all elements of the community in the planning process has been a difficult step for many to take. Provision in the voluntary and commercial sectors has to be interwoven into local cultural and sporting strategies to develop a framework for provision by all partners. New ideas to improve understanding of community needs have had to be developed. Many council officers are now embarked on community consultation exercises to ensure that these ideas can be fed into the planning process. This is in itself a logistically difficult and expensive process and there are clear concerns about the weight given to views expressed and how potentially short-term concerns may overtake the longer-term needs of diverse communities.

- ### Compare

Perhaps the most difficult element is the comparison of value for money between authorities. Previous attempts to produce satisfactory Performance Indicators (PI's) that gave accurate, clear and indisputable proof of performance have foundered ever since the Audit Commission's early attempts during the period of Conservative government. The failure to find any worthwhile forms of measurement was in itself some indication of the complexities involved in developing indicators that accurately measured both the financial cost and the quality of services being provided. If trying to deliver PI's for facility management was not problematic enough, there have been few if any attempts to measure the value of the services growing under the banner of more community or outreach sports development work. Lead agencies are immersed in new and imaginative ways of answering the previously unanswerable but there is still some way to go. The use of the Quest quality management system that was developed by the industry as one means of benchmarking performance is under constant review in relation to facility management. This is a system developed by the leisure and sports industry intended to contextualise, but only in relation to the operation of facilities, the generic concepts of Total Quality Management (TQM) and the process-based quality systems of BS5750 and ISO2000. A parallel model to be extended to other areas of sports development is in embryo. However, this seems to miss the essential premise relating to Best Value and joined-up thinking which looks at the whole picture of sports provision rather than separating it out into discrete arenas. It is surely not in the interests of the sporting community to continue with outmoded views of different elements of provision when what is sought is a more holistic view. The need for an overarching framework of sport indicators has spawned serious attempts to measure existing provision and use the information to change policy. Some of this work is potentially achievable by geographical mapping of facilities and sports. Use of data relating to gender, race, disability social deprivation and age may be interpreted to develop plans for sporting developments at all levels of the continuum. There are also options for mapping changes across Sport England's active programmes that will show if current policies are effective and where they might be built upon.

- ### Compete

  There is a clear compunction on local authorities to ensure the maximisation of resources across all services. This requires that due process be given to the most efficient and effective means of service delivery and that direct provision is only one of the options under consideration. The implication for sport is that partnership working between public, voluntary and commercial sectors should be a key element of local service strategies as discussed in Chapter 6. It may well be that an authority chooses to test its competitiveness through voluntary tendering having used a series of benchmarking exercises and ratings against local and national performance indicators.

Summary

The implications of the development of a new policy of 'joined-up thinking' in service delivery for sport is still in its infancy. It will be some time before it becomes clear if improved partnership working between the myriad agencies can bear fruit. Clearly all who have a stake in the future of sport often have differing aims and objectives and this will continue to create tensions.

There are real concerns amongst sports development professionals that in becoming more customer focused and accountable (about which there are very positive feelings), they may find themselves spending a disproportionate amount of their time counting and checking than on actually delivering. But accountability is both essential and desirable and there is a real need for a clarification of the value of strategic thinking, advocacy and justification for sport to be cascaded down to those who provide sporting opportunities at all levels in all sectors.

There is also an articulated concern that applies to all services subject to Best Value, not just sport, that continual reference to communities through consultation exercises may make long-term planning especially difficult if pragmatism and the disproportionate effect of pressure groups is allowed to have too much influence. To add to an already complex picture a further layer of context requires integration into the provision of Best Value – and that is the role and influence of Regional Cultural Consortia and Regional Sport Boards. The widening of the urge to work across geographical and service boundaries is clearly espoused in this newly emerging tier of policy development that will hopefully have more impact than its predecessors. A determined attempt to incorporate a strategic approach to a range of cultural and creative agencies and activities across regions is being developed. The provision for sport within wider areas is a serious attempt to plan sensibly for the needs of a range of communities. This broader overview should in theory be translated into the strategic plans for Best Value within individual authorities and the regional setting.

Best Value has appeared as the latest manifestation of government policy to affect the sporting scene and it is unlikely to be the last as the ever dynamic environment continues to evolve. There appears to be robust support through the stated strategies of Sport England and the Department for Culture Media and Sport. Time is required before a verdict can be passed on the performance of the new policies and their success in improving real effectiveness in the delivery of sporting opportunities across the whole country.

Case Study: Fairfax Metropolitan District Council

With a total population of 300,000 people to cater for, FMDC has since 1974 built four sports centres with swimming pools in the mainly urban central zone to complement the three joint-use facilities provided on secondary school sites. In the outlying rural and semi-rural communities attempts have been made to meet local aspirations by using existing social spaces for sporting activity.

With the advent of the Compulsory Competitive Tendering regime the Labour controlled council has decided that it would like to continue to maintain management control through its own workforce. It has therefore set up the structures that comply with the legislation but which are not encouraging of any private sector operators who may be interested in bidding for contracts. The council are very conscious that the neighbouring Conservative run Priestly Council has openly declared that it believes that ideologically it is not appropriate for it to be directly involved in the management function in sport and recreation and is therefore actively encouraging bids from the private sector. Priestly Council has told its workforce that the in-house Direct Service Organisation (DSO) will not be supported in bidding for their own current jobs and they will have to either bid as a newly constituted business or take their chances with whoever wins the contracts. There are mixed feelings about this scenario as some see this as a threat to secure local government jobs, whilst others see it as an opportunity to display their entrepreneurial skills in a welcoming new environment.

In preparing its defences against the threat of unwelcome predators, Fairfax MDC has developed a very complex contract specification and has excluded from the competition regime those sport and leisure functions that are not explicitly included in the legislation. This means that the joint-use and community facilities and the Sports Development Unit will be operated outside any contractual arrangements but could be in competition with those facilities that are put out to tender. Although a handful of private contractors show an interest in bidding in the initial stages ultimately none submit a bid on the final day due to the difficulties that could ensue in trying to operate in such a complicated and potentially hostile environment. The DSO breathes a sigh of relief and sets about trying to realise the predictions in its business plans in very difficult market conditions. FMDC is complicit in allowing some questionable variations to the contracts to allow the DSO meet its targets and avoid being reported for breaching the regulations.

Meanwhile over at Priestly the friendly contractors who were welcomed by the council have found that the same market conditions have made their own projections unrealistic. They are in the process of renegotiating the terms of the contract with an authority that is not keen on changing its position having put its trust in the free market to deliver the service it specified.

Fairfax MDC is pleased to see New Labour elected in May 1997 and enthusiastically embraces Best Value as a seemingly much more user-friendly policy. Priestly MDC also complies with the Best Value programme whilst continuing to encourage and develop new long-term partnership arrangements with private sector contractors to make substantial capital investment in the stock of facilities alongside a quality management operation.

References

Audit Commission, The (1988) *Sport for Whom? Clarifying the Local Authority Role in Sport and Recreation*, London: HMSO.

Audit Commission, The (1989) *Local Authority Support for Sport. A Management Handbook*, London: HMSO.

Collins, M. F. and Kennett, C. (1999) *Leisure, Poverty and Social Inclusion: The Growing Role of Passports to Leisure in Great Britain*, 1: 19–30. London: Sport England.

Department of Culture, Media and Sport (2000) *A Sporting Future for All*, London: DCMS.

Department of the Environment (1975) *Sport and Recreation*. Cmnd 6200, London: HMSO.

Department of Environment Transport and the Regions (1998) *Modernising Local Government. Improving Local Services Through Best Value*, DETR: HMSO.

Fromm, E. (1994) *The Art of Listening*, London: Constable.

Haywood, L. (1992) 'Community Recreation and Local Government in the 1990s', in *Leisure in the 1990s: Rolling Back the Welfare State* (LSA Publication No. 46). Eastbourne: Leisure Studies Association.

McIntosh P. (1984) *Sport in Society*, London: Macmillan.

McIntosh, P. and Charlton, V. (1985) *Action Sport: An Evaluation of Phase One*. London: Sports Council.

Sanderson, I. (1999) Unpublished presentation 'National Evaluation of Best Value Pilot Programme', Leeds Metropolitan University, Policy Research Institute (May).

Sport England and the Local Government Association (1999a) *The Value of Sport – Best Value Through Sport*, London: Sport England. Available HTTP: http://www.english.sports.gov.uk

Sport England and the Local Government Association (1999b) *Delivering Best Value Through Sport*. London: Sport England. Available HTTP: http://www.english.sports.gov.uk

Torkildsen, G. (1999) *Leisure and Recreation Management*, London: E & FN Spon.

Wolfenden Committee on Sport (1960) *Sport and the Community*, London: Central Council for Physical Recreation.

Chapter 4

Developing 'Sport for All?' Addressing inequality in sport

Kevin Hylton and Mick Totten

Introduction

The original 'Sport for All?' campaign was a creation of the early 1970s and has long since been succeeded by a multitude of subsequent campaigns and causes. But the ideals of 'Sport for All?' still have resonance today as a clarion call for all those involved in sports development. Despite this apparent consensus, the reality of 'Sport for All?' has never fully been achieved, and the successes remain incomplete and partial. Gains have been made, but massive inequalities still remain. However, tackling inequality must continue as a central premise and aim of Sports Development. In order to tackle inequality, inequality itself must be better understood. If the aim is to foster 'inclusion', then 'exclusion' and its social context must be better identified and understood.

Content and process

This chapter examines the nature and extent of inequality in sport, and outlines attempts to tackle inequality through sports and recreation development policy and practice. The first sections are used as a focus to draw out some of the challenges and issues that sports development workers have been engaged in when trying to provide 'Sport for All'. The chapter commences with an analysis of how inequality is exhibited, and how it can be identified, within sport. It then draws out how inequality is linked to broader social processes in society. Sport is directly influenced by society and consequently many of the wider processes of society express themselves in the realm of sport. Loosely translated, this means that where there is prejudice, discrimination, power differentials and social exclusion in society, these will be also manifest in sport.

The chapter considers how inequality can be understood in society. The use of *sociology* is viewed as an essential and important weapon in the armoury of an effective sports professional. The authors draw on sociological theory and interpretation to gain a deeper understanding of the issues. Four differing interpretations, (or perspectives) are contemplated to offer the sport and recreation development worker and policy maker alternative views to issues surrounding equality and inequality in sport. These are applied to sport, sports development and sport for all. These views enable the sports professional to understand that competing views or arguments are often grounded in the way that other people see the world and therefore sport and recreation development. Having established the social context of inequality in sport, the authors then analyse significant strategic policy responses and specific examples of practice in the light of previous theory and argument. The politics and policy implications are explored and explained in a case study of good practice, and other related examples, of the way in which different organisations have attempted to develop sport for all.

Inequality and sport

Sport and recreation development has been at the cutting-edge of what is seen as innovative and refreshing approaches to traditional sports provision. Despite constraints within their organisations, and within society, sports workers today are attempting to operate in a bid to bring more opportunities to the public. The house of sport and recreation development was built on the foundations of 'Sport for All' which has always been an ideal rather than a coherent realisable object. This ideal can be viewed from different perspectives to 'open-up' interesting views on sport and recreation and its development. Sports development professionals are challenged to plan, implement, and monitor equality work in sport. Furthermore, the cultural shifts that have to take place in organisations for long-term change need to go hand in hand with political and social change. Sustainable strategic planning only becomes a realistic proposition when resources and commitment are in close attendance.

Social Exclusion and 'Sport for All?'

The notion of 'joined up thinking' in 1999 (see Sport England, 1999) confirmed that sport is part of a broad diet of activity influenced by the government, which has an instrumental function. An agenda for social inclusion subsumes 'Sport for All?' and institutional equality work, at the same time as acting as a catalyst. A more equal society is something that most people would like to see in one form or another (Burden, 1998). It is a principle which changes over time (Jewson and Mason, 1986), and is fundamental to most people's idea of citizenship (Moore, 1993: 260). But a commitment to equality is not universally accepted; LeGrand (1991) suggests that equality is illusionary, impractical, inappropriate and immoral. Clarke (1994) suggests that some see it as secondary to efficiency, economy and effectiveness, and Coalter (1998) argues that due to the primacy of the market sport is not a right of citizenship. So, although working towards equality might be a priority for some within sports provision, it may not be as high on the agenda for others. Despite those occasional dissenters, this chapter advocates a commitment towards more equality development within sport as a primary responsibility for sports provision. Subsequent analysis will therefore consider more about the nature of inequality and how it can be tackled.

A number of authors (Rawls, 1971; Desai, 1995; Mithaug, 1996) have tried to articulate the evasive concept of equality, which consistently provides thinkers with a kaleidoscope of choices as to its constituency, and subsequent eventual achievement. Like academics, professionals in sport have competing views, which is one reason why there are inconsistencies in approaches. Bagilhole (1997: 7) prefers to use equal opportunities only in inverted commas as it is such a contested notion and subject to superficially shared and often tangentially related ideas. Similarly, the rhetoric in sports development, concerning 'Sport for All', is another indicator of a philosophy of provision which has been interpreted inconsistently.

There are different approaches to identifying inequality in sport. Inequality can be considered 'macroscopically' where it can be observed or tracked across large sections of society or comparatively between different societies. It can also be analysed 'microscopically' in relation to more specific local or group contexts. Inequality can be considered 'quantitatively' in terms of the numbers or percentages participating. But it can also be considered 'qualitatively' in terms of the reasons behind the who? how? and why? people participate and their experiences of participation or spectating in sport.

Trends in participation patterns: the quantitative analysis of sport

Quantitative analysis of participation relies mostly on surveys of participation in particular activities. Analysis can focus on sport as a whole, or on types of sports, or on specific activities. Participation rates are sometimes monitored in isolation, but perhaps more usefully when set against other 'variables'. Most commonly variables will include 'socio-economic' factors which characterise the 'demographic' composition of a population. These factors might include participants' age, gender, social class, and occupation, level of educational attainment, wealth, ethnicity, or access to car use. These variables when set against levels of participation reveal 'patterns of participation'. These patterns can be compared to average, or expectant, levels of participation. Where specific variables reveal levels of participation which are significantly above or below average, it can be concluded that that variable has an influence in predicting the likelihood of participation. For example, women, the physically disabled, or the unemployed, are significantly less likely to participate in snowboarding than men, the non-disabled, or the highly paid. Collectively, patterns of participation highlight trends which reveal 'inequalities in participation'. These can then be used to identify specific groups in the population who are less likely to participate – like the elderly, the disabled, many women, certain ethnic groups, the unemployed and others. These can then be considered 'priority groups' in terms of focusing initiatives to promote and increase participation. This common strategy of 'targeting' can concentrate efforts in attempting to 'include' the previously 'excluded'. In so doing participation can be increased by that group, so changing the pattern of participation, and decreasing inequality in patterns of sports participation. (See Table 4.1.)

Table 4.1 Trends in participation in physical activities (excl. walking) by socio-economic group, 1987–93

	1987 %	1990 %	1993 %	% point change 1987–93
Professional	65	65	64	–1
Employers and managers	52	53	53	+1
Intermediate and junior non-manual	45	49	49	+4
Skilled manual	48	49	46	–2
Semi-skilled manual	34	38	36	+2
Unskilled manual	26	28	31	+5

Source: Mintel (1997).

By analysing Table 4.1 it can be deduced that participation in physical activities varies by socio-economic group; the 'higher' the group, the more likely participation becomes. However, the 'lower' group appear to be increasing their participation. Overall, an individual's socio-economic status would appear to bear a direct relationship to the likelihood of their participation in physical activities. (See Figure 4.1.)

By analysing Figure 4.1, quite a few aspects can be deduced; participation in individual sports is more likely than in team sports irrespective of sex or age. Overall, men participate more frequently than women. Proportionately, men participate in team sports more often than women. Proportionately, younger people participate more commonly in team sports. Younger people participate in more sport overall. So both sex and age appear to have a strong influence on both the type and likelihood of participation.

Finally Figure 4.2 shows that different groupings of women participate differently in aerobics; younger women are more likely to participate. Mothers are less likely to participate. Working women are more likely to participate. There are also differences in the type of activities chosen by different 'types' of women. Overall, a variety of factors affecting women's lifestyles and status appear to influence their participation in aerobics. Quantitative methods of analysis are useful in identifying such broad patterns in participation, but don't really uncover their full *meaning*.

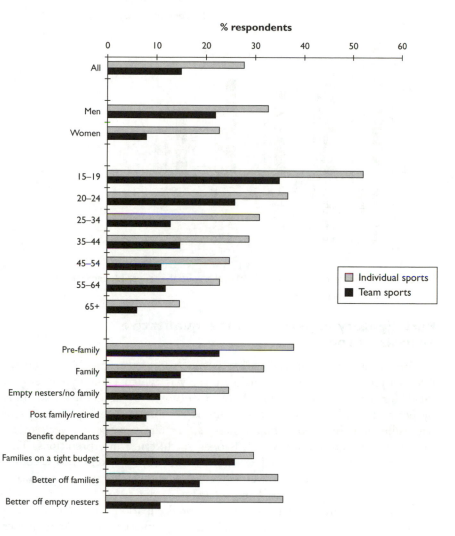

Figure 4.1 Individual and team sport participants by age, lifestage and special groups, November 1996. Base 1,003 adults.

Source: Mintel (1997).

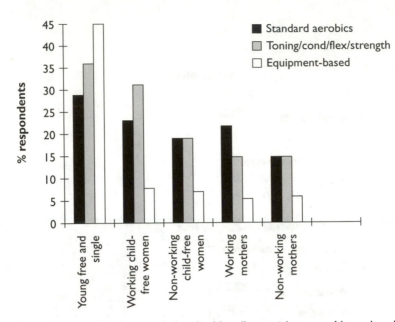

Figure 4.2 Profile of type of class by Mintel's special groups, November 1997.
Source: Mintel (1998).

Participatory experiences: the qualitative analysis of sport

Qualitative analysis of participation is much less common than quantitative analysis. As such it is a field of analysis which could be developed much further. It is much more likely to be used by academics than it is by policy makers or practitioners. This is because it is costly in terms of data collection time and human resources, but also because it reveals much more complex information which is open to differing interpretations. This complexity is often perceived as too difficult to be taken into account. Additionally its findings are often perceived as too challenging to be implemented and directly translated into changes in practice.

Qualitative analysis veers away from a preoccupation with numbers and concentrates on the *meaning* and *significance* of participation. It offers deeper insights into the motivations of participants and in the social significance of their participation. It often employs methods like semi-structured interviews, discussions or observations of practice to gain those insights. It focuses on the 'social relations of participation', how people behave, and what that behaviour means to them and to others. Understanding how and why people behave and relate to each other in particular ways, and what that means, is essentially at the root of participation and choice. Behaviour can be seen to be 'structured' in particular ways and linked to broader 'social influences'.

Society affects sport and sport affects society. The inter-relation of sport and society is manifest as social influences brought to sport, and as influences exported from it to broader society. The analysis of sport must also encompass other more informal manifestations such as recreation and play. 'Sport' is a social activity only partly composed of those elements which might involve some form of competitive activity. Analysis must extend beyond the playing field, into the locker room, and for some even into the bar afterwards as well! These are all a part of sport.

For example, if you were to observe behaviour in a badminton sports and social club bar you could focus on the influence of gender, class, ethnicity, disability or age. Sticking with gender, it is most likely, though not always the case, that women and men would behave differently, and adopt different behavioural roles in the same setting. Different groups and individuals of the same sex could also be seen to be behaving differently towards each other. Analysis would focus on the role of gender in influencing and determining that behaviour. Different views of masculinity and femininity can be determined to result in different 'engendered' role behaviours. The setting might be seen to be dominated by a specific gender, or a particular type of masculinity or femininity. This might differ in some way from another context like a rugby club bar; however, the resulting atmosphere might still make some groups or individuals feel more, or less, welcome in that setting. That in turn might lead to the partial exclusion of certain groups from that setting through a perception of discomfort, or simply a feeling that it is not for them. Those groups are unlikely to be attracted to that setting while those gender norms prevail despite best efforts to countenance an open-door policy. Fully including those excluded groups is unlikely to occur without first challenging, then changing, that prevailing 'gender order' or culture. The same observation but focused on class, ethnicity or disability, would be as likely to throw up similar results. A prevailing class or ethnic culture, or a prevailing cultural perspective, or attitude, towards disability could all be identified. These could be seen to include or exclude in a similar way.

The complexity of even beginning to address cultural change in practice deters many attempts at the offset. So in relation to gender, class or ethnicity, the prevailing order or culture continues, and with them so too does exclusion. The inherent difficulty in addressing participation in a qualitative way explains why it is less common. But until participation is addressed in a qualitative way, exclusion will continue to manifest itself – and therein lies a challenge for sports development!

Barriers to participation

Promoting inclusion and tackling exclusion involve identifying inequalities. Ultimately inequality is shaped by different social, cultural, political and economic influences. Using the previously identified quantitative and qualitative methods of analysing participation, the same influences crop up again and again. Key influences include disposable income, levels of educational attainment, occupational status, social class, culture, ethnicity, gender, sexuality, age, ability and disability.

These social influences can either encourage or discourage sports participation. In terms of exclusion, influences can also act as potential 'barriers to participation'. These can be further categorised as physical, economic, social, and political. Physical barriers to participation might include the location of facilities, activities and services, and physical access into and within those facilities, activities and services. Economic barriers relate to affordability, cost, and perceived value at that cost. Motivational barriers to participation can relate to the perceived absence of value in activity, or toward a conflict with self-image when viewed in the light of the perceived image of an activity. Cultural barriers to participation might include direct conflicts with the code, custom, convention or values inherent in an activity, or perhaps less directly, with a discomfort affiliating with the perceived cultural image of an activity. Political barriers to participation relate to feelings of alienation from, or lack of ownership over, the existing choice of provision. This may stem from a lack of representation, consultation or involvement in decision-making about provision which leads to feelings of being disenfranchised from that provision.

Alienation can occur at a very local level in relation to a particular facility. One example would be the aerobics group within an area of Leeds who preferred to participate in the local community centre rather than in the local sports centre. (The community centre was a blighted Portakabin in the *car park* of the sports centre!) Here the clients' perception of the centre and the negative class values that they associated with 'formalised' leisure needed to be addressed (Department of the Environment, 1989: 6). Another example, but at a more civic level, were the feelings of many of the people of Sheffield towards the provision for the World Student Games. Again perceptions of loss rather than gain clouded the community's views of this new provision; questions were asked about local access to the facilities and why local community centres were not being built or were being closed in the light of this massive spend on prestige capital investments. All the previously highlighted barriers can exclude and lead to feelings of 'this isn't for me'.

Remedying inequalities and overcoming barriers involves development strategies. These must challenge the inequitable nature of existing provision. There are limitations as to what can be achieved solely within sport. Many barriers draw their foundations from broader processes and institutions in society. But if the barriers are physical, economic, motivational, cultural and political, then so too are the solutions. If sports development strategies can address the structural issues, then they are on the way to establishing a 'cure' and treating the 'disease'!

Inequality and society

The social context of inequality

'Sport' is more than just an activity. It has far more meaning for the individual, and significance to society. It does not exist in a 'vacuum'. Unequal processes and practices in society are contributory reasons why sport and recreation development professionals have a difficult job in developing sport for all. Inequality exists on the field of play and it exists also in the rest of society. Analysis must embrace a more comprehensive social inquiry beyond the unique institutional framework which constitutes 'sport' itself; it must also consider society!

Inequality and discrimination

Institutions are constituted by members of society whose actions have varying degrees of significance for work towards, or indeed away from, equality in society. Amongst the groups who are traditionally excluded in society some have regularly been the focus for sports development. Gender, disability, 'race' and ethnicity have preoccupied policy makers, implementers and social commentators who recognise inequalities in the location of marginalised groups in the positions of power in sport. Class, age and sexuality have been considered less systematically, but their influence on life-chances should not be underestimated. There are fewer people from these excluded groups in managerial and administrative positions in sport and this has a clear qualitative impact on the opportunities for individuals from these groups to access sport and recreation (Sport England, 1999).

Inequality in sport and society can be caused through discriminatory practices and processes which can occur at different levels:

- Individual
- Institutional
- Societal.

All levels are inter-related in that everyone is part of, and contributes to, society. The industry of sport and recreation development is a small reflection of larger processes and practices which continue in wider society. The societal (macro) issues which impact on us all in our day-to-day lives are carried with us into sport. So where there are power and structural advantages which accrue for or against particular groups in society then they will be replicated in sport and recreation development in diverse ways.

For example: discrimination against disability in sport can be:

- Individual level discrimination (micro)
  Disabled people are regularly the focus of active direct prejudice and stereotyping by others through discrimination, and are therefore disadvantaged.
- Institutional level discrimination (meso)
  Disabled people are under-represented amongst the major institutions and policy makers of sport in society and this again is a mirror image of society.
- Societal level discrimination (macro)
  A 'disabling' society favours 'medical' rather than 'social' models of disability, which is reproduced in sport. This has the effect of stereotyping and problematising disabled people rather than problematising society's response to disabled people.

Another example (this time hypothetical!) which illustrates these levels could be 'Weatherfield Leisure Centre' (WLC).

Individual level discrimination (micro)

If a receptionist treated particular people coming into the centre unfavourably then this could be seen as a series of isolated incidents linked to a person going through a personal crisis. However, if this receptionist or any other member of staff at Weatherfield Leisure Centre frequently discriminates against people due to age, sex, ethnicity and disability they would be discriminating at a personal level. This behaviour might also be a combination of overt and/or covert discrimination and a further complication could be that it may be conscious or subconscious. Overt behaviour is the easiest to identify, although responses to any type of discriminatory action are never simple, and often inadequate.

Institutional level discrimination (meso)

Where WLC does not have in place policies and systems (remedies and/or sanctions) to ensure staff awareness of these discriminatory actions (or non-actions!), then it could be said to be encouraging institutional discrimination. Again this activity (or inactivity) by an organisation might be overt or covert.

Societal level discrimination (macro)

Society has practices and processes which are (to varying degrees) knowingly or unknowingly discriminatory. WLC draws its staff from members of society who (to varying degrees) reflect these broader predjudices.

Social exclusion and inclusion

Persistent barriers to participation can be understood as 'social exclusion'. Social exclusion was one of the major foci of the United Nations World Summit on Social Development in 1995. Social exclusion is typified by social and economic boundaries and the continual aggravation of differences and divisions in the life chances of members of the same society. For example, divisions can be expressed *socially*, in terms of gender differences in sport; *economically*, for example in terms of differences in income; or *culturally*, through ethnic differences. 'Exclusion' and 'Inclusion' affect individuals in different ways, but ultimately have a real impact on their overall quality of life. The setting up of a Social Exclusion Unit by the government in 1997 gave a clear indication of the need to use sport and sports development as a tool to encourage social inclusion.

Sports development workers need to be conscious of the evident common ground which sport shares with other 'social' services. Such recognition enabled New Labour to coin the phrase 'joined-up thinking and policy making'. This phrase emphasises the economies of scale that shared professional knowledge and integrated resources across departmental areas can afford to the client or local citizen. These mutual areas of interest which become fields for integrated coherent policies are often referred to as 'cross-cutters'. These cross-cutters enable workers from different professions to work together to reduce social exclusion and include:

- Community development
- Lifelong learning
- Social cohesion
- Community safety
- Active healthy lifestyles
- Social and economic regeneration
- Job creation
- Equal opportunities
- Crime prevention
- Environmental protection.

All of the above emphasise the idea that sport cannot be considered in isolation from other aspects of society.

Sociological approaches to understanding inequality

As indicated earlier, an understanding of the social context of sport necessitates some understanding of society itself (Coakley, 1994; Kew, 1997). In terms of sports development, the enlightened practitioner must embrace this social perspective and its analysis; namely 'Sociology'. Only then can they hope to have any significant understanding, and therefore impact, on the social context of sport. This prospect can seem somewhat daunting as society is so all-encompassing and the individual practitioner often feels isolated in relation to the enormity of it all. But sociology is not just about 'thinking'. Sociology is alive and breathing. Sociology also involves 'doing', and the enlightened sports development worker (whether aware of it or not) can be an 'active sociologist'! Social processes which create inequality, and solutions (albeit with limitations), must be pursued not just in sport but in society as a whole. Let's face it; 'You are either a part of the cure, or you are a part of the disease'!

Introducing sociology

Sociology is the study of society and is committed to developing a greater understanding of society. The 'Sociological Imagination' enables a deeper, more significant insight into society and how it works (Haralambos and Holborn, 1995; Giddens, 1997). Sociology attempts to explain, and sometimes predict, social behaviour. A grasp of sociology will enable the enlightened practitioner to more accurately understand the profound and complex influences which affect sports participation. The following analysis will employ sociological theory and apply sociological perspectives to the study of inequality in sport. For the uninitiated it may initially be challenging or cause mild befuddlement, but 'hang-in there' as it may prove quite illuminating! It begins with an analysis of how significant social influences are in determining participation in sport. It will then work towards offering different perspectives from which to understand 'sport for all'. But, in order to do so, it will establish what sociological perspectives are, what they explain, and how progressively they interpret society, sport, sports development, and then 'sport for all'.

Influencing participation

Social influences like gender, ethnicity and class, which can act as barriers to participation in sport, can be considered as 'structures' which permeate society. However, individuals attempt to make choices and exercise their free will in their leisure and in their sport. This is known as 'agency'. Social structures influence individuals as they make these choices. Structures inhibit total freedom from constraint. As much as individuals perceive themselves to be exercising free choice, they are either consciously or subconsciously constrained by the influence of these structures. Social structures can make certain choices more or less likely. As such they influence individual choice whether we are aware of it or not. So, individuals attempt to make free choices in sport based on their own unique opportunities and tastes. But these very opportunities and tastes are informed by the influences of social structures. So total free choice is illusory! But, we are still free to choose, even if we have little control over what our choices are. So choice itself is constrained by structures outside the immediate influence of the individual. In short, once again, society influences sport. The combined influence of structure and agency on choice can be described as a 'dichotomy'. Dichotomies, or seemingly real contradictions and tensions in policy and practice, were discussed in detail in Chapter 3.

Understanding society

Within sociology, different perspectives have emerged from which to view and understand social contexts and processes like sport. These perspectives put more or less emphasis on the role of structure and agency in determining choice. Furthermore, they offer different interpretations of the social world. To an extent they may overlap, but each believes its own interpretation is the most accurate; thus disagreement and argument ensue, and are inevitable.

The four most dominant perspectives are outlined below as tools that academics and practitioners may use to better understand sport and society. Ideally the four views should be utilised strategically by sport and recreation development professionals to interpret processes and practices in sport. Understanding the way people make sense of society, sport, sport development, and sport for all, enables reflective practitioners to balance the relative merits of competing or alternative views more effectively. If an individual were to imagine their day-to-day relationships at work, or at leisure, then just that small group of acquaintances could offer up (from their diverse backgrounds) different, very challenging, views on developing sport for all. This gives an indication of the surface to be scratched when four perspectives are offered as informative tools for analysis in contemporary sport and recreation development contexts.

As sociological perspectives consider much more than just sport, they will be introduced from a bigger picture, before working progressively towards more specific consideration of sport for all. Table 4.2 highlights four perspectives: functionalist (Loy, 1981), neo-Marxist (Hargreaves, 1986), feminist (Hargreaves, 1994) and post-modernist (Rail, 1998). The table offers a simplified version of those four interpretations of society. The reader can attempt to judge which perspective they find the most convincing. Ideally, you may find that one perspective seems to emerge as more compelling, or you may choose to apply different perspectives at different times. Whichever you choose, the adoption of sociological imagination and analysis offers a critical insight into how society works (or does not!).

In comparing the different perspectives it is worth noting their historical relationships to clarify their differences. Functionalism supports the most traditional view of Western society and sport. It is perhaps the most popular perspective amongst the political establishment and the wider population.

Table 4.2 Interpretations of society

Functionalist
Society is based on broad agreement (consensus). This consensus reflects a balance between different interests. The 'social system' regulates the smooth flow of these plural interests.

Neo-Marxist
Society is based on coercion and consensus. 'Social relations' are dominated by power struggles. The economically and politically powerful attempt to lead, and protect their dominance. The masses either consent to these arrangements or offer resistance against them.

Feminist
Society is based on male domination or patriarchy. Social relations exist within a gender order. Masculine values dominate society. Traditional femininity prescribes a subservient role for women.

Post-modernist
Society is fragmented and diverse. There is no universal truth, only individuality and different interpretations of reality. The only certainty is uncertainty! Society is in a perpetual state of change and flux. Traditional structure and order are things of the past.

Its ideals tend to be most dominant in current sports and social policy. But it is savagely criticised by Neo-Marxism for being at best, too 'rose-tinted', unconditionally positive and unrealistic, and at worst; for being ideologically divisive, conning the general public into believing in a leadership which ultimately works in its own best interests. Neo-Marxists draw more attention to power inequalities and conflicts which Functionalists overlook, particularly in the economics of society, and of sport. Feminism arose as a critique of the failure of the two previous perspectives to take account of gender divisions and power relations in their analysis. Feminists promote the influence of gender as the primary determinant in social relations and sport. Post-Modernism is the most recent of the perspectives. It critiques all of the three perspectives for clinging to any form of clear determination in an increasingly unpredictable world. In fact it argues for unpredictability.

Neo-Marxism could be seen as being adaptable enough to account for the massive changes in current society. Functionalism, on the other hand, could be viewed as over-simplifying the world, to be unrealistic and naïve. It is the world we would like to live in but do not. Neo-Marxism considers the power processes ignored by more simple social theories as well as the more constructive, empowering elements of society. Neo-Marxism can also be argued to encompass and account for the concerns of both Feminists and Post-modernists. Neo-Marxist analysis then takes into account cultural power as inclusive of concerns about gender division, as well as other dynamics such as ethnicity, class and disability. Neo-Marxism interprets

Table 4.3 Interpretations of sport

Functionalist
Sport is greatly valued as it has many positive benefits. It contributes to the smooth running of the social system. It acts as a form of 'cultural glue' which helps to hold society together.

Neo-Marxist
Sport can liberate or constrain. It largely serves the interests of dominant groups and institutions. But it can also act as a site for resistance or change by subordinate groups or individuals.

Feminist
Sport reinforces patriarchy and traditional masculine and feminine values. It promotes masculine values over feminine. But it can also act as a site for women, or men, to challenge these traditional values.

Post-modern
Sport is a paradox. It can be highly significant to individual self-image and lifestyle, but it is ultimately superficial. It can be highly symbolic of society, but it is ultimately unreal. It is in this sense 'hyper-real'.

Post-modernism as a context, not a perspective. It is the times we live in, not the way they should be understood, see how Table 4.3 helps to develop some of these ideas as they apply to sport and recreation.

Functionalists clearly place an enormous value on sport, but there are other important issues that have been considered in this chapter, but which are not as significant for functionalists. They are considerations of power processes. Views with a neo-Marxist perspective in sport (Clarke and Critcher, 1985) have recognised that sport, like society, can liberate; for example through offering opportunities, and at the same time constrain; through reducing choice through processes of discrimination. Feminist writers, and practitioners in the field, have also acknowledged power differentials in society. However, in this case the differences are due to a male dominated or 'patriarchal' system that results in a more oppressive society for girls and women than boys and men. So gender relations are a primary source of focus here. Other related areas and issues build upon many of the arguments by neo-Marxist and Feminist thinkers. 'Race' and ethnicity, class, disability and age, amongst others, are crucial concerns for the enlightened practitioner. These issues are not mutually exclusive in that individuals are identified by and identify with multiples of these socio-economic factors.

Table 4.4 applies perspective directly to sports development. Functionalism is one view which when used takes as its basic premise that broad agreement typifies the way that sport and sport and recreation development is structured and functions in society. The ability of individuals and groups to access opportunities in society and sport is based upon combined interest groups. Simply, if something has not been set up or established in society then individuals in

Table 4.4 Interpretations of sports development

Functionalist
Sports development polices gaps in provision and participation. It distributes social justice in the face of market trends. It circumvents barriers to participation. It spreads the benefits of sport. It presides over competing plural interests. It advocates on behalf of marginalised interests. It applies the glue to bind diverse strands into an integrated whole.

Neo-Marxist
Sports development reflects conflict between the 'top-down' interests of dominant groups and institutions, and the 'bottom-up' needs and wants of subordinate groups and individuals. It illustrates social tensions between 'structures' and 'free-agency'. It is a 'dichotomy'. It both perpetuates the dominant agenda, and can act as a site of resistance to that agenda.

Feminist
Overall, sports development perpetuates sport as a patriarchal institution. Token attempts are made to incorporate more women into sport without challenging the fundamentally patriarchal nature of its institutions and culture. But it does also offer some limited opportunities for women to infiltrate and reclaim previously masculine territory.

Post-modern
Sports development reflects an institutional anxiety to exercise control and impose order in an increasingly disorganised world. It attempts to navigate a complex map of diverse sources of provision and motivations for participation. It is prone to a layering of disparate influences at local, regional, national and global levels. It is insecure. The only constant is change.

society do not see a need for it. If this point is applied to lottery funding, then if particular groups in society are accessing funding and others are not, the funding should still be going to the right places because some groups are showing interest in terms of organisation and application, and others are not.

A neo-Marxist viewpoint accepts that there are constraints at the same time as there is a level of agency in sport and society. Even the local authority which is proactive in its sports equity work will be working with a backdrop of inadequate resources from past discriminatory initiatives, which causes the limitation of choice and opportunities. This is the context for many practitioners and policy makers in sport. This is also a challenge for the development of sport for all.

Post-modernists base their views on sport and recreation development and society on an analysis and description of the speed of change and de-regulation of society. They reflect upon how technology, structures, processes and practices today no longer resemble the form they had yesterday; for example the difference between the 1980s and the 2000s. In sport and recreation development the multi-agency, cross-departmental work that has become common in the achievement of best value for the customer is an example of symbolic change in the industry. Another example of the shift in practices is the way that proof of the worth of sports development is part of the move towards more accountability which was not part of its dominant discourse in the 1970s and 1980s.

Having taken a theoretical detour to set the scene, let us return specifically to 'Sport for All'. The different ways of interpreting 'Sport for All' in Table 4.5 are starting points to understanding why 'Sport for All's' objectives, and equality in sports development, are rarely acclaimed uniformly across the profession. The reader can analyse the following perspectives of 'Sport for All' and, as before, critically evaluate the worth of each. Subsequent sections of this chapter will turn more directly to consider policy and practice, but it is hoped that the reader will continue to exercise a little 'sociological imagination' throughout.

Table 4.5 Interpretations of 'Sport for All' and inclusion

Functionalist
In a maturing society, equity and inclusion are ultimately and inevitably achievable. Historical inequities in sport are gradually being eroded. Social consensus necessitates inclusion. The social system is committed to a project of inclusion. Exclusion is 'dys-functional' and undesirable.

Neo-Marxist
The need to redistribute opportunity is paramount to create a fairer society. But this is unlikely to happen against the backdrop of a capitalist society, which is based on competition and inequality. Sport reflects and reinforces this. Power struggles in sport mirror those in society. Sport is a site of cultural struggle. This struggle includes the vested political and commercial interests of the dominant culture, the diverse self-interests of communities, and the emancipatory interests of the oppressed.

Feminist
In recent years, there has been some partial success in terms of addressing numerical inequalities in participation. But women are still institutionally excluded from the governance of sport. Ultimately the quality of women's and men's experiences in sport are still vastly unequal. The culture of sport is still male-dominated. Gender equity in sport is impossible in the context of broader patriarchal society.

Post-modern
Concepts like sports equality and inclusion are outmoded. There is nothing objectively fixed to determine inclusion or exclusion. Society is increasingly influenced by global processes which lead to the redundancy of traditional social structures and inequalities. Class, gender and ethnic boundaries are collapsing. Lifestyle and identity are increasingly individualised and self-determined through consumption, like sport.

Sports policy addressing inequality

Equity and equality

The idea of fairness or equity is a term that is often used interchangeably with equality; however, equality has a more descriptive component. Edwards (1990) suggests that equal opportunities are, in effect, equal opportunities to compete for rewards, and hence to be unequal. Previous historical differences between groups must be taken into account in terms of who has, and who has not, got access to opportunities in sport. Sport England advocates sports 'equity' and has sports 'equity' trainers involved in working with national governing organisations and local authorities. Equity is a more arbitrary concept in that the individual or organisational view of 'fairness' is paramount rather than a universal view of equality. These trainers promote 'equal opportunities'. At the same time Sport England has initiated a project in partnership with the Commission for Racial Equality promoting racial equality in sport for black and ethnic minority groups called 'Sporting Equals'. Here is an example of one organisation whose lack of clarity in this area compounds the historical confusion in the sport and recreation development industry. Further, we have also established that they are not alone in their misunderstanding of terminology and problematic concepts. Clarity in this area must be reached if people in sport intend to work towards equality and inclusion, as positive outcomes. In addition, it is important to note that equality does not necessarily imply equity as equality may be advocated for reasons other than equity as we will see later in this chapter.

Equality in practice

Working towards equality in different contexts can take interesting turns depending on the strategy(ies) employed by the implementers. Equality of opportunity implies that all persons regardless of their background should be given equal access to the same facilities, services, employment and other social conditions. Statutes such as the Sex Discrimination Act 1975, the Race Relations Act 1976, and Disability Discrimination Act 1995, make it unlawful to discriminate in the provision of goods, facilities and services. Equality of opportunity, equality of condition, and equality of outcome are three significant issues in the journey towards understanding equality processes in sport and recreation development.

For example, if a sports worker were to adhere to these laws, yet some members of the community were still being excluded, then equal opportunities could still be seen to exist even though they are ineffective in this instance. However, if the excluded groups were filtered away from the sports worker's sessions because of a lack of transport, technical equipment, or for cultural reasons, but these socio-cultural gaps were *then* addressed, then the sports worker would have moved beyond *just* providing equality of opportunity. The sports worker would also be providing equality of condition in that considerations other than physical access would have been the reasons for a lack of participation by groups in this community. The worker would be moving towards what Cockburn (1989) terms a 'long agenda' rather than a short one. Jewson and Mason (1986) would argue also that the worker is moving from a liberal to a more radical agenda. The long-term implementation and monitoring of equality strategies is complex and involves more than policy statements and rhetoric, as we will see later.

A more radical view of equality in operation might come through the use of equality of outcome principles. Here more positive and explicitly differential provision will take into account some of the larger *structural* inequalities in society. Taking into account these structural differences will actively challenge them through new initiatives and strategies. Sports professionals occasionally find it necessary to focus on equality outputs (CRE, 1996) or positive action initiatives to refocus their work towards providing more equal and sensitive provision. Women only sessions, or work with young disabled people, are examples of 'positive action' strategies. Positive action, due to the statutes mentioned earlier, can also be applied to recruiting people to work in those areas of provision where they are under-represented. This basic regulation and distribution of resources is something that has been recognised as an essential aspect of progressive equality policies.

Equality policies

So, inequality is a significant cause of social exclusion whereby individuals, or communities, are unable, for a variety of reasons, to participate with others or in activities in society. In sports development unless there is a recognition of the needs and aspirations of diverse people in society and amongst client groups, providers will continue to maintain the inequalities in society. An example of work towards these ends is the Brighton Declaration (1994) which was written by national and international policy makers to develop a sporting culture that would enable and value the full involvement of women in every aspect of sport. The major areas of the Declaration revolve around the guiding themes in Table 4.6.

Sport then is not isolated from the inequalities in society. Sport and recreation development has an endless task if it has the primary responsibility of reducing social exclusion amongst people in the UK. The role of

---

Table 4.6 The guiding themes of the Brighton Declaration

- Equity and equality in society and sport
- Facilities
- School and junior sport
- Developing participation
- High performance sport
- Leadership in sport
- Education, training and development
- Sports information and research resources
- Domestic and international co-operation

sport as part of a broader social policy strategy might go some way in contributing to reducing social inequality, increasing community cohesion and acting as a catalyst for social regeneration. The creation of a social exclusion unit and its use of sport and recreation development as part of its strategy to increase social inclusion is an indication of, at the very least, the ideological significance of sport and recreation development in society.

Equality and sports development

Certain managerial and political perspectives have informed the practice of equality work since the late 1970s. Taylor's work (1994) encapsulates some of the thinking in this area. Two major competing views in this period have revolved around a New Right view which focused on the primacy of the market as the guardian of individual rights and natural justice. Whereas more recently the New Right view has been modified with elements of a social reformist agenda which has taken a more inclusive stance to public sector interventions, the social reformist perspective encourages a more 'active society' through proactive social support mechanisms which promotes community development, capacity building, social cohesion and the reduction of social exclusion. Sport England's 'Active Framework' which focused on Active Sports, Active Schools and Active Communities, is an example of individuals and organisations being empowered to meet their own specific needs. What is clear from either position is the value of rigorous practical management in any field of work and equality's place within it.

Equality in sports development

Ellis (1994) and Escott (1996) looked at the positive aspects of working towards equality within the 'bottom line' pressures of the commercial sector. One of the major drawbacks of the contracting process as a result of the Local Government Act (1988) is that social objectives or equality targets do not have to be tied into contracts. Equality targets in the political climate of 1988 were seen as non-commercial considerations. The then Sports Council's National Information Survey in 1993 on the first round of CCT bares testimony to this. It was established that out of many local authorities only a few incorporated social objectives into the clauses for contracts that went out to tender. However, more enlightened organisations have tied equality targets into contractor activities by inextricably linking them with quality targets and principles of Best Value. This is where the Commission for Racial Equality (CRE) and the Equal Opportunities Commission (EOC) have focused a lot of their attention in recent times.

In support of this view Taylor (1994) advocates the use of equal opportunities policies in any industry, not from a moral perspective (although there is an element of that), but from a business perspective as well (!) (see

Etzioni, 1961; CRE, 1996; EOC, 1996; Coalter, 1998). Taylor outlines the major skills that a manager needs to be successful in business. Five major considerations to develop management skills in this area are:

- human rights and social justice
- business efficiency
- quality management
- the labour market
- legal considerations.

So equal opportunities are not just the exclusive preserve of the social reformist agenda in the public and voluntary sectors; they can be a desirable aspect of the economics of the commercial private sector as well.

Research, equality and sports development

The case study at the end of this chapter focuses on a proactive local authority and considers the necessary steps that need to be taken where sports organisations have made a commitment to work towards equality. Documented experiences of sport and recreation organisations' inability to work consistently towards equality lead writers and practitioners to look in more detail at the reasons for this lack of success.

Carrol (1993) and Horne (1995) have concluded from their research into local government that there is a policy implementation gap between the formulation and implementation of equal opportunities strategies. This in itself has implications for the prospects of success in any organisation. Horne in particular developed three classic types of local authority provider and labelled them gestural, reactive and proactive. Gestural authorities had a policy or policy statement but did not feel it necessary to go beyond these steps, whereas the 'reactive' authorities would have a policy but would not have a rigorous and actively monitored plan to work towards equality. In fact they would react to the demands of their local communities which might have the effect of 'the louder you shout the more you get!' Proactive authorities had policy statements and plans and were actively working towards achieving their goals. Unfortunately only a few organisations were placed in the proactive category, most tended to be reactive to their local community and staff needs rather than plan ahead. Gibbon (1989) went a stage further in Sheffield in his summary of employment practices. He argued that employers in Sheffield 'possessed hazy ill-defined or contradictory goals [on equality] and that they were inadequately implemented'.

Analysing the impact of strategies in sport can often reveal some of the glitches in what many would see as a rational decision-making process. Young and Connelly (1984) categorised over a hundred local authorities in order to understand the work that they had conducted towards policy development and implementation in equal opportunities. They stated that there were those who:

1   As a matter of political preference set their minds against change and were prepared to ignore the requirements of their [statutory] duties.
2   Were reviewing their policies but were moving cautiously forward in a fairly conventional manner but with a willingness to accept the need for change.
3   Were aware of a changed social, moral and legal climate presenting a challenge to traditional practices but were not sure of the appropriate response.
4   Were testing out the political and legal possibilities and developing approaches aimed at giving a fair deal to people.

If policy approaches were to be considered from the previous sociological perspectives, the following conclusions could perhaps be drawn:

*   Functionalism would seem to support either conservative support for the status quo or milder liberal reforms. This underscores broad satisfaction with the current organisation of sport, and the value of the role that sport plays in society. Minor reform acknowledges 'dys-functional' exceptions in need of remedy, but their extent do not threaten the wider social order.
*   Neo-Marxism and Feminism would seem to support stronger liberal reform, but more likely increasingly radical reforms. This draws attention to the institutionalised and unequal distribution of power within sport, how that supports the interests of dominant groups, and how other groups' interests are marginalised or even oppressed.

*   Post-modernism would appear to support less paternalistic reforms, which empower individuals rather than specified groups. The collapse in influence of the traditional institutions are envisaged, and the growth, and importance, of individualised cultural choice is predicted – and championed.

Addressing inequality in practice

A sports organisation in context

Each sector and organisation has its own unique context, economies of scale and organisational culture which will impact upon the implementation of equality initiatives. The Badminton Association of England is a national governing organisation that saw a need to implement an equality strategy which would assist the sport in becoming more representative of the society it operates in. The organisation's staff decided that there was a problem and that the problem itself needed some form of definition. What brought the Association to this point was a series of acknowledgements by the staff (see Table 4.7).

In addition to these internal drives the external reality for the governing body included a funding mechanism from Sport England whose more recent conditions on funding, ensured that there would be consequences for organisations who did not adhere to principles of equity. Reactive or gestural organisations would need to consider their practices in the light of their financial support being reduced as a result of their lack of consideration of social objectives and strategic planning. An understanding of the catalysts for change are important for governing organisations as change can occur under duress and possibly without a sustainable force. However, if these principles are taken on as part of an individual or an organisation's goals, there is more of a chance of success in the long term. The governing body may need to challenge its existing power structures. This would result in a focus on its dominant practices and processes and enable a robust opportunity for the long-term implementation of proactive equality outcomes.

According to the BAofE some of the explanations for their actions have included the following needs:

- to develop an understanding of sports equity
- to evaluate the benefits of a sports equity approach
- to identify exclusionary factors
- to identify issues and target groups
- to draft an equal opportunities statement.

This has had the effect of shedding some light on the practices that the Association had been engaged in for some years. It has also motivated it to draw in related experts to advise on how to make itself more accessible to those hard-to-reach groups and communities.

If the BAofE's journey is considered from the perspective of a simple policy process model it would in effect be at the stage of now having to identify responses to its major problems before evaluating the options open to it. The next stages after evaluating options are, selection of policy option, implementation and then active monitoring and evaluation of action as shown in Figure 4.3.

Table 4.7 Badminton Association of England – catalysts for action

Factor	Observation
Image/Profile	Predominantly white male middle class, stuffy, all white kit.
Administration/Coaching	Very few black and ethnic minority coaches, women and disabled people.
Executive members	Are not close to reflecting the population mix.
No equal opportunities strategy or monitoring	Unable to get an accurate profile of coaches and players.

Jabeer Butt (1994: 77) established in her work that equality strategies needed to have a work programme, a timescale and needed to be monitored and reviewed. Even though the BAofE has agreed a policy statement on equal opportunities it has not yet established a coherent plan of action:

1.1 The Badminton Association of England is fully committed to the principles of equality of opportunity and is responsible for ensuring that no job applicant, employee or volunteer receives less favourable treatment on the grounds of age, colour, disability, ethnicity, parental or mental status, and sexual preference.

1.2. The Association will ensure that there will be open access to all those who wish to participate in the sport and that they are fairly treated.

The policy statement shows a positive intention from the BAofE However, for it to move from being a gesture of intent to a concrete policy with action the organisation must make purposeful steps in a direction which will allow it to best utilise its resources. This will ensure effective equality outputs as a result of the process.

In 'Anyone for Cricket?' (1998), research commissioned by the Essex Cricket Association and the London Cricket Association, their task was to find out why black and Asian teams tended not to affiliate to the County Association. The research helped them to recognise that institutional systems were not enough to effect lasting change, but that a critical mass needed to be motivated to change the culture of the sport, as was attempted with the Brighton Declaration. In fact the research gave an indication of starting points but due to the size of the task, was not assured enough at the end of an exact course of action. The English Cricket Board followed up this work in 1999 with further research 'Clean Bowl Racism' where it reinforced the notion that the majority of those researched (58 per cent; p.8) believe that there is racism in the sport.

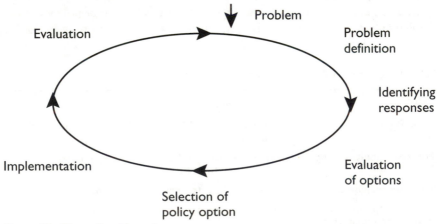

Figure 4.3 The policy life cycle.

All organisations vary in their ability to implement all-embracing equality initiatives. Hylton (1998) looked at three local authorities in England and compared their operational environments. The three authorities varied in size, location, history, industry, wealth, demography, politics and policies, although they were similar in their diversity of local people especially where 'race' and ethnicity were concerned. Each authority was publicly committed to 'equal opportunities'. After further analysis it was found that, through comparing each authority, their political and professional commitment to equal opportunities work was not the same as the initial rhetoric. Differences in perception and focus on equality of opportunity, local politics and policies and related variables, all impacted upon the place of equal opportunities work in each organisation.

The CRE have recently attempted to move local authorities on a stage further by presenting a common standard framework based on quality with which 'to identify and acknowledge achievement made and to plan systematically for improvement'. This template is useful as a guide for other equality work. The following case study shows how Kirklees MBC have adapted in a bid for an all-inclusive service which embraces the principles of quality and equality, and the basic steps outlined by Butt (1994). The drive from the centre of the organisation ensures that all departments are aware of the corporate vision and where the parameters of their work should fall.

Case Study: Proactive equality work in sport and recreation development

'We remain committed throughout our services, to the core values of quality and equality' – 'Our Vision for Kirklees'

The 'Vision' for the authority has three primary goals:

* A thriving economy
* A flourishing community, and
* A healthy environment.

The whole authority has taken on board an all-embracing equality strategy which is based upon frameworks from the CRE (1996) and the EOC (1997). The new framework adopted by all Council departments is called Equality 2000 and it enables equality principles to be mainstreamed and achievable objectives set, monitored and evaluated according to strict criteria.

The CRE established a Standard Framework which has five levels to be achieved. Once a level has been achieved a department progresses to the next. Kirklees have stipulated that where one department has not achieved its objectives then all departments will be held back from progressing to the next level. Thus an integrated supportive environment of mutual working is developed over time.

In addition to the five levels there are five focus areas which include:

1. Policy and planning
2. Service delivery and customer care
3. Community development
4. Employment; recruitment and selection, and developing and retaining staff
5. Marketing and corporate image.*

* A useful example of this is the Council's commitment to working competitively as a market oriented enabler by using techniques to identify markets differentiated by age, gender, ethnicity and locality. Marketing is seen as a crucial tool of the Council's equal opportunities policy although it emphasises how aware workers must be in keeping its social objectives close to everything that happens in implementation.

The Leisure and Recreation Services in this authority are implementing a five-year plan to achieve the Council's main themes within this leisure and recreation context.

The Sport and Recreation department in Kirklees is trying to sustain a 'Sport for All' ethos and intends to target disadvantaged groups such as young people in order to 'provide accessible community and facility based activities and opportunities which strive to meet the needs of young people'.

Statements, in this authority, relating to women, people with a disability, the fifty plus and black and ethnic minorities, continue in a similar vein to the work with young people, i.e. there is a recognition that discrimination and disadvantage are key factors which influence the nature and extent of [the target group's] involvement in sport. It is also suggested that this work cannot be completed quickly and that it is part of an ongoing development process.

Where interdepartmental partnerships are formed to work towards the authority's vision there is more chance of a concerted effort towards the ends of equality of opportunity. Councillors, senior officers, external partners and the local community become important components of a successful action plan.

Conclusion

This chapter has attempted to invigorate the sustained and contemporary relevance of the quest for 'Sport for All'. It has identified the continuing inequalities which permeate sport and society, and therefore the failure to realise sport for all. In drawing attention to the social nature of inequality in sport, the chapter has advocated the importance of 'active sociology' to practical sports development. It has considered policy approaches to addressing inequality and finally it considered aspects of good practice.

Practitioners still occupy distinct and different roles and responsibilities in the delivery and development of sport. This can cause strategic tensions in provision of sport and recreation, and a perennial competition for resources. Sport and recreation development can be viewed in a number of different ways by a variety of practitioners, policy makers and academics. The significance of sport in society is beyond question. The future of sport and recreation development in society is also beyond question. Its exact role, however, is in particular dispute when it comes to developing 'sport for all'. Concepts such as 'Sport for All', 'equality', 'social exclusion' and 'equity' are problematic. This compounds the complexity of policy decisions and the practices that sports development workers aim to implement. Sports development workers and policy makers have a variety of challenges facing them in the twenty-first century. The continued development of opportunities for people in sport is consistently being questioned where practitioners have differing aims, objectives, and basic philosophies, in their role and place in developing sport and recreation.

It was previously stated that 'sport affects society and society affects sport'. This relationship can be described as reflexive, or symbiotic. Essentially, it cuts both ways. Sport and society both reproduce inequality, but they can both also challenge it. A fairer arrangement cannot be achieved in one and not the other. So the marriage of sports and social policy is more than just of convenience. According to the Social Exclusion Unit, social exclusion is impacting society, and therefore sport and recreation development. Sport has a role to play in reducing the constraints which excluded groups experience. Sport and recreation development can help to reduce exclusion by enhancing community development opportunities, social cohesion, equal opportunities, crime prevention and community safety, lifelong learning, active healthy lifestyles, social and economic regeneration, job creation, and environmental protection.

Significantly there is no clear consensus on the importance of unconditionally increasing access for disenfranchised groups in sport. This is due to competing viewpoints and causes. Sociological perspectives should begin to stimulate the sociological imagination in a bid to illustrate different ways of seeing sports development and inclusive sport. Effective sport and recreation development workers (active sociologists!) should be able to use the appropriate analytical tools and research available to them to ensure that they 'work smart' in trying to address inequality.

References

Bagilhole, B. (1997) *Equal Opportunities and Social Policy*, Harlow: Longman.

Burden, T. (1998) *Social Policy and Welfare*, London: Pluto Press.

Butt, J. (1994) *Same Service or Equal Service?*, UK: HMSO.

Carrol, B. (1993) 'Sporting bodies: sporting opportunities', in C. Brackenridge (ed.), *Body Matters Leisure Images and Lifestyles* (LSA Publication No. 47), Eastbourne: Leisure Studies Association, pp. 106–14.

Clarke, A. (1994) 'Leisure and the new managerialism', in J. Clarke, A. Cochrane and E. McLaughlin (eds), *Managing Social Policy*, London: Sage.

Clarke, J. and Critcher, C. (1985) *The Devil Makes Work: Leisure in Capitalist Britain*, London: Macmillan.

Coakley, J. (1994) *Sport in Society: Issues and Controversies*, London: Mosby Year Book.

Coakley, J. (1998) *Sport in Society: Issues and Controversies*, Singapore: McGraw-Hill International.

Coalter, F. (1998) 'Leisure studies, leisure policy and social citizenship: the failure of welfare or the limits of welfare?', *Leisure Studies*, 17: 21–36.

Cockburn, C. (1989) 'Equal opportunities: the long agenda', *Industrial Relations Journal*, 20(3): 213–25.

Commission for Racial Equality (1996) *Racial Equality Means Equality*, UK: CRE.

Department of Culture Media and Sport (1999) *PAT 10 – A Report to the Social Exclusion Unit*, London: DCMS.

Department of the Environment (1989) *Sport and Active Recreation Provision in the Inner Cities*; Report of the Minister for Sport's Review Group, London: DOE.

Desai, M. (1995) *Equality*, London: LSE.

Edwards, J. (1990) 'What purpose does equality of opportunity serve?', *New Community*, 7(1): 19–35.

Ellis, J. (1994) 'Developing sport through CCT', *Recreation*, 53(9): 31–3.

English Cricket Board (1999) *Clean Bowl Racism: a report on racial equality in cricket*, London: ECB.

Equal Opportunities Commission (1997) *Mainstreaming Gender Equality in Local Government*, UK: EOC.

Escott, K. (1996) *Equal Opportunities Strategy for CCT*, UK: Centre for Public Services.

Etzioni, A. (1961) *A Comparative Analysis of Complex Organisations*, New York: Free Press.

Gibbon, P. (1989) *Equal Opportunities in Sheffield: Policies and Outcomes*, Department of Employment and Economic Development and the Race Equality Unit, Sheffield City Council.

Giddens, A. (1997) *Sociology*, Cambridge: Polity Press.

Haralambos, M. and Holborn, M. (1995) *Sociology: Themes and Perspectives*, London: Collins.

Hargreaves, J. (1986) *Sport Power and Culture*, New York: St Martin's Press.

Hargreaves, J. (1994) *Sporting Females*, London: Routledge.

Horne, J. (1995) 'Local Authority Black and Ethnic Minority Provision in Scotland', in S. Fleming, M. Talbot and A. Tomlinson (eds), *Policy and Politics in Sport, Physical Education and Leisure* (LSA Publications No. 55). Eastbourne: Leisure Studies Association

Hylton, K. (1998) 'Equal opportunities and the sports policy process, paper presented at the Sport in the City Conference, Sheffield Hallam University.

Jewson, N. and Mason, D. (1986) '"Race" employment and equal opportunities: towards a political economy and an agenda for the 1990s', *Sociological Review*, 42(4): 307–34.

Kew, F. (1997) *Sport Social Problems and Issues*, Oxford: Pergamon Open Learning.

Kirklees MBC (1997) 'Young people and sport policy', in *Kirklees the Vision.*

LeGrand, J. (1991) *Equity and Choice*, London: HarperCollins Academic.

Loy, W., Kenyon, G., McPherson, B. (1981) *Sport Culture and Society*, Philadelphia: Lea & Fabiser.

McDonald, I. (1998) *Anyone for Cricket?*, UK: University of East London.

Mintel (1997) *Leisure Trends – Market Factors and Trends* (January), downloaded on 16/7/99 from http://www.mintel.co.uk

Mintel (1998) *Profile of Type of Class* by Mintel's Special Groups, downloaded on 16/7/99 from http://www.mintel.co.uk

Mithaug, D. (1996) *Equal Opportunity Theory*, London: Sage.

Moore, S. (1993) *Social Welfare Alive,* London: Stanley Thornes.

Rail, G. (1998) *Sport and Postmodern Times*, USA: State University of New York Press.

Rawls, J. (1971) *A Theory of Justice*, Oxford: Oxford University Press.

Sport England (1999) *The Value of Sport: Executive Summary*, London: Keldia Printing Company.

Sports Council (1993) *Compulsory Competitive Tendering Sport and Leisure Management: National Information Survey Report*, London: Sports Council.

Sports Council (1994) *The Brighton Declaration,* London: Sports Council.

Taylor, G. (1994) *Equal Opportunities*, London: The Industrial Society.

Young, K. and Connolly, N. (1984) 'After the Act: Local Authorities' Policy Reviews Under the Race Relations Act 1976', *Local Government Studies*, 10(1): 13–25.

Chapter 5

Community Sports Development

Kevin Hylton and Mick Totten

Introduction

Community Sports Development is a form of practice that conveys a philosophy and spirit which addresses many of the themes raised in Chapter 4. It arose as a response to concerns about issues around equal opportunities and participation in sports. An understanding of the precise meaning of Community Sports Development (hereafter most often referred to as CSD) will be progressively developed throughout this chapter, but an initial glimpse would acknowledge that CSD is a form of provision which addresses social concerns about the nature and extent of inequality. Its history is also referred to in the following pages, so other than pinpointing its genesis as being concurrent with the development of 'Sport for All' in the early 1970s, that too will be passed over for now.

This chapter aims to analyse the theory, policy and practice of CSD. Significant tensions and issues in CSD will be discussed and delivery models ranging from top-down to bottom-up will be considered. The chapter will also view CSD from social, cultural and political perspectives. Theoretical concerns about policy, process and practice will be illustrated throughout by reference to specific case studies.

The following analysis commences with an exploration of key concepts and issues such as sports development, community development and 'community' itself. It then examines the complexity of the different sectors, levels, and partnerships inherent in CSD Provision. Next, CSD Policy is considered with a historical overview of the development of community sports policy leading to its contemporary context. Analysis will then shift to a more macroscopic view of different policy models and their rationale. These will be contextualised in the light of a case study of Action Sport in Leeds. CSD Practice is then critically analysed against the policy backdrop in the light of two further case studies of practice; the Bradford Sports Web project and the Leeds Sporting Communities Unit. At that juncture CSD will then be reconsidered to accommodate the diverse conceptual dynamics of discussion raised in the chapter. The social theory of hegemony will be used to aid this analysis. In so doing a holistic and more coherent concept of CSD will be offered.

CONCEPTUALISING COMMUNITY SPORTS DEVELOPMENT

Community sport is often subsumed under the title of community recreation. This is in recognition that practice often reflects quite inclusive informal activities which blur the boundary between sport and recreation, and some which on first glance seem hardly to constitute sport at all. Community sport is provided through many different types of organisation. It is not solely the preserve of local authority leisure services or of sports development officers. It is mostly located in the public sector, often also in the voluntary sector, but seldom in the commercial sector. It is practised in youth and community work, social services, probation services, schools, and many other realms as well. Community sport originally arose out of the realisation that traditional participation patterns were dominated by advantaged sections of the population and that an alternative approach was needed. In attempting to conceptualise community sport, it must be understood that it can be described as a contested concept (Haywood, 1994; Lentell, 1994; MacDonald, 1995; Coalter and Allison, 1996) In this sense it could be said to have multiple meanings. Due to organisational contexts, politics and changes in terminology over time, 'community sport' is interpreted by different bodies and individuals, in different ways.

To complicate matters further, there are often instances where it is claimed that community sport is being practised when in fact it is not. It could be argued that certain agencies have 'hijacked' the prefix 'community' as a flag of convenience because of its perceived feel-good value, and therefore currency with policy makers (Butcher, 1993: 3). This has variously been described as using community as 'a fashionable label with virtually no recognition that a particular set of practices and values is implied' (Haywood, 1994: 27) and as 'often sprayed on purely to lend legitimacy and positive feelings, credence and acceptability' (Plant et al., 1980). Many of the most senior providers nationally and locally are prone to such accusation. In order to progress for the time being, community sport will be referred to as a form of intervention in sport and recreation provision which in some way addresses inequalities inherent in more established, mainstream, sports provision.

Sport, development and community

The term sports development (also taken to include more informal aspects like recreation) dictates that something is indeed being developed. This implies either some form of professional intervention or localised voluntary action. Various models have been developed to characterise the nature and intent of these interventions. Chapter 1 illustrated various sports development continua. What each of these continua share is a distinction in type or levels of development within sport. They further imply a hierarchical progression through these levels from participation towards performance and excellence, so the primary focus of development is very much specific, established sports. However *Community Sport Development is not solely concerned with the development of sport*. It is not simply 'sport *in* the community'. It also encompasses the realm of 'community development'. Therefore an alternative continuum can be drawn upon (see Figure 5.1).

As this Community Sports Development continuum implies, different aspects of practice can be located with different degrees of emphasis at different points on the continuum. At one extreme is pure 'sport' development, or 'sport *in* the community', where the practice of sport is an end in itself. Here practice does not stray beyond the primary focus of participation in sports, as sports development beyond participation is best catered for by other mainstream agencies. At the other extreme is sport as 'community development' where sport is simply a means to a human development end. Accusations of the use of the term community as a flag of convenience are mainly aimed at initiatives and organisations that fall into the left-hand side of the spectrum, Sport Development. Haywood and Kew (1989) are critical of sport in the community. They describe it as 'old wine in new bottles'. It is the same 'sport' as practised in the mainstream, but repackaged. Community sport implies a much more fundamental adaptation or change of approach and practice. So what does it mean when sport engages in elements of community development? A further examination of what is meant by the terms 'community' and 'community development' is where we now turn.

Community

The term community, like community sports development, is also contested and can be interpreted to have multiple meanings. Community implies some notion of collectivity, commonality, a sense of belonging, or of something shared. A community can be self-determined by its members, or it can be a label externally constructed and defined by some statutory agency. Either way, community can be imagined as much as it can be 'realised'. It

---

Sports Development ⟺ Participation ⟺ Community Development

Figure 5.1 Community Sports Development continuum.

can be 'inhabited, as 'place', a specific locality, or a geographically defined area. It can be an 'experience', through a gathering, an interest, or affiliation to a social, leisure or sports activity. It can also be experienced as a shared 'identity', history or nostalgia, or as an action when engaged in some form of interactive process. It can be 'protective' of a way of being, or 'expansive' in terms of some aspiration (Butcher, 1993; Popple, 1995; Chaskin, 1997; Popple and Shaw, 1997).

The analysis of community by place, or locality, is diminishing in the eyes of many academics as society and social relationships transcend locality due to increased mobility. But this deterministic model traditionally, and still, courts more favour from CSD policy makers and is in greater evidence in working practice. In this approach the state has traditionally taken a leading role in identifying disadvantaged communities and in targeting groups of disenfranchised people. This also links with notions of community as shared identity. This deterministic concept of community has connotations of working-class, shared experiences, and the inner city. The inner city itself is further characterised by special social needs, high unemployment, high density, poor quality housing, social disadvantage, and concentrations of marginalised groups. Community and community development are of course neither exclusively urban nor exclusively working class, but these are the dominant images.

Community development

Community development can be viewed on a developmental scale based upon a level of intervention. This scale ranges between the external imposition and the internal formulation of community action. The external is a top-down deterministic model of intervention like the initial, nationally driven, Action Sport initiative (Rigg, 1986). The internal is a bottom-up interactive model of intervention, through community self-help mutually organised with enabling agents or professionals. The Bradford Sports Web project (see Case Study 1) is an example of that approach. There is a whole spectrum of positions between those two extremes (Arnstein, 1969; Torkildsen, 1992; Haywood, 1994). Any individual initiative can be interpreted as located at a given point on that spectrum. But all initiatives will ultimately place more emphasis on one of the two extremes. The concept of community as a process, or dynamic, and its incorporation into forms of community sports provision is suggestive of an interventionist direction towards community development:

> Community development is about involving the people themselves in the context of the community's overall needs and developing responses for themselves. It is not simply the delivery of services to the community . . . (it) can empower local people to take an active part in

defining both needs and solutions . . . (engaging) local people directly in dialogue and partnership.

(AMA, 1989: 8, 11)

A good example of community sports practice is the Action Sport project. It was originally implemented nationally, but in this chapter reference will largely be confined to research on the project based in Leeds (Totten, 1993), unless otherwise indicated. When Action Sport workers were asked how much their work was community work as opposed to sports work, they saw a very large and significant part of their work as being community work. In balance, they saw sports work as fractionally dominant, though one worker described community sport (conceptually) as a part of community work. All concerned concluded there was a lot of overlap. It has been said that outreach community sports leaders need to possess counselling skills in greater measure than sporting skills (DOE, 1989). Community sport is recognised as a valuable tool with which to pursue community or socio-cultural development (AMA, 1989, Coalter and Allison, 1996).

COMMUNITY SPORTS DEVELOPMENT PROVISION

CSD provision operates at different levels: local, regional, national, and even transnational. The lens that is taken to view CSD must also take into account the different economies of scale, tensions, organisational and personal demands that the different levels must impose on any CSD organisation:

Transnational CSD

Transnational refers to organisations and processes which occur across, or beyond, national boundaries. The clearest example of this for CSD is the increasing influence of the European Commission (EC) on policy and practice. This is especially true in relation to the funding of projects and initiatives. For example, EC funding work with priority initiative areas often ties in with areas that have been identified in the UK as areas of social and economic deprivation. Therefore the EC funding in some settings for CSD can be seen as the difference between failure or success.

National CSD

Nationally, the Department of Culture Media and Sport (DCMS), the Department of Education, and the Department of the Environment, are the three government departments mainly involved in setting influential policy direction for CSD. Further Sports Action Zones (SAZ) have concentrated government support for CSD activity in under-resourced or disadvantaged areas. The impact of the DCMS on sport in particular through the 'Active Sports' framework (which includes the 'Active Communities' initiative) is crucial in understanding the range of influences on CSD in the UK.

National Governing Bodies (NGBs) and quangos also have a major influence on sport in the UK. There are approximately 112 sports recognised by Sport England and nearly 400 NGBs ranging from the All England Netball Association to the forum for NGBs; the Central Council of Physical Recreation (CCPR). This gives an indication of a significant part of the policy community that make and affect CSD policy at all levels.

Regional CSD

Governing bodies and quangos tend to set policy at a national level; however, specific policy implementation strategies mainly occur regionally. The National Coaching Foundation (NCF) serves coaches and recreation consortia such as the Yorkshire and Humberside Federation of Sport and Recreation which co-ordinates work at a regional level. They are also examples of organisations that operate at different levels.

Local CSD

Ultimately CSD is delivered at a local level often in a specific geographical area. At this point there are greater differences in delivery as CSD focuses, and sets priorities, to support specific local needs. Policy may have trickled down from organisations working at 'higher' levels, but practice and micro-policy has been adapted to suit those specific needs. There are also organisations and individuals who work at a purely local level like Action Sport Leeds, or a local Youth worker, or Sports Development Officer.

Levels of provision

The different levels of provision can be plotted as a continuum as shown in Figure 5.2. Different organisations can then in turn be plotted on the continuum as shown. From their own knowledge the reader might consider where other organisations would be plotted.

The mixed economy of provision

Another important aspect of the analysis of CSD policy is that it occurs in all three sectors of the economy: Private, Public and Voluntary. Some organisations operate exclusively in a single sector. Figure 5.3 incorporates the three sectors of provision as well as levels of provision. Five organisations from specific sectors are shown. Once again the reader might consider where other organisations would be plotted.

Figure 5.2 Levels of provision continuum.

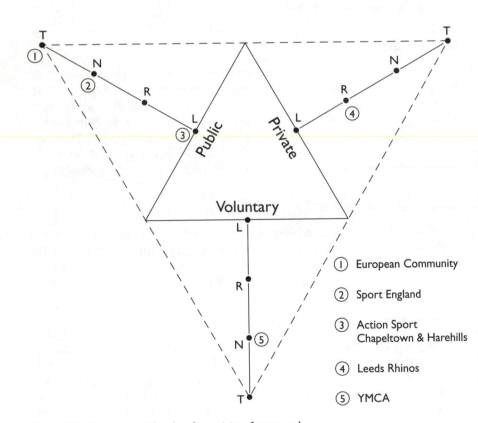

Figure 5.3 Sectors and levels of provision framework.

Partnerships

Increasingly, specific initiatives involve partnerships and incorporate involvement from organisations from different sectors. A hypothetical initiative, 'X', with an equal involvement from all three sectors is shown in Figure 5.4. The hypothetical initiative is placed at the centre of the diagram. An initiative with more emphasis from one sector would be placed closer to that particular axis. Another hypothetical initiative, 'Y', is placed to demonstrate stronger involvement from the public and voluntary sectors, with only partial involvement implied from the private sector.

Structure and organisation of provision

An ideal model should be able to incorporate elements of each of the previous diagrams. Such a model would enable a vigorous analysis of the structure of CSD policy provision, and enable comparative analyses of organisations, initiatives, and partnerships. Such a model, is shown in Figure 5.5.

To follow the matrix the reader should recognise that a pyramid has been assembled from the previous diagrams. An appropriate metaphor would be 'Origami'. Imagine the base of the pyramid is the 'Partnership domain of the mixed economy of provision' diagram (Fig. 5.4), which can also be seen as the central triangle in the 'Sectors and levels of provision framework' (Fig. 5.3). Next the outer triangles of the 'Sectors and levels of provision framework' are folded up to form a pyramid. And finally, the 'Levels of provision framework' appears as a supporting internal column in the centre of the pyramid.

As technology develops the reader might have access to this model through virtual reality. They could explore the matrix as though they were excavating

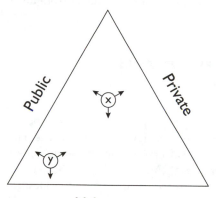

Voluntary

Figure 5.4 Partnership domain of the mixed economy of provision.

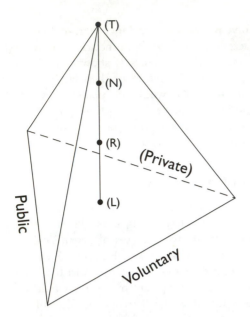

Figure 5.5 Structural dimensions of provision matrix.

one of the ancient pyramids! Different CSD organisations and initiatives could be understood, or located, at different points, and levels, in three dimensions. The matrix offers a holistic, all round, way of understanding each of the previously discussed elements of structure, provision, and policy. So, despite the limitations of two dimensions, it is perhaps worth while to dwell and consider where further analysis would locate initiatives from areas not considered here.

COMMUNITY SPORTS DEVELOPMENT POLICY

Historical overview

Community Sports Development is a practice, a policy direction, and in particular a philosophy of provision, which has developed since the late 1970s and early 1980s. It is now maturing after years in the early 1990s where news of its passing had been premature! (MacDonald, 1995; Lentell, 1994). CSD occurs in a number of diverse settings and contexts. Despite political shifts, which resulted in macro policy trends and which made CSD policy seem less fashionable in some quarters, continuity existed elsewhere. In darker times the CSD torch was often carried by other non-sports specific practitioners, like youth workers, or by specific sports initiatives at a very local level. The idea that CSD occurs only in local government sport and recreation departments is an error that is easy to make as the most prominent face of CSD is local and often in that context; however, this is a narrow view of CSD: there is a need to sketch a bigger picture for practitioners and students alike. Awareness of the way people and organisations work in this network is often how good practice gets communicated. In some cases these links might seem as though they have cut across unconnected parts of the service sector, when in reality there is much more in common than at first glance.

Community sports development grew out of the roots of post-1975 Howell *angst* which was critical of the massive local authority and Sports Council led facility build-up in the country which was to the detriment of the personal 'community' provision. 'People not bricks' was an ideal which came through quite clearly in London where it transpired that the major users of the Brixton Sport Centre were mainly white, middle class males from outside the area. Many of the local community felt the centre unwelcoming and not a facility that they could identify with (Murray, 1988).

Lessons like those learnt in Brixton were occurring all over the UK. However, it took a dramatic series of events culminating in severe social disturbances and a reaction from the government before massive resources were poured into what many practitioners saw as the first recognisable community sports projects. It was no coincidence either that young people were 'targeted' in the rush to reduce actual and perceived threats of crime and anti-social behaviour. Ironically, a closer look at the areas affected by the disturbances showed that they were, in reality, deprived of most social welfare services. The Midlands and London were set up as areas for the pilot projects of Action Sport to see if there was a way for sport to defuse the inner city areas which were the scenes of civil unrest in the early 1980s.

At this time, the use of focusing on target groups came to prominence, although for practitioners involved in good practice this was no surprise. Young people, the unemployed, women, black and other ethnic groups, disabled people, and the elderly were targeted in a combination of partnerships between local government and central government which has rarely been seen since.

The success of the pilots was such that they became national projects wherever partnerships like those with Action Sport could be formed. Indeed, evaluations of Action Sport nationally and regionally were very positive (MacIntosh and Charlton, 1985a; Rigg, 1986). Overall they were unanimous in saying that the skills of the leaders, and techniques used such as outreach and active consultation, meant that they were the most successful way of identifying low and non-participants to encourage their participation.

National Demonstrations projects built on the success of the Action Sport and Community Recreation initiatives. Target groups were strategically mapped on to each initiative in an effort to reproduce the success of these projects in different contexts. The Coventry Active Lifestyles project, the Solent Sports Counselling initiative and the Scunthorpe Black and Ethnic Minority project are three examples of the evolution of CSD policy, process and practice in recent years (Sports Council Research Unit, 1991).

Contemporary policy

CSD was initially seen as a challenge to traditional ways of approaching provision for disadvantaged groups, almost a counter culture. The change in emphasis from facility based sport to community oriented sport and recreation was shown to be effective and most of the partners took on board these ideas and either mainstreamed their projects, or the project philosophy, in their more established units. Consequently, in recent times the demarcation between the established and, what was the emergent way of providing sport and recreation opportunities for most priority groups in society, is much less clear. In reality these days the use of the term 'community sports' is almost as generally used as the term 'community' in other areas as it invokes positive images of considerate client oriented practice.

The public, private and voluntary sectors all have an input into the path that CSD takes. Voluntary groups, clubs and societies are often the independent face of community sports development. The scale of voluntary sector organisations is such that they range from small local organisations such as the new 'Little London Baseball Club' to national/internationally linked organisations such as the YMCA and YWCA. The voluntary clubs provide a safety net for people who engage in activities which tend to be niche oriented. This often means that the private sector does not see a profitable market there or the public sector cannot provide a rationale for fully supporting those activities.

Private sector CSD is often a more extrinsically driven affair where organisations such as professional football and rugby clubs work with schools, and other breeding grounds for talent identification, talent development, income generation and public relations. Some clubs have, in addition, also established community units as charities which then allows them to draw on the concessions and economies that this mode of operating affords to its owners. For example, Leeds Rhinos RL have used their community links to promote an anti-racist message through rugby. Links with 'communities' for professional clubs have been successful in forging close relationships and can also be seen as effective marketing opportunities.

The public sector, where most CSD work occurs, is often actively implemented at a regional, and in particular at local level. Still, the range of interested parties is diverse. Sport and recreation from a sport specific view, but with a complementary social policy focus may emanate from youth work, community work, housing, the police, sports and recreation departments, arts workers, education, the health services and other related organisations. (Discussions on the value of partnerships intra- and inter-sectorally are developed in Chapter 6.)

Models of community sports development policy

The overwhelming majority of community sports initiatives have been funded by the state. This has been directly from central government, indirectly through the leisure quangos, and most often from local government. The former Sports Council has played a role as a lead body developing policies and directing provision. Community sport has operated as an arm of the Sports Council's aim of 'Sport for all' (Hargreaves, 1986). But community sports provision has seldom been funded for its own ends and has been legitimated for more instrumental reasons (Glyptis, 1989). Sport has been viewed largely from the standpoint of the social function it fulfils (Council of Europe 1971), and, as such, is as much a part of 'social policy' as it is of 'sports policy' (DOE 1989, PAT 10, 1999). Nationally, Action Sport has been a demonstrative project showing the legitimate role sport can play in urban regeneration by 'super-concentration' on a few streets (Glyptis, 1989). This social agenda for community sports has already been well documented (Sports Council, 1982; MacIntosh and Charlton, 1985b; DOE, 1989; Haywood and Kew, 1989; Yorkshire and Humberside Council for Sport and Recreation, 1989).

As has already been discussed, Community Sports Development can be understood as a form of 'socio-cultural' intervention. Different policy models have characterised this intervention. Subsequently four models will be explored; two 'social' models which illustrate the 'instrumental' use of sport; Social Control, and Social Welfare, and two 'cultural' models which illustrate attempts to extend the participatory franchise: Democratisation of Culture, and Cultural Democracy. A fifth 'political' model, which characterises the political motivations of some practitioners, will also be explored: Radicalism. Once again, the previous case study of Action Sport, Leeds, will be used to contextualise theory. It is not the intention for these models to be contrasted against one another exclusively, but for them to be seen as operating simultaneously, and to varying degrees of influence. In this respect they reinforce the notion of CSD as a 'site of cultural and hegemonic struggle' (Hargreaves, 1982; Hargreaves, 1986) rather than as a static consensus (hegemony will be discussed in detail later). The state is able to form a coalition of support for its policies and unite diverse interests behind a dominant project. This approach offers an 'economy of remedies'; a single solution to a variety of issues, within one policy, and with a broad base of support (Coalter *et al.*, 1986: 92).

Social control

Social control is performed by the state directly and indirectly, manifestly and institutionally. The state intervenes directly to legislate for and against particular leisure forms. Sport is used explicitly as a form of social control. The Sports Council (1982: 3) openly believes, 'Kids in sport don't throw bricks'. It could be said that this philosophy continues within the Bradford Sports Web project. Research reveals that the sports player tends to be conformist in nature (MacIntosh and Charlton, 1985b; Coalter, 1991). The police have taken an open interest in involvement in community sport (Haywood, 1983). So much so that Carrington and Leaman (1983: 10) state; 'Community policing and community sport would appear to share an identical logic and perform an identical ideological function'. Sport is used as surrogate violence, channelling aggression into a socially acceptable activity. Hargreaves (1986) describes how community sport defines various categories of potential user; but it is clear that the main concern is the 'potentially troublesome'. Hargreaves goes on to describe how a cadre of sports leaders are developed, who are 'co-cultural' with users, to enable infiltration and the exercising of influence by the dominant culture.

The salient impetus for Action Sport, nationally, has been a response to the urban riots of the 1980s (Totten, 1993). The Action Sport workers from the inner city of Leeds were overwhelmingly in agreement that they owed their existence to the fact that there had been riots there. One worker commented ironically that if there was another riot their budget would be doubled and applied the following metaphor: 'We act a little like community policemen. . . . We walk the beat. We go back to our station house and fill in our forms'. Another worker said he felt responsible to motivate people to get a job. Yet another said that because Chapeltown (in the inner city) is known as a racially 'black' area, politicians were responding in an institutionally racist way; by providing community sport *because* they were 'black'! Despite being overwhelmingly aware of their use as a potential instrument of social control, Action Sport workers were uncomfortable with this and recognised their own ability for resistance and to carry out their own objectives: 'We're not just a bunch of "jolly non-whites" doing the bidding of faceless bureaucrats!'. One also pointed out that drug pushers went back to their trade after doing their sport, a rather morbid failure of control over agency. Despite the fact that Action Sport workers were insistent that they promoted sport purely for fun, one worker observed that 'we may have far less freedom than we think'. Conscious of the controlling role of the state, and the role of Action Sport in that process, he commented that for community sport in the social context of the community as a whole: 'There are certain ways of behaving and attitudes towards people that have to be fostered, that are of paramount importance to the survival of the community, survival of the people.'

Social welfare

Sport England has always sought to integrate sport and social policy and much attention has been drawn to the importance of community sport as a form of social welfare (Lentell, 1994). Bernard Atha, when Vice-Chairman of the Sports Council (1978: 14) stated:

> Deprivation takes place in many forms – social, educational, cultural, housing, emotional, and recreational to mention just a few. This deprivation exists at great cost to our society, a cost most easily seen in terms of crime and vandalism, but more serious in terms of loneliness and alienation.

In this mood, Glyptis (1989) points out that the 1975 *White Paper on Sport and Recreation* (HMSO, 1975) heralded a shift from policies of 'recreational welfare' to the use of 'recreation *as* welfare'. Denis Howell (cited in Coalter *et al.* (1986), when Minister of Sport) declared that without a social purpose; sport would be irrelevant. The Association of Metropolitan Authorities (1989) viewed community sports as vital to community development. And at the start of a new millennium, nothing much has changed as Chris Smith (1998), Secretary of State for Culture, Media and Sport, stated that:

> Sport offers direct economic benefits. It contributes to the regeneration of towns and cities, improving health, productivity and quality of life. It contributes to savings in the cost of health care and leads to a reduction in crime and vandalism. It offers local environmental benefits that can change the image of a city or community and lead to increased inward investment.

Action Sport workers paid great attention to the value of their work in terms of social welfare and the contribution it could make to the quality of life of their users (Totten, 1993). Workers described how people gained a sense of achievement and self-determination which they could apply to other areas of their lives. People were able to enjoy themselves, to self-actualise and increase their feeling of self-worth. Action Sport workers agreed that they were facilitating people's rights to the opportunity to participate. Community sports initiatives certainly have the potential to bring about change in people's lives, but individual projects are more likely to stimulate personal change than effect any structural change.

Democratisation of culture

The democratisation of culture model is most commonly talked of in relation to community arts, but it can equally be applied to community sports. The concept of the democratisation of culture presumes that there is a single national culture. This culture though not fully appreciated, understood or participated in by large sections of the population can be spread from the top downwards. This process can be described as the demystification, or clarification, of the value of participation. Sport is promoted as a source of national pride. Community sport can act as a tool to overcome social barriers and demystify through participation. Some community sports initiatives are premised on the idea that the community is a homogenous entity and aim to integrate those unattached into participation (Hargreaves, 1986). By extending the franchise to participation through CSD and its 'soft' integration into sport, the then enlightened participant can cultivate the sports habit. Their continued participation might then lead them towards mainstream provision, which propagates the dominant culture through institutionalised sport. This would appear to reinforce the old wine in new bottles argument (Haywood and Kew, 1989).

Two workers felt that Action Sport could be a 'stepping stone' or 'foundation' towards integration into mainstream sport (Totten, 1993). Another example would be the way that Sport England gives preferential treatment towards approving 'certain' sports for funding like the Outdoor Basketball Initiative. In macro-policy terms, this has the overall effect of lending greater legitimacy to some forms of activity than to others.

Cultural democracy

The model of cultural democracy is, in part, a critique of the democratisation of culture which is seen as a paternalistic and elitist idea (Simpson, 1976a; Parry, 1986). The democratisation of culture can thus become, 'a foredoomed and wasteful effort to graft an alien culture onto tissue where it cannot thrive' (Simpson, 1976b: 50). Cultural democracy describes a more fundamental challenge to the means provision. It interprets provision as going beyond the consumption of traditional institutionalised forms of sport. It also advocates a devolution of power away from centralised agencies and back to the people. It argues for a plurality of access to the means of provision, and against passive consumption. Cultural democracy supports the finding of the 'Leisure and the quality of life experiments' (DOE, 1977: 161) that, 'The lessons of the experiments may be that a true community applies its development opportunities across the whole spectrum of interest groups rather than in trying to provide a homogenised mass leisure'. It is in recognition of the specialised needs of sub-cultures and sub-groups that a cultural democracy is proposed. It calls for a decentralised and more democratic and representative structure of sport and leisure management, allowing for effective participation in decision-making by the community (DOE, 1989). Devolved strategies promote 'ownership' by, and 'co-authorship' with, the community. Outreach sports leaders and animators have gone out into the community to assess needs and demand. Cultural democracy, so far, has largely been more a proactive than a reactive pursuit (Yorkshire and Humberside Council for Sport and Recreation, 1989). Simpson (1976a: 66) believes a proactive stimulus has been needed because, 'A stimulus of this kind seldom arises spontaneously in modern urban or even rural societies, and it has to be contrived as something additional to the normal circumstances of everyday life'.

Action Sport workers described how they have provided an 'organisational framework' for the community and have employed animation techniques to give people 'the drive to get up and go', a 'sort of injection' (Totten, 1993). One worker described Action Sport as being like a 'Local Sports Council'. Workers were critical of the notion of a homogenous national culture and of policy which is over-prescriptive. A worker pointed out that integration could be oppressive for groups like Asian women who could see it as infringing on their rights to their beliefs: 'People should be aware of others' cultural needs. If people were aware of those differences it helps, not just sport, but many other things as well'. Workers described how, over time, the project has become much more community-led. 'Representation' has been valued, particularly in relation to ethnicity and gender, and has been promoted in appointments, decision-making, programme planning, and activity leading. In this way the project strives to remain 'co-cultural' with its community.

Radicalism

In contrast to the four previously state-sanctioned models of community leisure, radicalism represents an intervention in the community which is politicised *against*, rather than on behalf of, the state. Whereas cultural democracy represents a challenge to cultural values, radicalism represents a challenge to social values. Radical cultural agendas in this country have mainly been carried out by small groups or individuals. Perhaps the only significant attempt to implement a radical cultural agenda by the state was that of the Greater London Council between 1981 and 1986 (Bianchinni, 1989). This was cultural action by the local state against the national state. Baldry (1976) and Simpson (1976a) have both described a certain inevitability that cultural programmes concerned with community development and concepts of change can become political programmes. There is a history of radicalism in the community arts which is not equalled by the history of community sports (Kelly, 1984). This does not mean that there is not a potential for radical action in community sports. These activists exist in CSD, but their profiles are predominantly covert. Sport does not share the historical tradition of protest that the Arts do. Many still believe 'Sport and Politics don't mix'. So activists in CSD may jeopardise their longevity if they raise their heads too high above the parapet. For many it is about 'infiltration and subversion' rather than revealing their true colours. So for a theoretical framework from which to view radicalism it is more profitable to consider community arts.

Kelly (1984) maintains that the role of community arts is to 'topple capitalism'. Kelly advises that community artists should explore alternative modes of cultural production, distribution and reception, and have a clear analysis of their work as part of a revolutionary programme committed to cultural democracy:

> Storm the citadels, and tear them down brick by brick; to demolish the oppressive and imperialist structures and to build in their place a series of smaller haciendas where activity and participation are encouraged and welcomed, and the only activity which is prohibited is the building of citadels.
>
> (Kelly, 1984: 138)

Kelly's analogy applied to sport would imply a programme of infiltration by workers with political motivations, and subversion by those workers and participants against the dominant institutional culture within sport. Examples would include: Marxists committed to the re-distribution of sporting resources towards the working class, Feminists committed to working with women towards challenging the prevailing gender order in sport, and also Black Activists committed to the advancement of Black culture, representation, and countering racism in sport.

Action Sport workers did not fully see what they were doing as being radical despite the fact that its community led approach could be described as a radical departure from mainstream provision (Totten, 1993). One worker did see himself as 'infiltrating' with an agenda to change. He was conscious of his ability to resist and interpret 'top-down' policy and carry out his own mission saying, 'the bosses don't visit the coal face'. At a later interview he corrected, 'it's not radical at all. It's very liberal'. He went on to say that there was a potential for radicalism but it can't be made public! He described using 'dual language' as 'one for bureaucrats and one for practitioners'. Action Sport illustrates a potential for opposition to the dominant hegemonic order, but also highlights the difficulties of resisting assimilation, or even marginalisation or expulsion.

COMMUNITY SPORTS PRACTICE

CSD is characterised by its approach to service delivery and practice. CSD is a movement away from mainstream, or dominant, sports provision with their focus on performance and excellence, and historical failure to reach all. CSD is focused at the initial threshold to participation. CSD is a reaction against elitism and inequality, and is person or community centred. There is a recognition of the structural barriers to participation discussed in Chapter 4. Access and inclusion are promoted. Disadvantaged groups are identified, and prioritised or 'targeted'. Haywood and Kew (1989) emphasise the flexible, proactive style and process of community sport. Community sport is more 'empathetic' and focuses more on the participant and the participatory process. As such, sport is often merely a means towards these developmental aims. Consultation is valued to determine, and be responsive to, expressed needs and wants, and so to extend the 'participatory franchise'. In that sense Community Sports tends to adopt a distinct, less formal more flexible, management style. It is a movement away from 'top-down', deterministic models of provision towards 'bottom-up' community led provision. Decision-making is more devolved to enable community participation in that decision-making process. In that sense the community and provider may become co-authors of destiny, or partners in policy and practice. In the main, community sport workers attempt to empower through advocacy, facilitation and enablement.

Action Sport conforms fairly comfortably with this common understanding of community sport (Totten, 1993). It promotes a sense of informality and a feeling of ownership amongst its participants: 'We try to cater for people on their own terms'. Action Sport started offering mainstream activities, but left space and has successfully provided for other activities like 'chairobics' and kabbadi. Action Sport is about enjoyment. That is stressed repeatedly as the bottom line. Workers were critical of 'serious' participation. They described how Action Sport brings people together, contributing, in a general sense, to community spirit (although it was pointed out that competing concepts of 'community' were not discussed). Workers saw Action Sport as promoting socialising and interaction, and making people happier. Action Sport is concerned with the development process from start to finish although participation is the most important thing as ultimately that determined if people came back again. The basis of Action Sport is social and the consultation process is important in developing the sense of ownership. Action Sport provides an organisational framework sometimes lacking in a local community. It emphasises an initial pitch of low ability requirements as the threshold to participation. Any ability fostered towards excellence is channelled towards other forms of provision. Through its outreach work, Action Sport bridges the gap in participation between people and facilities, which are predominantly local and may be unconventional. The challenge for CSD is to promote its philosophy that participation in sport and recreation is positive, and to extend the participatory franchise within the local community.

Bradford Sports Web

The Bradford Sports Web initiative gives a picture of a CSD context which can be considered in the light of the previous 'Structure and organisation of provision matrix'. The partners involved are:

Public Sector: the Department of the Environment through SRB funding, Bradford CC's Sport and Recreation Division Sports Development section, as well as the Education Department's Youth and Community Youth Sports Development Project, and the West Yorkshire Police linked to the diversionary 'Dynamo Project'.

Voluntary Sector: the Manningham area community.

Further, the *Levels* of involvement could be explained using the idea of the project's complementary social function where a key objective is that of social regeneration and inclusion. The issues of social regeneration through sport is an ideal which has come through the sports policy community strongly from the **Transnational** European Community especially through European Social Funding. **Nationally** a key policy influence, in this case study, has come via the government's social exclusion policies and **Regionally** through West Yorkshire Police's inclusion in the **Local** (Bradford) Sports Web project.

So, the Bradford Sports Web can be contextualised as a local community sports development project with local, regional and national partners, mainly, in the public and voluntary sectors. Similarly, influences for the project could be logically traced back to the EC.

CSD has been subject to pointed questions for many years concerning the utilitarian way in which key agents approach provision. Questions which suggest that CSD engages in *ad hoc* and piecemeal provision might be given some credence here where the objective of working towards 'social regeneration' through one project in an area of high social and economic deprivation would seem beyond their sole responsibility. In addition to this, diversionary projects are regularly asked to prove how they have enhanced the capacity for young people to move away from crime or local trouble. This has often been seen to be very difficult for most!

Community sports development for the Senior Outdoor Development Manager in Bradford's Sports Web is about empowering the community to take control of their own needs (see the Alternative CSD Continuum p. 68). This is done by training them to run activities for themselves or at the very least to develop a healthy lifestyle as a result of contact with the project. The notion of redistributing power and quality of life benefits is an important aspect of community development which sometimes provides the common ground for multi-agency working. Liddle (1988: 199) develops this point when giving an overview of youth and leisure services in Avon County Council.

The idea of sustainable sports programmes has come through good practice in CSD from the very first Action Sport programmes in the early 1980s.

What programmes like Action Sport failed to do, in some cases, was to make individuals and sessions independent of themselves quickly enough. This often meant that the overall input of resources needed to work towards this objective was very high and many organisations found that they could not sustain the level of commitment needed even though many successes were evident.

Case Study 1: Bradford Sports Web Project

The Bradford Sports Web Project is a partnership between the West Yorkshire Police, Bradford Recreation Service, Youth Sports Development Project and ostensibly the local Manningham Community.

Manningham is a multi-cultural area with a high minority ethnic population. The project is part of a Single Regeneration Budget (SRB) bid which focuses in on areas of disadvantage.

It is intended to use sport here as a tool for social regeneration and inclusion in what is planned to be a long-term strategy and commitment by a number of key agencies in the managing and development of sport in Bradford.

Main objectives:

To plan, deliver and develop a **sustainable programme of sport, recreational** and **diversionary activities** which is appropriate and accessible to the whole community and **delivered by the community**.

- To consult and provide support to the community (Manningham, Bradford) to ensure that their sporting needs are catered for.
- To promote new and innovative lifestyle messages within the local community.
- To encourage provision of educational and training opportunities in sport and recreation within the local community.
- To ensure equality of opportunity for everyone but particularly target young people from excluded groups.

Consultation

The project partners intend to consult local people with an overview of the project. Outcomes which include identifying local people to (a) run sessions where they have the skills, (b) be trained up where they do not have the skills or there are personal development issues.

Outreach

The Web Project plans to use the techniques of outreach working which has always been seen as effective in sports development. Outreach working in geographical areas has been seen as most successful and cost effective where local facilities, services and people are utilised as often as possible. This has the added benefit of less formal systems and pricing policies being introduced which are conducive to flexible working and positive local word-of-mouth promotion.

The Police intend to direct young people onto the programme where they have been convicted or are on probation as part of a subsidiary 'Dynamo' project. These young people will be counselled into the project as participants and, where they show potential, eventually as motivators and leaders.

Leeds Sporting Communities

In this next case study, CSD is very much local government oriented. Partners in other sectors and at different levels are drawn upon according to the specific needs of a local geographic community. CSD in this Leeds unit involves a mixture of objectives, in particular opportunities for young people across the city and black people in the inner urban areas. The scale of Sporting Communities is much larger than Bradford Sports Web, in that it is a city wide, mainstream unit, building upon the vast experience that has come out of its Sports Development Unit and Action Sport. Both have a long history of work from sports specific development to community development through sport and recreation.

Sporting Communities is influenced at all Levels and across all Sectors in diverse ways according to the setting of the activity/initiative in the city. For Example the Evans Sports Programme involved partners from the **Private Sector** (Evans) **Public Sector** (Leeds CC's Sporting Communities, and 'Sports Match'), **Voluntary Sector** (South Leeds Community). The Levels involved included **National** Sports Matching, and **Local** through the Council services and community interest.

Shared practice

The notion of 'sport' and 'recreation' is problematised in both case study organisations in Leeds and Bradford, and seems to take a wider emancipatory view of purposive leisure activity, and diversion, where young people are concerned. This generates another accusatory chorus of CSD workers being 'soft police'; indeed doing a policing job on behalf of concerned citizens and controlling the way young people behave and act. In the past providers have argued that giving people the opportunity to play sport away from their daily activity allows them to do something different in the time; however to presume that this will alleviate crime, or act as a palliative for negative social and economic conditions involves a large leap of faith! In 1977 this functional view was adopted in a Department of the Environment report on recreation and deprivation in inner urban areas and it was a message coming through clearly from the government in 1999 where community sport was being seen as a way of tackling serious social problems (Banks, 1998). Indeed Glyptis (1989) suggested that this view has been prominent in sport for a number of years when she asserted that:

> The promotion of opportunities for enjoyment has long been paralleled by a belief that recreation opportunities can help to contain urban problems, to build a sense of community, and to overcome class and other social conflicts.
>
> Glyptis (1989)

What has in fact been missing from many claims like these are the causal relationships between project aims and activities, and any significant coherent change. Chapter 4 discussed the merits of qualitative information gathering as a means of understanding the collective experiences of individuals and community members. Here information can be gathered to test ideals like active citizenship, social regeneration, social cohesion, and capacity building. CSD practitioners and policy makers who move beyond sport's reliance on quantitative measurements will have a more rounded view of the success of a project which has such ambitious objectives. These points were endorsed by the recommendations on sport and social exclusion in 1999 (PAT 10): qualitative measures were being advocated as ways to get an understanding of the impact of projects from the experience of participants and from a social impact perspective. They were seen as an essential part of the monitoring of active community initiatives.

Both of the case study organisations above espouse a bottom-up way of working or client-led delivery/facilitation. The imperative on both organisations to continually consult and work in tandem with local people is paramount. Active citizenship in each case means people in Leeds and Bradford reclaiming their access to resources for sport and recreation. It also means taking ownership of their own and other people's sport and recreation and working towards addressing quality of life and lifestyle issues in a bid to enhance social inclusion and cohesion. Is it enough to gain an understanding of this personal and social change through collecting statistical data?

Elsewhere, will measuring throughputs enable the Cleveland 'Reach for Success' basketball project claim that they have reduced levels of boredom, vandalism, peer pressure and intimidation as their aims state? The project is attempting to get 20,000 young people to play basketball in five years: will they be able to support their claims unless they use qualitative means of gathering information? The Policy Action Team (10) might argue otherwise and clearly this is a challenge for all sports development professionals to grasp (Freeman, 1999: 13).

In summary, both case studies have differing pressures on them. What is clear from the 'Structure and organisation of provision matrix' however is that when professionals discuss community sports development, there is now a clear need to clarify whether it is policy, process or practice which is the focus of the discussion. In addition, scale, context and levels are important factors in the way organisations and individuals operate in community sports development.

Case Study 2: Sporting Communities

The Sports Division in Leeds is split up into three sections:

1. Facilities (The Direct Services Organisation)
2. The Sports Development Unit (one of the biggest and most established in the country)
3. Service Development (Sporting Communities and Action Sport).

The Sporting Communities Unit in Leeds is an important part of the overall sports strategy for Leeds. The unit enhances the link between the Sports Development Unit which has a remit to develop excellence and facilities (DSO). Leeds is a city in the north of England with a diverse population of 750,000 who occupy 33 wards which have been split into seven areas of responsibility for the community sports development officers.

The seven areas range from inner urban areas to rural ex-mining villages. This range of areas and priority groups means that each development officer in each ward must be very sensitive to the demands and needs of their wards.

Main aims:

*   Inform policy and strategy development through effective community consultation (outreach/'bottom-up').
*   Co-ordinate sports information at a local level (community sports directories, help-lines).
*   Facility development planning and community needs (provide assistance with lottery bids, sports education, school to community links).

When Sporting Communities started the Development Officers spent 12–18 months solely gathering information about the 33 wards in Leeds. Development Officers were given the remit to 'know their area' so that plans and strategies would be informed in consultation with local communities and meet local needs. There was seen to be 'no quick fix' for success and it was accepted that where similar projects in the past which have almost been panicked into producing results immediately therefore not having a solid foundation for long-term developments. Sporting communities have taken on board evaluations of good and bad practice and have moved forward confident that their information and plans have a grounded rationale.

Recent work with the diverse geographical and priority groups have been:

- Village Link – A sports bus for rural villagers unable to access facilities outside of their own area.
- 'Families of Schools' combining their budgets to provide sporting opportunities for 60–80 young people outside of school hours. Taster sessions between 4 and 5.30 p.m. have enabled pupils in schools to try sports and be channelled into clubs and teams as a result.
- SPARKS project – partnership work with the West Yorkshire Playhouse to enable multi-agency access to the arts, youth service, drama, dance and sport.
- 'One Stop Shop' – a multi-agency partnership which enables local people to access information on sport, social services, education, health, and citizens advice.
- Evans' Sports Programme – A local business sponsorship 'Sportsmatched' and the budget used to provide opportunities for a local community to access sport at little or no cost.
- African-Caribbean and Asian communities sports development through information, training and direct provision.

Re-conceptualising Community Sports Development

So far this chapter has discussed key concepts and considered key dimensions to provision, policy and practice. In so doing it has revealed a complexity in attempting to pinpoint exactly what CSD is, how it works, and what it does? Having already explored some of these dynamics in passing, the following sections will endeavour to increase the depth of analysis to pull these strands together into a holistic and coherent whole. To do so it will employ the social theory of 'Hegemony' as central to the analysis of CSD.

There are various key themes, highlighted earlier, which the following analysis must take account of:

- The fact that CSD is a 'contested concept' which has sometimes been used simply as a 'flag of convenience'.
- That the policy community ranges from local to regional to national and even transnational.
- That provision is often a partnership between organisations with different motivations.
- That there is a capacity for different individuals engaged in the same work to have politically opposite motives.
- That policy and provision can be orchestrated either as top-down or bottom-up.
- That there are tensions between social welfare and social control, community empowerment and soft policing.
- That there are tensions in provision between social and cultural policy, between community development and sport development.
- And finally, that CSD is such a 'dynamic' concept that all the previous interpretations are possible!

Hegemony

Before addressing all of these key themes and issues, and launching into analysis, the concept of hegemony itself must be outlined in brief. Hegemony is a 'socio-cultural' process which also takes account of political and economic processes (Hargreaves, 1982). It is central to theorising around CSD. Hegemony implies some form of dynamic or dialogue between the provider and the community. It encompasses cultural relations between the powerful and weak (Sport England and the individual sports club), the dominant and subservient (the Local Authority SDU and the individual CSD worker). Hegemony is a 'lived system of meanings and values. . . . It thus constitutes a sense of reality for most people in society, a sense of absolute because experienced reality. It is, that is to say, in the strongest sense a "culture" which has also to be seen as the lived dominance and subordination of particular classes' (Williams, 1977: 110). As a socio-cultural process, hegemony permeates all aspects of the theory, policy and practice of CSD.

Hegemonic groups

There are different types of hegemonic groups who represent different interests in CSD and who have varying degrees of influence. Williams (1977) categorises these groups as dominant, residual and emergent. These groups in turn can be evidenced either as traditions, institutions or formations. This taxonomy is applied to CSD in Table 5.1. The exact location of various initiatives within this framework is open to some debate, but it does provide a useful starting point for the analysis of the hegemonic dynamics of policy and practice. However, a notable absentee is the community itself! This reflects the historical marginalisation of localised communities from the policy making process. The notion of hegemonic 'groups' or influences could be expanded to incorporate other aspects such as policy.

From their own knowledge of policy and practice, the reader may attempt to locate other CSD 'players' in the taxonomy shown in the table. This will enable their position to be identified in the hegemonic process, and for future analysis.

Freedom and control

CSD is a paradoxical combination of control, through state intervention and planning, and freedom, as expressed by the individual in sport, or 'at leisure'. Sport is an aspect of life over which people are believed to exercise considerable autonomy and freedom. If not, is it sport at all? This interpretation of sport as freedom is at some odds with the evidence of state planning and particularly of social control. There is an ambiguity of rights to participate in sport being provided for in co-existence with more prescriptive concerns to use sport more instrumentally. Gamble (1981); Long (1981) and Coalter (1989), have described how all leisure, including sport, operates as a dichotomy riddled with *conceptual couples*; 'liberation and control',

Table 5.1 Taxonomy of hegemonic influences in community sports development

	Dominant	Residual	Emergent
Tradition	Sport for All	CCT, Action Sport (Nationally)	Best Value, Active Sports
Institution	Department of Culture, Media and Sport, Sport England, Leeds City Council (LCC), Bradford City Council (BCC)	CCPR, NCF, Commission for Racial Equality, YWCA	Lottery Sports Fund, Bradford Sports Web, Sporting Equals
Formation	TOPS, SRB, LCC Sports Development Unit, BCC's Youth Sport Development Project	Women's Sports Foundation, NGB of Sport Disability Project, Action Sport (Local)	Active Communities, Sports Match, LCC Sporting Communities, Sports Action Zones, Little London Baseball Club

'freedom and constraint', 'the public and private sphere'. Long (1981) is satisfied that a coherent theory should be able to encompass dichotomies; so sport can be 'both a tool for community development and an opiate' which ameliorates deprivations. The sophisticated 'hegemonic state' is quite aware of this dichotomy and does not hesitate to take cunning advantage of its utility. So it aims to exercise *control* over sport, and to promote *freedom* to participate in sport at the same time!

CSD must be understood in the context of both structure and agency as described in Chapter 4. Social structures influence the social context of sport as do the discriminatory powers of individual human agents to choose their own sport. Structure and agency work with and against one another to influence outcomes. CSD is sensitised to the needs of the community as perceived by the providers, and as expressed from within the community. CSD is influenced structurally by provider organisations, like Sport England or a Local Authority SDU, and also by wider social reality, but it is flexible to adapt and respond to human agency determined from the community itself.

Hegemony accounts for those inherent contradictions, or dichotomies, apparent in the policy and practice of CSD. It acknowledges the role of both 'structure' *and* 'agency' implicit in the 'sphere of exchange' between the provider and the community (Bennett, 1981a). It reconciles the tensions between 'planning' *and* participant 'autonomy' in practice. It also describes a dialogue between 'top-down' and 'bottom up' dimensions of provision. So CSD is 'dichotomous'. It simultaneously spans different intervention policies, and so achieves an 'economy of remedies' (Coalter *et al.*, 1986). This combination of rationales demonstrates the hegemonic power of dominant groups like Sport England.

The previously cited 'models of CSD policy', four of which are most often forms of state driven intervention (Social Control, Social Welfare, Democratisation of Culture and Cultural Democracy), describe attempts by dominant cultures, manifested in institutions like Sport England and Leeds City Council, to influence the sports culture of the community. Historically, the Sports Council(s) have hardly ever legitimised sport as the carefree enjoyment which it is to most people. It has been preoccupied with externalities like the social ends, rather than the cultural meaning, of participation. Hegemony describes sport as a site for cultural struggle. This struggle takes place both independently in each of the previous intervention models, and also interactively between them. The dominant culture is contested locally by workers in the field, and by the community itself. For that reason the radical model of CSD was also cited. It can be understood as a hegemonic sub-culture oppositional to the dominant order.

This perpetual conflict is acted out in CSD between the dominant, residual and emergent cultural traditions, institutions and formations identified in the previous taxonomy. Community sport can be a concession of power by the dominant hegemonic order. This can be seen as a means towards the incorporation of other more marginalised groups into the dominant culture. This position is supported by Hargreaves (undated: 60):

> Leisure is unique in its capacity to provide surrogate satisfaction for an alienated mass audience, while at the same time perpetuating its alienation and functioning as a means of political socialisation into the hegemonic culture.

Dominance, resistance and incorporation

Hegemony describes incomplete attempts by dominant cultural groups to incorporate opposition, as well as the resistance by that opposition (Williams, 1977). CSD is sited directly in the midst of cultural struggle, whereby the dominant order, like Sport England and Leeds City Council, through projects and initiatives, like Active Communities and Sporting Communities, attempts to enfranchise dissociated sections of the population. Practitioners are conscious, at times, of being the middle-person between policy makers and the community. They are conscious of carrying out the aims set by policy makers, and yet are responsive and supportive of leadership and self-determination from within the community.

But, dominant groups do not rule society, they merely lead it. Dominant groups attempt to engage the support of others fostered around the dominant values. So Sport England 'sells' 'Active Communities' as a framework for all major providers to work within. And Leeds City Council 'buys' into that, and 'sells' 'Sporting Communities' to its own, more localised, co-providers. So dominant groups mainly lead by consensus rather than by coercion. But can resort to more overtly directive forms of coercion, or social control, by exercising their power: to *support*, or not to?; to *fund*, or not to? The state shapes and directs a 'national culture' and so enables the construction of a specific dominant culture. Popular cultural forms, alternative to the dominant culture, are 'incorporated' through market forces like commercialisation, or directly by the state itself (MacDonald, 1995).

> Hegemony works through ideology but it does not consist of false ideas, perceptual definitions. It works primarily by inserting the subordinate class into the key institutions and structures which support the power and the social order of the dominant order. It is above all in these structures and relations that a subordinate class lives its subordination. (Gramsci, 1971: 164)

The tendency of dominant groups to structure or frame the conditions for CSD practice does not enable them to dictate results. So, 'We operate within constraints, which we are free to change, but we are not free to abolish the principle of living within constraints' (Kelly, 1984: 4). Individual agents still ultimately 'make' their own 'sport' by responding to their own situations. 'Resistance' is as much a part of hegemony as conformity and control. The capacity for interpretation and reaction, agency itself, is dependent upon the situation. Individuals and groups find alternative, sometimes radical cultural expression, in opposition to the status quo despite the centralising tendencies of sports policy and provision. Sport (as leisure) has provided 'a more negotiable space' for agency than other spheres of life (Hall and Jefferson, 1976). Sport has emancipatory potential; the 'extent to which the politics of the popular provides a point of resistance to bourgeois hegemony' (Hargreaves, 1986: 220).

The state preserves its position as the dominant hegemonic culture in CSD by pursuing its own hegemonic project and responding to hegemonic opposition. The state maintains the mainstream market in which inequalities in choice occur, and intervenes 'in pursuit of distributive justice' (Roberts, 1978) without fundamentally changing the mainstream infrastructure. The responsive state is the hegemonic state which incorporates resistance and preserves the mainstream order. In relation to 'community arts', Kelly concedes that a radical programme, lacking co-ordination, has been diluted by assimilation into the arts establishment in a legitimated form, in which radicals have become foot soldiers in their own movement; 'we came as invaders, but without a language of our own we were soon acting and talking like the natives of the citadel' (Kelly, 1984: 29). The same fate has no doubt been met by many of those radical idealists working within CSD. This polemic analysis demonstrates the hegemonic power of the dominant culture to incorporate and disarm even the most radical of opposition. It also illustrates the potential for alternative and oppositional hegemonic cultures to emerge in a sub-cultural form.

Dynamic

So hegemony accommodates elements of both resistance and control, and must therefore be seen as a dynamic concept. The controllers of CSD policy and provision seek to impose control, and subordinate groups offer resistance. CSD is an arena in which this cultural struggle can be acted out. Hegemony is a continual process. It is continually assembled and re-assembled, reproduced and secured (and setback!) (Bennett, 1981b). Hegemony is never completed; 'it has continually to be renewed, recreated, defended and modified. It is also continually resisted, limited, altered, challenged by pressures not all its own' (Williams, 1977: 112). In hegemonic terms, that position, in limbo, will never be resolved. The struggle is ongoing; top-down control and bottom-up resistance. Individual CSD workers are able to discriminate, within certain confines, on the balance they wish to achieve between these contradictory aims, but hegemony itself is perpetual and all-encompassing.

Conclusion

This chapter commenced with an examination of key concepts and tensions in CSD. It then offered a vigorous analysis of the complex nature of CSD provision, policy and practice. In so doing, it raised many issues and debates about *that* very nature. It therefore concluded with a theoretical re-conceptualisation of CSD which could account for previously noted ambiguities in practice.

The conceptual complexity of CSD is compounded by its diverse range of provision. Its 'true' nature and meaning are therefore 'contested' in theory, policy and practice. For some, the content is very much conventional, institutionalised, sport. For others, it is a more informal manifestation of sport or recreation, and much else that may not be sport at all! For some, the central focus *is* 'sport'. For others, who may not bear any particular allegiance to sport; the key focus is very much 'the people', or community. So, CSD practice reflects these tensions between both sport development and community development.

The diverse range of CSD practices, and therefore its policy community, is reflected in the 'Structure and organisation of provision matrix'. This model accounted for policy formulated and driven at different levels; transnational, national, regional and even local. It drew attention to different styles of the management of provision ranging from top-down to bottom-up. It plots the involvement of all three sectors of the mixed economy engaged in provision; mostly public or voluntary, and occasionally private. It drew attention to the fact that many individual initiatives are often partnerships between organisations from different sectors, perhaps at different levels, who, in turn, are 'in partnership' with local communities. It further alluded to the different types of practitioners who may all share some interest in CSD: SDOs, Facility managers, Youth workers, Education workers, Social workers, Probation officers, and others.

This broad range of practitioners is further reflected in the range of policies interests which rationalise or legitimise provision. CSD is orientated around different and overlapping social, cultural, political, and economic concerns (Totten, 1995). It can be analysed from either of those perspectives. CSD accommodates a range of different philosophies, policy rationales and practices. They all share some concerns about either inequality, access and inclusion, marginalised groups and exclusion, democracy and participation. So, CSD is a form of socio-cultural intervention in mainstream provision, and in the everyday lives of communities. Five overlapping 'Policy Models' were evidenced in practice; Social Control, Social Welfare, the Democratisation of Culture, Cultural Democracy, and Radicalism. Each are a part of the full picture, and their compound effect is to underline the broad appeal of CSD to policy makers. CSD is 'dichotomous'; it is about liberation and control. Its agenda ranges from tokenism, to manipulation, to emancipation.

All of the complexities considered above underline the fact that CSD is conceptually dynamic; a hegemonic 'cultural struggle' between the varied institutions, organisations and interest groups who all share some commitment to this unique approach to provision. Best practice in CSD is varied, but what makes it so valuable and unique is its philosophy of approach, or process. Community Sports Development is a flexible, adaptable, informal, consultative, people-centred approach, aimed at the initial threshold to participation, to address the deficiences of mainstream provision.

References

AMA (1989) *Community Development – the Local Authority Role*, UK: AMA.

Arnstein, S. (1969) 'A ladder of citizen participation', *Journal of the American Institute of Planning*, July 1969.

Atha, B. (1978) 'The Sports Council and recreation deprivation', in *Quality of Life – the Contribution of Sport and Leisure*, Greater London and South East Council for Sport and Recreation.

Baldry, H. (1976) 'Community Arts', in J. Haworth and A. Veal (eds), *Leisure and the Community*, London: Lepus Books.

Banks, T. (1998) *Sport – The Strategic View*, http://www.coi.gov.uk/coi/depts/GHE/coi8450e.ok

Bennett, T. (1981a) 'Popular culture and hegemony in post-war Britain', *Politics, Ideology and Popular Culture* 1, Milton Keynes, Open University.

Bennett, T. (1981b) 'Popular culture: History and theory', in *Popular Culture: Themes and Issues* 2, Milton Keynes, Open University.

Bianchinni, F. (1989) *Urban Renaissance? The arts and the urban regeneration process*, University of Liverpool, Centre for Urban Studies.

Butcher, H., Glen, A., Henderson, P. and Smith, J. (1993) *Community and Public Policy*, London: Pluto Press.

Carrington, B. and Leaman, O. (1983) 'Sport as community politics', in L. Haywood (ed.), *Sport in the Community, the Next Ten Years, Problems and Issues*, London: LSA.

Chaskin, R. (1997) 'Perspectives on neighbourhoods and communities, *Social Service Review* (December).

Coalter, F. (1989) *Freedom and Constraint*, London: Routledge.

Coalter, F. (1991) 'Sport and anti-social behaviour', in J. Long (ed.), *Leisure, Health and Wellbeing*, London: LSA.

Coalter, F. and Allison, M. (1996) *Sport and Community Development*, Scotland: Scottish Sports Council.

Coalter, F., Long, J. and Duffield, B. (1986) *Rationale for Public Sector Investment in Leisure*, UK: ESRC.

Cooke, G. (1996) 'A strategic approach to performance and excellence', in *Supercoach, National Coaching Foundation*, 8(1): 10.

Council of Europe (1971) *Planning the Future VIII*, Council of Europe.

Department of Culture Media and Sport Policy Action Team (10) (1999) *PAT 10 – A Report to the Social Exclusion Unit*, London: DCMS.

DOE (1977) *Recreation and Deprivation in Inner Urban Areas*, London: HMSO.

DOE (1989) *Sport and Active Recreation Provision in Inner Cities*, Crown copyright.

Freeman, A. (1999) 'Exclusion zone', in *The Leisure Manager* (May).

Gamble, A. (1981) *An Introduction to Modern Social and Political Thought*, London: Macmillan.

GLC (1986) *Campaign for a Popular Culture*, UK: CRS.

Glyptis, S. (1989), *Leisure and Unemployment*, Milton Keynes: Open University.

Gramsci, A. (1971) *Selections from Prison Notebooks*, New York: Lawrence & Wishart.

Hall, S. and Jefferson, T. (1976) *Resistance Through Rituals*, London: Hutchinson.

Hargreaves, J. (undated) *State Intervention in Sport and Hegemony*, University of London: Goldsmiths.

Hargreaves, J. (1982) *Sport, Culture, and Ideology*, London: Routledge.

Hargreaves, J. (1986) *Sport, Power and Culture*, Cambridge: Polity Press.

Haywood, L. (1983) *Sport in the Community . . . the Next Ten Years, Problems and Issues*, UK, LSA.

Haywood, L. (ed.) (1994) *Community Leisure and Recreation*, London: Heinemann.

Haywood, L. and Kew, F. (1989) 'Community sports programmes: old wine in new bottles', in P. Bramham, I. Henry, H. Mommas and H. Van der Poatt (eds), *Leisure and Urban Processes*, UK: Routledge.

HMSO (1975) *White Paper on Sport and Recreation*, London: HMSO.

Kelly, O. (1984) *Community, Art and the State*, UK: Comedia.

Kingsbury, A. (1976) 'Animation', in J. Haworth and A. Veal (eds), *Leisure and the Community*, CURS.

Lentell, B. (1994) 'Sports development: goodbye to community recreation', in C. Brackeridge (ed.), *Body Matters: Leisure Images and Lifestyles* (LSA Publications, No. 47) Eastbourne: Leisure Studies Association.

Liddle, D. (1988) 'Youth and community services as part of local authority leisure provision', in J. Benington and J. White (eds), *The Future of Leisure Services*, Harlow: Longman.

Long, J. (1981) 'Leisure as a tool for community development and the opiate of the masses', in A. Tomlinson (ed.), *Leisure and Social Control*, UK, LSA.

Long, J. (1991) *Leisure, Health and Wellbeing*, Leeds: LSA Publications.

MacDonald, I. (1995) 'Sport for all – RIP?' A political critique of the relationship between national sport policy and local authority sports development in London, in S. Fleming, M. Talbot and A. Tomlinson (eds), *Policy and Politics in Sport, Physical Education and Leisure* (LSA Publications No. 55). Eastbourne: Leisure Studies Association.

MacIntosh, P. and Charlton, V. (1985a) *Action Sport (MSC): An evaluation of phase one*, London: Sports Council.

MacIntosh, P. and Charlton, V. (1985b), *The Impact of the Sport for All Policy*, London: Sports Council.

Murray, K. (1988) 'The Brixton Recreation Centre: an analysis of a political institution', *International Review for the Sociology of Sport*, 23(2): 125–38.

Parry, J. (1986) 'The community arts, an arts revolution incorporated', in J. Parry and N. Parry (eds), *Leisure and the Arts* (LSA Publications No. 30), Eastbourne: Leisure Studies Association.

Plant, R., Lessen, H. and Taylor-Gooby, P. (1980) *Political Philosophy and Social Welfare*, London: Routledge, Kegan Paul.

Popple, K. (1995) *Analysing Community Work*, Buckingham: Open University.

Rigg, M. (1986) *Action Sport – an Evaluation*, London: Sports Council.

Roberts, K. (1978) *Contemporary Society and the Growth of Leisure*, London: Longman.

Simpson, J. (1976a) *Towards Cultural Democracy*, Strasbourg: Council of Europe.

Simpson, J. (1976b) 'Notes and reflections on animation', in J. Haworth and A. Veal (eds), *Leisure and the Community*, London: Lepus Books.

Smith, C. (1998) *The Comprehensive Spending Review: New Approach to Investment in Culture*, London: DCMS.

Sports Council (1978) *Sport and Recreation in the Inner Cities*, London: Sports Council.

Sports Council (1982) *Sport in the Community: The Next Ten Years*, London: Ashdown Press.

Sports Council Research Unit (1991) *National Demonstration Projects: Major Lessons and Issues for Development*, London: Sports Council.

Torkildsen, G. (1992) *Leisure and Recreation Management*, London: E & F Spon.

Totten, M. (1993) 'Birds of a feather: a comparative analysis of community sports and community arts', unpublished MA dissertation, Leeds Metropolitan University.

Totten, M. (1995) 'Conceptualising community leisure: unravelling the rationale', in J. Long (ed.), *Nightmares and Successes: Doing Small Scale Research in Leisure*, Leeds Metropolitan University.

Williams, R. (1977) *Marxism and Literature*, Oxford: Oxford University Press.

Yorkshire and Humberside Council for Sport and Recreation (1989) *A Sporting Chance*, Yorkshire and Humberside Council for Sport and Recreation.

Chapter 6

Partnerships in sport

Stephen Robson

> We want to use . . . new partnerships to modernise and professionalise
> the way sport is run.
>
> (Department for Culture, Media and Sport, 2000)

Introduction

Many feel anxious about working with others in professional and organisational life. However, sport and recreation development work is such that
organisations can no longer expect to be able to function and thrive in
isolation. The need for partnership working has been emphasised by the
successes of many joint ventures and the failures of many individual pursuits.
This has led to an increasing compulsion for sports organisations to perform
effectively in concert in order to obtain cultural, financial and political
support, as confirmed by Slack (1997: 146):

> No sport organization exists in isolation from the other organizations
> in its environment, the source of the material and financial resources a
> sport organization needs to survive.

The range of alliances now in existence in sport and recreation management is immense. They span the entire spectrum, from major national
consortia preparing and implementing the Manchester 2002 Commonwealth
Games, to local authority sports development professionals assisting the
local netball team in its attempts to attract new players. As a more strategic
approach to partnership working develops, the professionalisation of sport
and recreation development work has witnessed the growth of managerial
posts, specifically to oversee the partnership process. Operating in seclusion
is clearly something of the past in the sport and recreation field.

Partnership working centres on the idea that agencies make a commitment in terms of what they are able to *input* into the relationship, on the
basis that some or all of the *outputs* will help them to achieve their overall

goals. This issue of mutual benefit permeates the chapter, although examples will be drawn from selected partnerships where the rewards are not always clear or shared.

The purpose of this chapter is to explore the benefits and problems experienced by organisations working together. It also provides practitioners and students with means to analyse and optimise such working relationships by drawing on relevant organisation and management theories. A brief historical perspective details the growth in strategic partnerships encouraged in these 'new times' of more flexible state and government agencies. Partnerships predominantly involving the public and voluntary sectors have primacy, as the majority of organisations with a responsibility for developing sport and recreation are located within these sectors. Political and strategic dimensions are intrinsic to much collaboration, as is exemplified in a highly complex multi-agency initiative in the Midlands of England. This provides practitioners with a critical edge to aid their own planning, and students of sport and recreation with the means to develop their own critical skills.

It is useful, initially, to reflect upon accepted definitions of the term 'partnership', and to consider how these may or may not be applied to the world of sport and recreation development.

Key terms

Throughout this chapter, a number of terms will be used interchangeably. Expressions such as 'alliance', 'networking', 'collaboration', 'joint working' and 'working together' carry the same emphasis as the key concept 'partnership'. The Collins Gem English Dictionary 5th edition (1981: 383) defines 'partnership' simply as 'association of persons for business'. In the context of the sport and recreation development professions, this definition accommodates the gamut of alliances to be considered. Thus, any coming together of organisations (through their people) or interested individuals, to further the cause of sport, can be considered to constitute a partnership.

Given the scope of possibilities for partnerships within and between organisations throughout the public, private and voluntary sectors, across all walks of life, it is odd that the majority of related literature in the business and management areas makes reference to partnership only in the commercial context. However, it is helpful to start with the concept of alliances as provided by business discourses in order to refine definitions. Yoshino and Rangan (1995: 5) assert that characteristics of 'strategic alliances' are that two or more organisations unite in the pursuit of common goals, to share both the benefits and the assignment of tasks. Importantly, as is reinforced by Dussuage and Garrette (1999: 2), there is no loss of 'strategic autonomy'; in other words, the organisations remain independent from one another. They offer a 'representation' of an alliance for further clarification (see Figure 6.1).

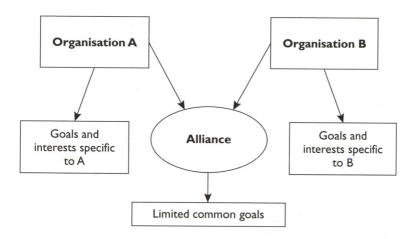

Figure 6.1 Representation of an alliance (adapted from Dussuage and Garrette, 1999).

Figure 6.1 clearly illustrates that a partnership or alliance, in this context, is distinct from a merger, where two organisations are replaced by a single new entity. The alliance is constituted to deal with issues relevant to goals that the organisations have in common; meanwhile each organisation will be engaged in its core work elsewhere.

It is possible to generate a definition of partnerships, which is specific to the sector of interest. For example, many alliances in sports development will involve local authorities, particularly in light of the government's Best Value initiative. Newchurch and Co., on behalf of the Department of the Environment, Transport and the Regions, developed a working definition of local authority partnerships that encapsulates the key issues discussed earlier:

> A local authority partnership is a process in which a local authority works together with partners to achieve better outcomes for the local community, as measured by the needs of the local stakeholders, and involves bringing together or making better use of resources. This working together requires the development of a commitment to a shared agenda, effective leadership, a respect for the needs of the partners, and a plan for the contributions and benefits of all the partners. The dynamic aspect (is) to be evaluated, (alongside an) . . . assessment of the continuing fit between partnership activities and community needs and priorities.
>
> (1999: 6–7)

Note the key themes of co-operation and fit – the relationship between partnership organisations and their environments will be dealt with in depth elsewhere in the chapter.

The nature of partnerships

Partnerships in sport and recreation take on a myriad of forms – 'there are almost as many types of partnership as there are projects' (DCMS, 1999). This section considers the factors involved in characterising any given partnership.

The first of these is *timescale*. A collaborative venture may be temporary or permanent, may involve a relatively long lead-in and negotiation period, or may be instigated rapidly once a need or common interest has been identified. The staging in England of the 2005 World Athletics Championships, for instance, is a temporary partnership between the government, UK Athletics, local authorities, sponsors, stadium developers and the many other partners; but the planning and implementation phases are relatively long term. By contrast, a permanent arrangement between a national governing body of sport and a university, aimed at providing performance analysis of elite performers, may be established much more quickly and be sustained for many years.

The second factor to consider is the *type* of partners. These may be drawn from any combination of public, voluntary and private sectors. In a local authority-led alliance, for instance, there should be a strong emphasis on *stakeholder* involvement. In other words, the citizens of that area have a dual role as customer and partner of the authority. Elsewhere, organisations such as Premiership Rugby Union teams and sportswear manufacturers enter into arrangements located purely in the commercial sector.

It is also important to recognise that partnerships occur *within*, as well as between organisations. In the context of Compulsory Competitive Tendering (CCT), local authority sports facilities were often managed according to a client–contractor arrangement where all the actors were employees of the same organisation.

Power distribution is the next factor to consider in characterising a partnership. Whilst many alliances are entered into with all partners on an equal footing (for example, a high profile sponsorship deal, where the benefits to each partner are tangible and relatively commensurate), others have a dominant or lead agency. Arguably, the politicisation of the failed England 2006 World Cup bid resulted in the government becoming the agency holding the reins of power, whilst not necessarily engaged in the bulk of the day-to-day operational work. In alliances involving the public and voluntary sectors, it is important in an era of social inclusion initiatives that all stakeholders have the opportunity to influence decisions (see DCMS, 1999).

The *scale* or size of partnerships varies greatly. From the 2005 example, where millions have an interest with new sports facilities as a multi-million pound national legacy, to a joint venture between a community gymnastics club and the local church, there is scope for joint working at every level. Partnerships exist at transnational, national, regional and local levels; certain alliances are local or regional manifestations of national partnership initiatives.

The scale is often determined by the *aims* of the partnership. Once again, there are as many possible motivations for entering into collaboration with others, as there are projects. The *raison d'être* for the majority of sport and recreation alliances is, of course, the attainment of some social objectives. However, especially in elite sports, commercial considerations attain increasing importance. Sponsors' profit motives often cross over with political, cultural and social goals at local and regional level, as sports development officers court commercial support for worthy initiatives. Numerous Youth Games managers have generated vital operating revenue, but have had to make concessions in the process. Political aims also instigate many partnerships from national to local level. The recent high level of governmental interest in national sporting achievement has led to the World Class programme, whereby national governing bodies of sport can access National Lottery funding to support athlete development. A key criterion they must fulfil is to work in partnership. It is therefore important to note that not all partnerships are entered into voluntarily, as pragmatism also produces unforeseen and unintended consequences. Some ramifications of enforced partnership working will be considered later.

Historical perspective

Since the focus of this chapter is on the strategic use of partnership in working towards sport and recreation development goals, the countless *ad hoc* or informal alliances between individuals and organisations in sport cannot possibly be considered in depth. Instead, the discussion will focus on those associations with a national impact, those fledgling partnerships which helped to establish a framework for the current trend of increased collaboration.

Contemporary sport and recreation workers are accustomed to a high level of interest on the part of the state in their affairs. Central government now has an explicit role as a *partner* in major national initiatives. This, however, has been a relatively recent development. Pre-1960, the story of organised sport and recreation provision was one of a disparate band of national bodies with a remit in this area. There has been a steady but not dramatic increase in governmental interest in the area, with largely voluntary or private provision of sporting opportunities. Public sector sports services, other than in the educational setting, were a rarity. The large number of highly organised and heavily subscribed voluntary groups rendered that sector important to successive governments, who were able to use it as a medium through which their goals could be attained (Henry, 1993: 149). Key sports organisations in this era included the Central Council for Physical Recreation and Training and the National Playing Fields Association, but collaborations between such bodies were characteristically limited and unsophisticated.

From its inception the Sports Council indicated a willingness to address the issue of the lack of structure and co-ordination in UK sport, evident in mass participation and international performance in that era. During the early 1970s, it promoted the 'Sport for All' message through a range of organisations. It was apparent that this could not be achieved through the traditional structures of the national governing bodies of sport. Henry (1993: 21) identifies that 'the vast expansion of facilities and services which occurred in the 1970s was largely a product of local government support'. Note Henry's use of the term *support* – the growth in public sector provision ultimately resulted in a period of the 1980s where, arguably, local authorities defined their role as direct providers and facilitators of sport and recreation opportunities.

This situation arose in no small part because of the inception of the Action Sport schemes of the 1980s (see Chapter 5). Building upon the Sports Council's experimental initiatives of the mid–late 1970s, funding was identified for the establishment of schemes designed to address the problems of unemployment and disillusionment amongst the youth, manifested in the inner-city riots across England in the early 1980s. A core intention of these projects was to provide free daytime sports activities as a diversion from less socially desirable modes of behaviour. Whilst evaluation of the pilot Action Sport programmes was patchy and inconclusive, it cannot be disputed that they were instrumental in establishing a foothold for sports development in the very heart of the public sector provision. From these schemes sprung numerous full-time, often mainstream funded, sports development units, leading to increasingly strategic and refined partnerships formed between the public and voluntary sectors.

Henry (1993: 118–20) charts the changes in the approach to public sector sport and recreation provision over this period, highlighting moves towards partnership (with the community as well as other organisations) and advocacy. The mood of 'economic realism' induced by the fiscal policies of the Thatcher government meant that, whilst individuals with the capacity to stimulate others into sports participation were finding gainful employment in the public sector, imaginative and flexible ways of achieving this within a tight budget would become ever more necessary.

Into the 1990s, with the onset of Compulsory Competitive Tendering (discussed in Chapter 2), local authority sports development teams reported a range of experiences. A continuum existed where, at one end, some were fully consulted and had a major input into the design of facility contracts, whilst, at the opposite extreme, many found themselves marginalised. CCT undoubtedly increased management innovation and entrepreneurialism but also reduced sports development activity in many cases (Sports Council, 1993). The requirement for successful 'in-house' partnership working came to the fore, illustrating to those in sport and recreation development that they could only truly prosper if they could forge profitable relationships with their colleagues in facility management. A complaint often expressed by sports development professionals is that facility managers do not appreciate their crucial role in the sports development process, as they see sports development as a discrete function. The client–contractor relationship under CCT regularly served to exacerbate this problem, and even the most gifted sports development workers had their work cut out to secure quality facility time and other support, as the contractors' financial imperatives established primacy in many negotiations.

Labour's Best Value initiative (see Chapters 2 and 3) places the most explicit requirement yet upon local authorities to operate in a flexible, democratic and collaborative manner. This policy initiative is one of the icons of New Labour's third way and its vision of a stakeholder society. The onus now is on the public sector to negotiate and develop partnerships with the voluntary sector, local community groups, users and non-users and so on. Indeed, their performance will be in part measured with reference to their ability to develop strategic alliances with related organisations and, crucially, the communities they are charged to serve.

Partnership working is now part of the political landscape. It has had its role upgraded from a desirable tactic for the advancement of sport and recreation development to its current status of a *necessity* for prosperity and survival. Given the political and professional significance of partnerships, the paucity of academic material dealing with this area is perhaps surprising. The next section provides a conceptual discussion of the benefits and problems of working collectively. It is based on personal-professional experience and that of others working in the field.

Benefits of partnership working

In an atmosphere of enforced partnership, it is all too easy to lose sight of the numerous benefits to be gained from collaboration. Prior to the introduction of a regulatory framework demanding that partnerships become the focus of local authority work, many far-sighted practitioners were actively engaged in fruitful arrangements with partners from a wide range of organisations. This section will provide an overview of the benefits such alliances have realised, with particular reference to a successful multi-agency initiative at local level – Middlesbrough Council's Get Active On Prescription (GAP) scheme. Chapter 7 of this book accentuates the role of positive health messages in developing sport, and vice versa, and this section will consider that in the context of a prosperous strategic partnership.

GAP was established in the mid-1990s, and is now a mature and well-respected service, which has become part of the vocabulary of many healthcare providers in the Middlesbrough area. In order to attain that status, a relationship of trust and understanding between key personnel of Middlesbrough Council's sports development team and Tees and District

Health Promotion had to be forged. The two agencies worked in concert to convince healthcare providers, initially in primary care (GP surgeries), and later elsewhere (e.g. occupational therapists, physiotherapists), of the benefits of referring patients into a programme of sport and physical activity. The story of the GAP will be told alongside a discussion of the advantages of partnership working. A selection of examples from elsewhere is presented to enhance wider understanding of issues.

Pooling of resources

As has already been indicated, agencies in sport and recreation development have generally experienced resource constraints in recent times. In addition to the constriction of local authority finances by successive governments, many national governing bodies of sport have seen declining membership lists result in reduced subscriptions. Direct Sports Council grant aid to voluntary sector organisations has been superseded by more demanding funding regimes, e.g. National Lottery World Class Fund. This has made agencies such as national governing bodies more accountable to their paymasters. Pressured resources demand greater innovation in order to achieve organisational objectives. Working in partnership can lead to the realisation of goals even in financially lean times:

- *Duplication* in two or more agencies' work can be identified and eliminated which reduces the financial burden on both and still enables desired outcomes to be attained. For example, many community police officers around the UK have used sport as a vehicle for improving opportunities for young people in disadvantaged areas. This is a shared aim of sports development professionals, a number of whom have developed ties with the police service to streamline provision and enable the young people to access wider provision. This allows both parties in the alliance to refocus their work into new areas and realise new projects. Non-financial resources such as facilities and equipment can be shared in a strategic arrangement of relevance to all partners. Consider the numerous local authority sports facilities which are used by governing bodies for the staging of 'centres for excellence' (swimming, cricket and athletics are three common examples). The governing body is able to provide vital links for the progression of athletes towards excellence, whilst the local authority can report heightened usage of the facility. Such sports development success in terms of the partnership with a voluntary sector agency, and possibly even social inclusion achievements, depends on the strategies involved, location of the facility and the demographic make-up of the participants.
- *Human resources* can be maximised. As well as enhancing projects, sharing this particular resource base can be the saviour of otherwise

unattainable goals. Around the UK, many sports development professionals have created links with local Probation Services, whose responsibilities include the provision of client activities which deter further criminal activity, but also help with personal development. Sports development teams have often provided training opportunities, such as Community Sports Leader's Awards, on the basis that probation clients are encouraged, suitably supported and supervised to practise their new skills in recreational settings (e.g. a mixed sports club at the local leisure centre). Thus, the sports development team may, through such a partnership, be able to contribute to social order, increase the sports leadership base and stabilise a labour-intensive activity session.

- *Expertise* is another aspect of human resources that can be pooled. Complex projects requiring a range of knowledge and competencies, as with the above examples, may not be able to be staged without the organisers having access to experts from outside their own organisations. A large proportion of local authority sports development professionals are familiar with staging sizeable sports events, such as the Youth Games for their localities. Each event incorporates the technical and developmental requirements of a diverse array of sports, coupled with complex marketing and logistical requirements. Without the co-operation of local schools (the identification and selection of athletes), voluntary sector clubs and the regional governing body (technical knowledge, officiating, links to opportunities for progression), other council departments (e.g. marketing, parks, facilities management), and private sector companies (sponsorship in kind can involve logistical support), it is hard to imagine such events coming to fruition.

In the Middlesbrough GAP scheme, all the above benefits were achieved through strong partnership established at the outset and consolidated in current practice. At the outset, the health promotion and sports development officers concerned pooled their expertise. The health promotion officer had a background in physical activity, and was adept at communicating its benefits at all levels from community to senior managerial. This was considered important, as, curiously, not all senior healthcare managers were convinced that physical activity could be beneficial to all. The sports development input focused on how physical activity could be achieved readily through appropriate sport and recreation participation, and on suitable opportunities which could be accessed or created in order for this to occur. Shared knowledge of the make-up of the Middlesbrough community, including health profiles, was applied to the design of the programme. Sports development professionals were able to identify suitably qualified leaders, some from within their own team, to lead the proposed activities.

Financial commitments were initially shared, with a significant contribution in cash and kind identified by Health Promotion to 'pump-prime' the scheme. Another arm of the local authority, in the shape of the facilities management team, relaxed charges to enable the programme to be as financially accessible as possible. Facility managers also demonstrated their commitment to the scheme through flexible programming, enabling GAP to access timings sympathetic to the needs of the target market. Thus, whilst the Middlesbrough Council input into GAP was driven by sports development, further internal collaboration was necessary for the scheme to get off the ground.

Alongside the fusion of physical and human resources, allied organisations, such as the GAP partners can each bring something more subtle and intangible, yet no less crucial, to the table. Every individual at every level in a given organisation is able to exert some measure of *influence* over certain situations.

Pooling influence

Partnership working often facilitates otherwise unattainable goals. This is as much the case in terms of getting favourable decisions made, or approval for projects to go ahead, as it is in the context of sharing vital resources. The governing body regional development officer, for example, who wishes to promote her/his sport in all of the local authorities within a given region, does not have direct access to the senior managers who may need to ratify development initiatives. Equally, the local authority officer may not have a communication channel open with the national marketing manager of the commercial concern s/he wants to sponsor her/his event. In either case, strategic links need to be forged in order to exert influence over the decision-makers. Influence can be exerted upon key figures in partner organisations in a number of different settings:

- As stated above, links between individuals at similar levels in partner organisation 'open doors'. Productive personal relationships lead to mutual commitment to the project, from which point it is relatively straightforward for people in senior positions to be informed of plans. Barriers caused by technical language and jargon can be overcome by the presence of an advocate within an organisation. The credibility of the intended activity is enhanced in this way. For example, in areas where the local authority has a relatively poor profile in local communities (e.g. because of high council tax), the sports development worker attempting to promote a new activity to a community group may be met with suspicion. Securing the support of a member of the group, prior to visiting, may be vital in gaining the members' respect before the initiative can progress.
- *Political* power can be exercised in ways which have productive or destructive effects upon sport and recreation development. As is clearly

highlighted elsewhere in this book, politics and politicians are intrinsically linked to the management and provision of sport at all levels. It is always desirable, and very often essential, to be able to influence politicians whether they are local authority elected members, executive members in a national governing body or Members of Parliament. The various mechanisms by which this can be achieved include the formal reporting systems of local authorities and governing bodies of sport, where ratification for activities is sought through a voting process, and *lobbying*.

- Lobbying involves interest groups making representations to politicians in order to secure support on issues of consequence. This can take place on a very localised basis. For example, one local authority in the North of England, when the sports development team wished to withdraw direct resourcing to a community bowls league (which had demonstrated the capacity to operate independently), found the officers in regular discussions with ward councillors who had been approached by league members. Had the partnership between professionals and community been more fertile, they may have been in a position to *jointly* approach the politicians for support. Lobbying also plays an important role in the political process at national level. Such manifest power can be exemplified by the formation of the Countryside Alliance with its efforts to persuade vociferously and demonstrate to the government that fox hunting was crucial to the rural economy and culture. On another issue, that of access to the countryside, the Ramblers' Association, in concert with similar interest groups, has been similarly boisterous in its campaign to compel landowners to allow use of public rights of way.

- Having access to important people is important at an interpersonal as well as organisational level. In this context, effective working together means sharing *contacts*, whereby tactical use is made of each partner's professional relationships. This is another example of the ability of alliances to open avenues to resources. Contacts range from community leaders to senior politicians. In certain communities, for example Muslim and other religious groups, certain figures possess the status of 'elders', who often must be consulted by sports development workers before further inroads can be made. In such instances, operating in collusion with community workers who already have credibility, and who can provide access to the relevant community leaders, can be of great value.

- Partnerships can enable those in less senior, but strategically vital, positions in organisations to elicit support for their extended work amongst their own senior managers and politicians. For instance, sport can be a powerful means for non-sporting organisations to achieve their goals. In the current climate of the key governmental agendas cutting across all aspects of life, and of sports development anxious to maintain its identity in local authorities in the Best Value climate, this theme needs to be embraced by those working in sports development. They can only benefit from developing cogent arguments for the role of sport in social inclusion, economic regeneration and other priority areas (see, for instance, ISRM website). Better yet, successful projects such as Bolton Metro's Pathways initiative, tackling deprivation and exclusion in some of the most disadvantaged communities, as well as achieving meaningful results in their own right through involving the community as equal partners, impress those in power and open avenues to further support.

The GAP scheme is a case in point of a venture mobilising shared influence to its fullest potential. A significant number of healthcare professionals remain sceptical about the benefits of physical activity. At the time of the instigation of GAP, communication channels at an operational level between the Middlesbrough sports development team and the health authority were very limited. The health promotion professional, however, had good standing with many managers and practitioners alike, due to the success of a pilot scheme in a neighbouring area. He was able to persuade GPs to refer patients to the programmes of recreational physical activity. As the worth of the scheme became shared, the momentum gained meant that it became possible later for sports development professionals to negotiate independently with other branches of the health authority (e.g. back pain clinics, services for disabled people, etc.).

The sports development team exerted influence not only on colleagues within the leisure department but also on elected members. A presentation to the Leisure Services Committee, involving the health promotion officer, was successful in securing political endorsement for the project.

Perhaps the most telling aspect of the GAP story in this regard, though, is the influence of GPs and other healthcare practitioners. The whole point of referral schemes is that they enable the sport provider to gain access to potential participants who are not necessarily predisposed towards active recreation. For many people, the opinion of the trusted GP, physiotherapist or other practitioner is highly valued and they are more likely to participate, if encouraged by this person. Thus, the healthcare professionals are pivotal partners in the undertaking. In many ways, a scheme such as GAP can be said to have been specifically *designed* around the influence they are able to have over their patients.

Accessing resources

Accepting that many public and voluntary sector organisations in sport and recreation face financial restriction, and drawing together the themes of resources and influence, partners with a joint mission can use their combined strength to attract finance for programmes. Indeed, the current financial and political climate dictates that, when it comes to obtaining major funding support, partnership working is a necessity rather than merely an advantage. This applies equally at all levels of sport, from participation initiatives at local level to the support mechanisms aimed at developing and nurturing elite performers. The issue of accessing resources is one upon which the narrative on the successes of the GAP scheme can be neatly concluded.

Whilst both of the GAP partners input a small amount of direct and indirect financial revenue, it was necessary to attract external support for the scheme. A joint bid to the healthcare purchasing authority, which, had it been submitted by either partner in isolation, would not have received such a sympathetic hearing, was successful in securing significant financial support at a crucial point in the growth phase. GAP continues to flourish at the time of writing; its stable base, created in the first instance by individuals' willingness to embrace 'outsider' philosophies, has been consolidated by subsequent incumbents of the sports development team.

In conclusion, GAP and thousands of other prosperous ventures are not solely improved by partnership working, they are *predicated* upon it. As has been illustrated, GAP would not have taken place without the opportunities presented by the sharing of motivation, expertise, financial and physical resources and influence. There is a powerful case that the vast majority of sports development objectives can be attained more readily, and to a higher standard, through partnership working.

It would be foolhardy in the extreme to assume that joining forces with another organisation cannot also present problems of its own. By acknowledging what can go wrong, the professional with vision can anticipate potential difficulties and take steps to overcome them – 'The true test of a relationship is not that it can solve problems but that it can function *despite* problems' (Drucker, 1990: 125).

Partnership problems

In the interests of positive thinking, this section will be shorter than its more optimistic counterpart. A realistic appraisal of some difficulties encountered through partnerships will be presented, but always with one eye on the overwhelming case in favour of collaborative working. To reinforce that even fruitful partnerships can experience pitfalls, relevant examples from the GAP scheme will be presented. Emphasis will be given to means of *overcoming* identified problems.

First, consider the point, made at frequent intervals in this chapter, that by no means all alliances are entered into voluntarily. This is often due to the requirement to work collectively to access resources, but other factors can lead to individuals being required to work together. Politicians or senior managers may have demanded that a particular initiative is embarked upon, or public clamour may have been acceded to. Whatever the reason for their inception, enforced partnerships are inherently problematic, at least in the initial stages.

Enforced partnerships

As two distinct organisations will undoubtedly possess differing structures, cultures and methods of operation, so it follows that individuals within and between partner agencies will be inherently different. The experience of countless individuals asked to align significant aspects of their work to that of 'outsiders' bears this out. First consider how these issues are manifested at an organisational level:

- Organisational *priorities* may be very different between the players in the partnership. These conflicts can centre on such factors as financial imperatives, social objectives and political direction. Discord between the organisations may be so great that, rather than overcoming the issue, at best, an *accommodation* may be achieved which enables the initiative to move forward. In such instances, what underlies the partnership is the fact that irreconcilable differences exist. For example, the language of partnership is commonly employed in sponsorship arrangements between public/voluntary and commercial sector organisations. Whilst many of these satisfy the needs of all partners, there is a clear dissonance between the sports organisation's social goals to improve the provision of sport in some way, and the commercial organisation's profit motive. Manipulation of sports events/rules/protocols, etc. to suit the marketers is now an accepted feature of contemporary sports management, although many of those who consider themselves to be 'purists', with the interests of their sport at heart are often opposed to such measures. Clashes in organisational priorities can also occur at local level. For example, a comprehensive school leading on a bid to the National Lottery to develop dual-use sports facilities may be informed by the regional Sport England office that, to enhance the bid's prospects of success, a strategic arrangement with the local cricket community should be entered into. A high quality coaching facility was desperately required. The school's original plan to generate much-needed income through evening use of the facility may be partly hampered by the requirement to offer low-cost use for cricket coaching on three evenings.
- *Political* obstacles may also be met in so-called enforced relationships. Elected officials may have personal or party political agendas at the forefront of their thoughts. Contemporary governmental interest in sport is at an unprecedented level and it is inevitable that the political cycle (e.g. approaching elections) will have some impact on decision-making. Personalities of those in positions of political influence can also have a

major impact on matters. In the context of the major partnership initiative to design and resource the new Wembley Stadium, it was revealed by former Minister for Sport, Tony Banks, that he and his successor, Kate Hoey, had 'not had a conversation' about the project in the six months following his departure from the post. This was despite well-documented problems, which almost derailed the project. The Wembley saga was further complicated by the personal and professional roles of Ken Bates, chair of the consortium responsible for the development of the stadium facilities.

- *Initiative overload* is a real issue for many workers in sport and recreation development. During the 1990s and into the new millennium, a bewildering and seemingly endless array of 'products' emanated from Sports Councils, Youth Sport Trust, National Coaching Foundation and other national and regional organisations. In almost all cases, an emphasis was placed on partnership working. In these circumstances, pressured local authority sports development professionals are faced with an almost impossible task of deciding which of the 'essential' products to embrace and which not to, and so face alienating key partners in prioritising certain initiatives.
- *Culture* is another organisational factor that may differ greatly between partner organisations. Organisational culture can be considered to be 'the way of life in an organization' (Hatch, 1997: 204), or meanings and norms shared between individuals within the workplace. Some national governing bodies of sport have been criticised for demonstrating cultures of snobbery, social exclusivity and paternalism (Houlihan, 1997). Sports development professionals in organisations with a modernising agenda (e.g. local authorities, National Coaching Foundation, etc.) encountered obstructions in implementing the raft of new initiatives introduced in the 1990s. The divergent cultural values of the recently graduated development officer and the governing body representative with many years' service to her/his sport are not necessarily conducive to working together effectively.

Whilst key players in the GAP alliance shared similar motivations, problems did arise. A new manager, appointed in the health promotion service, was not as predisposed toward the benefits of physical activity as the previous incumbent (physical activity is but one element of the wider health promotion agenda, and is in conflict for resources with issues such as drug and alcohol awareness, healthy eating, etc.). In one sense, the new manager could be seen to be experiencing the effects of an enforced partnership as by this stage GAP was well established and had a positive profile. When the original health promotion officer left the service, the partner agency, Middlesbrough Council, lacking a strong advocate within health promotion, subsequently saw a diminution in financial and professional support to GAP.

Further obstacles may be encountered even in operations between willing collaborators. In many cases, a mechanism for resolving such issues has not been agreed in advance, and this can be a source of difficulties.

Planning problems

A multitude of management texts exhorts managers to plan rationally and effectively. For a variety of reasons, this does not always occur. *Bounded rationality* (see for instance Cherrington, 1989) dictates that individuals take decisions under a number of external and psychological constraints. All relevant information is not available, and even if it were, decision-makers would be unable to process it all nor would they necessarily want to. Thus, the individuals in the sports development partnership cannot be expected to plan effectively for every contingency.

However, it is extremely naïve to assume that difficulties will not arise. Despite this, in some partnership settings, potential problems are not discussed at all at the outset, resulting in situations, all too familiar to experienced practitioners:

- *Delegation* of the workload should be carefully considered and conducted at the commencement of the relationship. Particularly in multi-agency undertakings, the nature and scope of the tasks to be performed will be large and complex. Yoshino and Rangan (1995: 126) highlight that some organisations hold back their best people for internal activities, and that partnership managers need to monitor this type of activity carefully. Strong leadership is needed to determine who is responsible for which tasks, and by when they should be completed. Leadership can be thought of as a combination of effective command and motivation. Command, according to Fayol, is 'maintaining activity among personnel, getting the optimum return from all employees in the interests of the organisation' (Fayol, cited in Mullins, 1996). Motivation constitutes 'getting members of the team to work effectively and carry out properly the activities allocated to them' (Brech, cited in Mullins, 1996). An added dimension in multi-agency partnerships is that leaders may not have direct authority over other key individuals who may need to surrender elements of their internal organisational status for the benefit of the alliance. Youth Games provide a good illustration of this issue. In some areas, professionals have been specifically appointed to deliver regional events; in others, an officer of one of the partner agencies has been nominated. In either instance, trust and responsibility is conferred upon the event manager, who must then exercise effective leadership to deliver the event to the satisfaction of all parties.
- In the event of problems, individual and organisational *responsibility* must be negotiated. This may not always be conferred upon the

organisation of the 'lead' individual in the partnership. Conversely, if the lead organisation is initially identified, it does not always follow that the lead individual will be drawn from that agency, although that will often be the case. In any event, as and when problems are experienced, it is vital to have agreed in advance who will 'carry the can', and deal with those situations on behalf of the partnership. If a positive approach is taken to difficulties, the likelihood of a *blame culture* will be diminished. This avoids expending energy assigning liability for the issue, which could be better spent rectifying problems.

Returning to the GAP scheme in Middlesbrough, whilst it is generally regarded as a success, there have undoubtedly been times of adversity during its life span. For example, there were inevitable instances in the early days of patients reporting a 'bad experience' to their referring agents, usually GPs. It would be unreasonable to expect that all participants would enjoy the exposure to active recreation offered by GAP, and the scheme managers accounted for this at the outset. When healthcare professionals raised concerns, there was no temptation on the part of the health promotion officer to point the finger of suspicion at practitioners from within Middlesbrough Council. Instead, a united response to the issue could be made. In this way, fears of current and potential referrers could be assuaged, and the scheme was able to proceed in a positive vein.

To conclude this section, it is as well to reinforce that it would be unusual for any sport and recreation partnership not to experience some form of obstacle at some stage. Consequently, partners can plan for a number of contingencies and tackle them maturely and productively as and when they arise. Relationships built on genuine trust are far more likely to thrive than are those where a hidden agenda, or a mood of suspicion, is allowed to prevail.

The merits and shortcomings of joint working have been presented from a personal-professional perspective due to the lack of academic theoretical writing, specifically on the nature of partnerships. It is, however, useful to the student and practitioner alike to consider how generic theoretical analysis may be applied to understanding the dynamics of partnership working.

Partnerships and organisation theory

Numerous fields of study lend themselves readily to the academic scrutiny of sport and recreation partnerships, for example, sociology, psychology, political sciences and *policy* studies. It is then somewhat surprising that, given the growth in the use of partnership working in recent times, so little academic work has been undertaken in this area. This section illustrates how some of the key components of one field of study can be usefully applied to understanding partnerships. *Organisation theory* has been chosen, as it can encapsulate key debates underpinning joint working. Other disciplinary approaches could also just as readily be applied, but organisational analysis is the most compelling.

This section applies organisation theory to the partnership aspect of sport and recreation development. For those unfamiliar with the field of study, organisation theory boasts an immense body of work. Theories of organisation offer 'abstract images of what an organization is, how it functions, and how its members and other interested parties interact with and within it' (Hatch, 1997: 7). This notion of organisation theory provides for the study of partnerships, particularly at the level of examining interactions between people. Branches of theory include the design and structure of organisations, management of organisations, decision-making, culture, conflict and the management of change. All can provide a critical lens through which to view the issue of collaborative working. Due to restrictions of space, however, the focus of this section will be on one central issue – how organisations interact with the environment. Although this topic will be dealt with discretely, as with most aspects of organisational life, it is interconnected with a host of other factors.

The organisation and its environment

Every organisation is located within an environment in which are situated all 'other organisations and people with whom transactions have to take place' (Pugh and Hickson, 1996: 52). The organisational environment for a sporting body incorporates national and regional governing bodies, government and other political institutions, the public, commercial and voluntary sectors, current and potential sports participants, suppliers and so on. The environment is subject to changes (demographic, cultural, technological, political, etc.) to which the organisation needs to be able to respond. From this it can be deduced that all of the inhabitants of the environment are potential partners.

Mary Jo Hatch's comprehensive and accessible text, *Organization Theory*, tackles this arena with clarity and vision. Her perspectives on environment, with contributions as appropriate from other writers, will be used to shed light on how application of this branch of organisation theory can foster a critical understanding of partnership working. Hatch argues that organisations can be characterised as occupying a place within a network of interacting and competing organisations, and that managers traditionally perceive their own organisation to be at the centre of such networks. This is represented in Figure 6.2.

Theoretical material can be applied from a number of perspectives. The aforementioned manager's viewpoint is of the organisation at the centre of the network, and this viewpoint allows for any of the groups in the network

Figure 6.2 The organisation at the centre of a network (Hatch, 1997: 66).

© Mary Jo Hatch (1997). Reprinted from *Organization Theory: Modern, Symbolic and Postmodern Perspectives*, by permission of Oxford University Press.

to provide partnership opportunities. For example, if we take the organisation to be the English Table Tennis Association (ETTA), then the types of relationships which can be developed would include sponsorship deals (perhaps with *suppliers*), coach development initiatives (with the ETTA's *customers*) and scientific studies of athlete performance with Leeds Metropolitan University (a *special interest* group). Equally, we could take the organisation at the centre to be a *partnership*, such as Durham Sport, a conglomerate of (principally public and voluntary sector) sports organisations. All of the above relationships could be developed in respect of this wider 'organisation of organisations'. Thus, it is possible to view partnerships in the context of one organisation's interactions with its environment, or to consider the partnership itself to be an organisational network, which interacts with a revised environment.

As well as the network of organisations, wider forces impact upon the organisation/partnership. These have been categorised by Hatch (1997: 67) as the *general environment*. Hatch locates the organisation, and the network, within the general environment as shown in Figure 6.3.

As with the example in Figure 6.3, the partnership can be considered to be impacted upon by the stated external forces. The partnership manager can conduct an *environmental analysis* (see for instance Johnson and Scholes, 1999: ch. 3), to assess the forces outside the control of the partnership

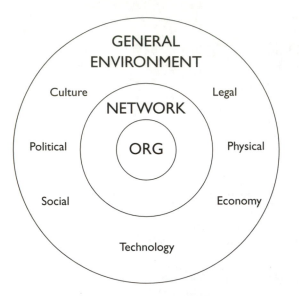

Figure 6.3 Sectors of the general environment (Hatch, 1997: 68).

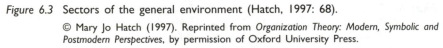

© Mary Jo Hatch (1997). Reprinted from *Organization Theory: Modern, Symbolic and Postmodern Perspectives*, by permission of Oxford University Press.

which have a bearing on its operation. In the Durham Sport example, some of the salient factors to arise from this would include:

- *Political* trends towards partnership work. The likelihood that partnership will be an ongoing theme can be recognised and treated as an opportunity by the consortium.
- The *cultural* dominance of football. This can be embraced by the partners to promote wider sports participation, whilst those with an interest in developing other sports could prepare for battle, so to speak, to engage with local dominant cultures and subcultures.
- *Economic* trends should be identified, both locally and nationally. In times of financial restriction, opportunities should be co-ordinated between the partners which do not discriminate on grounds of price; cross-subsidisation of partnership activities may be deemed necessary.

A full environmental analysis would clearly involve all elements and necessitate much greater depth, and the reader is encouraged to attempt this in relation to a partnership with which s/he is familiar. The above gives an indication of how such an appraisal helps the manager to locate the place of the partnership within the environment, and to identify the key issues to be addressed.

Numerous writers have developed theories on the ways in which the interaction between an organisation and its environment take place (*organisation–environment relations*), and these are summarised by Hatch. Early writers on *contingency theory* made an assertion that we today take for granted – that managers should organise as a response to the demands of the environment. There are, of course, instances where powerful organisations are able to *shape* the environment (e.g. Nike as market leaders in the sportswear industry). Usually in sports development, however, the environment has a powerful influence over organisational activity. There are three principal perspectives within contingency theory, detailing the options for *how* to respond to the environment:

- *Resource dependence* – this assumes that organisations are controlled by their environments, due to the need for resources like knowledge, labour, equipment, customers, political support and so on. A resource dependence analysis begins by tracing each of the needed resources back to its source; the levels of dependence can then be categorised. Pfeffer and Salancik (cited in Pugh and Hickson (1996)), who developed this theory, determined that an organisation should attempt to create a 'counter-dependency'; in other words, it should endeavour to render elements of the environment dependent on it. Powerful dominant coalitions inside organisations can shape environments and strategically choose which environment to operate in . . . see for example Microsoft, McDonald's or Nike. Another tactic proposed is to work in partnership with other organisations. From a sport and recreation perspective, the resources upon which organisations are dependent are not always tangible, physical commodities. For instance, in the current climate political support at local and national level is crucial to local authority sports development teams. By entering into partnerships with, for example, social workers servicing socially excluded young people, the team can deliver on a key aspect of the government's modernising agenda, making itself indispensable in that regard. The counter-dependency thus induced, through partnership working, helps the team to contain the effects of its own vulnerability to the environment.
- *Population ecology* – this starts from the same perspective as resource dependence theory. The difference is that population ecology takes a perspective of the relative success and failure of all the organisations competing in a given 'resource pool' (Hatch 1997: 81). The environment has the ability to select from all of the organisations competing for its resources. Writers such as Hannan and Freeman (cited in Pugh and Hickson (1996)) see the world of organisations from a Darwinian 'survival of the fittest' standpoint. Specific areas within the environment, called *ecological niches*, and not the environment as a whole, are examined. These are resource pools on which groups of organisations

depend. The focus of interest is on patterns of survival and not on links between organisations and their environments. Maintaining the Darwinian theme, population ecologists are interested in the evolutionary processes of *variation* (the entry of new organisations into the population, or the adaptation of existing ones), *selection* (by the environment on the basis of fitness) and *retention* (the attrition or survival rate of organisations). The implication is that much of what happens to an organisation is the result of chance or external forces. Sport and recreation organisations can be said to be in just such a situation in terms of their jostling for external public funding. The National Lottery Sports Fund, for example, was more than three times over-subscribed at the time of writing (Sport England website). As well as simply conforming to the requirement to work in partnership (variation), under the population ecology model, organisations bidding for funds would do well to be able to demonstrate the *strength* and *quality* of the partnership in order to prove their fitness to the environment, increasing the prospects of selection (i.e. a successful bid).

- *Institutional theory* – environments place social and cultural demands on organisations, forcing them to adapt to play specified roles and maintain desired outward appearances. The *institutional environment* represents the shared values of a society to which certain organisations are expected to conform. Slack and Hinings, 1994 (cited in Slack (1997)) investigated Canadian sports organisations from an institutional perspective, and identified increased structural homogeneity (i.e. similar outward appearance) brought about by the pressures imposed by Sport Canada (see also his arguments about professionalisation and changing leadership styles). It could be argued that Best Value will result similarly in local authority sport and recreation providers becoming obsessed with harmonising their image to suit the government criteria for quality. In a partnership sense, this could lead to some of the problems of enforced joint working, discussed earlier, as local authorities team up with other organisations for the wrong reasons.

In summary, the three perspectives all offer valuable insights into partnership working from the viewpoint of organisations' interactions with their environments. Hatch (1997: 88) emphasises that the greatest benefit to the manager or student is to examine an organisation or partnership through each of the lenses provided, and to be prepared for surprises when the findings are collated.

Finally, environmental theory provides for managers to defend the organisation against the uncertainty inherent in most environments. Hatch (1997: 88–9) characterises the environment as having properties of complexity (number and diversity of elements) and being subject to constant change. These factors lead to uncertainty in the minds of managers who lack the information they need to make robust decisions. Arguably, the environment for managers in sport and recreation is highly complex, with a baffling array of structures and organisations, subject to a high rate of change and innovation. Uncertainty occurs when, far from having the required information, the manager does not even know what type of information is needed.

One response to uncertainty is *isomorphism*, when the organisation attempts to match the complexity of the environment. Two techniques, suggests W. Richard Scott (cited in Hatch, 1997: 91) employed by organisations to achieve this, involve structural differentiation or re-ordering aspects of the organisation to deal with specific aspects of the environment:

- *Buffering* – this is usually applicable to manufacturing organisations, whereby certain personnel are assigned to insulate the remainder of the workforce from shocks in the environment, for example, resource shortages or increased demand (Slack, 1997). However, the notion can be applied to essentially service-oriented sport and recreation organisations, and to partnerships within this context. For instance, the manager of an Active Sports partnership may provide a buffer between the operational staff delivering coaching on the ground, and the possibility of subtle or sweeping changes in the priorities prescribed by Sport England, which would otherwise serve to distract them from their objectives. Through an appropriate response to the institutional environment in this way, cosmetic changes can be steered through without affecting service provision.
- *Boundary spanning* – this role is at the heart of partnership. Boundary mechanisms deal with the transfer of information between the organisation and the environment, so in one sense individual members of a partnership are acting in this role on behalf of organisations. The duality of the role is central to joint working – first, the boundary linkage provides decision-makers within her/his organisation with information relating to the environment. If a partnership is to succeed, the boundary spanner must be personally committed. Second, s/he represents the organisation in the partnership setting. In this instance, the image portrayed must be professional and contribute to the *counter-dependence* the organisation wishes to instil in the environment, by being a valued party to the alliance.

This section has introduced but one aspect of organisation theory and demonstrated how it can be applied to the study of sport and recreation partnership working. Those working in the field should be encouraged to read independently and widely around the subject to stimulate a deeper critical awareness of the strategic role of partnerships in modern sport and recreation organisations. The final section draws together the key themes of the chapter through the critical examination of a partnership case study.

Case Study: Derbyshire and Peak Park Sport and Recreation Forum

The Derbyshire and Peak Park Sport and Recreation Forum was proposed by the Derbyshire Local Authorities and instigated in 1995. It is a large and complex organism, incorporating the County Council, the City Council, eight district authorities, the Peak District National Park, the education sector, numerous voluntary sector organisations and regional representation from national organisations such as Sport England. Each local authority partner has committed over £10,000 per annum (using a per capita formula) to finance Forum initiatives. Its stated mission is to:

> Promote and influence provision for sport and recreation in the County and Peak National Park and to encourage greater involvement in this process.
>
> (Derbyshire and Peak Park Sport and Recreation Forum, 1998: 3)

The rationale for the partnership needed to be strong, given the geographical scale of the county and the diversity of work already undertaken. The reasons given in the Forum's strategy document for working in closer alliance mirror those discussed throughout this chapter:

- to improve co-ordination of effort and expenditure on the development and delivery of sport and recreation
- to be in a position to apply for both capital and revenue funding support from the Lottery Sports Fund
- to better develop sport and recreation opportunities for young people and the population as a whole
- to reduce unnecessary duplication of sport and recreation facilities and their programming (Derbyshire and Peak Park Sport and Recreation Forum 1998: 4).

In particular, the second point relates to the *population ecology* perspective, demonstrating an awareness of the conditions to be met for resources to be attained. The Forum is in a strong competitive position when compared to other organisations in its *ecological niche*. The final point relates to the earlier discussion of the benefits of partnership working that duplication is an unnecessary drain on pressured resources. It is apparent to any observer that the Forum has been designed with an appreciation for the general environment, and principally its political dimension.

The structure of the Forum has been deliberately designed to mirror political processes at local authority level, to the extent that all meetings under its auspices are chaired by elected members of the ten constituent councils – a working example of *isomorphism*. These members have been purposely invited on the basis of their interest in sport and recreation. Note the attempt to win political support and to influence the political process.

The remainder of the Forum structure also closely resembles the rigid hierarchical organisation found in local government. A simplified version is shown in Figure 6.4.

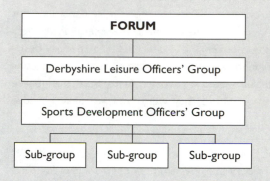

Figure 6.4 Simplified structure of the Derbyshire Forum.

The sub-groups are working parties, comprised of representatives of the three higher layers, plus representatives of the voluntary and other sectors that act on behalf of their peers. Politicians represent the Forum itself, at whose meetings only they can vote on issues. One sub-group deals with the management of implementation of the Active Sports initiative across Derbyshire, and a closer examination of the workings of this group will illuminate key issues relating to the partnership as a whole.

Active Sports sub-group was responsible in 2000 for co-ordinating a complex and strategically crucial Lottery bid, for over £1.25 million over a seven-year period to finance the Active Sports programme. In attempting to determine how the funds would be allocated, which sports would be implemented in which district, the group had to tackle issues which have resonance to the discussion throughout the chapter:

* Sport England launched a new product after the bulk of the work had been done on the bid. Concerns were felt that the threat of initiative overload was still real and this can have a negative impact, even when workload is shared.

- The issue of partners representing their professional counterparts from other authorities was a concern. The partnership had not matured to the extent that everyone gained the confidence of everyone else. It was common knowledge amongst professionals in the partnership that some sports development officers were at best ambivalent, and at worst, openly hostile to the Forum. As *boundary spanners*, would they make negative representations to their superiors and potentially undermine the Forum?

- When the Lottery grant was constructed, resources would need to be allocated to the districts on the basis of *readiness criteria*. Some authorities would be in a stronger position to begin implementation, but *all* had had a financial input into the Forum, and those allocated less could feel aggrieved. Thus, a *buffering* exercise utilising a specially designated *partnership services* fund would be undertaken. Those not meeting the readiness criteria in full would be allotted funds from this source to support them to a stage where they were ready to deliver Active Sports.

The scope for analysis of the Forum, using the tools provided in this chapter alone, is huge. Organisation theory provides limitless opportunities for partnerships in sport and recreation to be examined critically.

Conclusion

The range of benefits which accrue from working together is immense. Whilst problems of some form are inescapable, committed and trusting partners can plan for them and overcome them. National and local agendas are shifting so that, where partnership working was once a discretionary activity, it is now essential. There are possibilities for those with a scholarly interest to develop new areas of study around this topic. Indeed, in the contemporary climate, specific performance indicators, which measure the quality of partnerships, will surely arrive soon and become an important part of the policy discourse (Eady, 2000).

References

Cherrington, D. (1989) *Organizational Behavior: The Management of Individual and Organizational Performance*, Boston: Allyn & Bacon.

Collins Ltd (1981) *Collins Gem English Dictionary*, 5th edn, London: Collins.

Department for Culture, Media and Sport (1999) *Policy Action Team 10: A Report to the Social Exclusion Unit*, London: DCMS.

DCMS (2000) *A Sporting Future for All*, London: DCMS.

DCMS website at www.culture.gov.uk

Department for Environment, Transport and the Regions (1999) *Implementing Best Value: A Consultation Paper On Draft Guidance*, posted at DETR website www.local-regions.detr.gov.uk/bestvalue/bvindex.htm

Derbyshire and Peak Park Sport and Recreation Forum (1998) *Derbyshire & Peak Park Sport & Recreation Strategy: The County Strategy for Sport and Recreation 1998–2003*.

Drucker, P. (1990) *Managing the Non-Profit Organization*, Oxford: Butterworth-Heinemann.

Dussuage, P. and Garrette, B. (1999) *Co-operative Strategy: Competing Successfully Through Strategic Alliances*, Chichester: John Wiley.

Eady, J. (2000) 'Performance indicators for best value', paper delivered at ILAM Chester 2000 conference 'Contemporary Issues in the Development of Sport' on 13 April 2000 © Knight, Kavanagh & Page.

Hatch, M. J. (1997) *Organization Theory: Modern, Symbolic and Postmodern Perspectives*, Oxford: Oxford University Press.

Haywood, L., Kew, F., Bramham, P., Spink, J., Capenerhurst, J. and Henry, I. P. (1995) *Understanding Leisure*, 2nd edn, London: Stanley Thornes.

Henry, I. P. (1993) *The Politics of Leisure Policy*, London: Macmillan.

Houlihan, B. (1997) *Sport, Policy and Politics: a Comparative Analysis*. London: Routledge.

Institute of Sport and Recreation Management website at www.isrm.co.uk

Johnson, G. and Scholes, K. (1999) *Exploring Corporate Strategy*, 5th edn, Hemel Hempstead: Prentice-Hall.

Mullins, L. (1996) *Management and Organisational Behaviour*, 4th edn, London: Pitman.

Newchurch & Co Ltd (1999) *A Working Definition of Local Authority Partnerships*, posted at DETR website www.local-regions.detr.gov.uk/bestvalue/partnerships/definition.htm

Pugh, D. and Hickson, D. (1996) *Writers on Organizations*, 5th edn, London: Penguin.

Slack, T. (1997) *Understanding Sports Organizations*, Champaign, IL: Human Kinetics.

Sport England website at www.english.sports.gov.uk

Sports Council (1993) *Compulsory Competitive Tendering, Sport and Leisure Management*, National Information Survey Report, London: Sports Council.

Yoshino, M. and Rangan, U. (1995) *Strategic Alliances: An Entrepreneurial Approach to Globalization*, Boston: Harvard Business School Press.

Chapter 7

Sport and health

Stephen Robson

Introduction

Participation in sporting activity is often associated with improvements in the health and fitness of the player. Sports providers frequently extol the health benefits of taking part in regular physical exercise. Externalities of sport, physical activity and exercise have not been lost on politicians, policy makers, professionals and local communities. This chapter will examine how participation in all forms of sport and physical exercise can enhance individual well-being in a variety of different ways. It will also explore how professionals in the field can work in partnership to generate opportunities for people from all walks of life to enjoy the health benefits of sport.

The chapter will conclude by developing the use of a theoretical model of physical activity participation, which can be of great value to both the sports development professional and the student alike.

Key terms – health and fitness

In many settings, the terms such as 'health' and 'fitness' are often used interchangeably, although they carry distinct meanings. Consequently, it is helpful to establish working definitions of these and related terms to help our understanding of this growing aspect of sports development. The distinction between fitness and health is an important one. It is most useful to think of fitness as a component of health, with health as an all-embracing term used to describe the state of a person's overall well-being. Various established definitions of health, including that of the World Health Organisation, emphasise an holistic approach; health is not merely the absence of disease, but complete and optimal physical, mental, social and spiritual functioning. To quote Bouchard *et al.* (1990: 6–7), health is a

> ... human condition with physical, social and psychological dimensions, each characterized on a continuum with positive and negative poles; positive health is associated with a capacity to enjoy life and

withstand challenges, it is not merely the absence of disease; negative health is associated with morbidity and, in the extreme, with mortality.

Experts consider health then to be an all-embracing concept, which cannot be measured simply by objective physical criteria, but also must take into account an individual's subjective perception of his or her status. The concept of fitness is therefore but one important dimension of health, and deals specifically with the capacity to perform given tasks, such as to perform work satisfactorily.[1] Whilst fitness is conventionally thought of in terms of the capacity to achieve physical goals, most definitions accommodate ideas of mental fitness. 'Mental toughness' and other psychological factors such as commitment, motivation, coping with stress, anxiety and so on now occupy a vital role in the preparation and performance of elite sports people.

The physical aspects of fitness (speed, power, strength, endurance and flexibility – see for instance Paish (1998)) can be developed in elite performers to a high degree and they are specific to the particular demands of sport. Fitness can also be achieved by the 'ordinary' sports participant to benefit individual health; for example, an older person taking up cycling may experience gains in endurance and leg strength, and subsequently be able to undertake daily tasks with increased ease and vigour.

Fitness is clearly a relative term. It is shaped by individual needs and wants but is also dependent upon political, economic, social and cultural contexts. For example, compare a young Premiership soccer player with a slight injury, unable to play on in a crucial Saturday fixture and described by his coach or physiotherapist as 'unfit', with the condition of a middle-aged smoker with obesity, discharged from hospital and described by doctors as 'fit' to return to work.

The footballer is significantly fitter in general terms, but weighed against his individual and team needs, has been declared unfit. The above distinction leads to concepts of *health-related fitness*:

> ... an ability to perform daily activities with vigor ... and demonstration of traits and capacities that are associated with a low risk of (movement restricting) diseases and conditions. (Bouchard and Shephard, 1994: 81),

and *performance-related fitness*:

> Fitness necessary for optimal work or sport performance ... (that) depends heavily upon motor skills, cardio-respiratory power and capacity, body size, motivation, etc. (Bouchard and Shephard, 1994: 81).

Everyone's fitness needs are personal and unique, and other than in the case of the competitive performer, need not be measured against others'.

Consequently, sports development professionals should be seeking to enable people at all echelons of life and physical capacity to access the benefits of sports participation. People need not be put off from sports participation simply on the grounds of competition and fear of failure in comparison with others.

So, health is an all-embracing indicator or expression of a person's state of being, whilst fitness is one aspect of this which deals with capacity to perform tasks. Neither is solely confined to physical condition.

Another area of terminology often subject to confusion is the consideration of those activities that develop aspects of health and fitness. In particular, the terms 'sport' and 'exercise' are frequently interchanged, when their meanings have very different emphasis. We shall examine these below. The concept of physical activity will also be introduced at this stage. A key theme of this chapter is the numerous ways in which sports development professionals can work to change many people's negative perceptions of involvement in sport, through the manner in which sport is packaged and promoted.

Key terms – sport, exercise and physical activity

> Exercise is bunk. If you are healthy you don't need it; if you are sick, you shouldn't take it.
> (Henry Ford, cited in Geddes & Grosset, 1997: 114)

> I get my exercise acting as a pallbearer to my friends who exercise.
> (Chauncey Depew, cited in Geddes & Grosset, 1997: 113)

These homilies to idleness are acerbic reminders that for many people the notion of indulging in any activity offers nothing but negative connotations. Those with the responsibility of encouraging and enabling sport participation should therefore be familiar with the language or discourse of activity, and be able to articulate the different elements of sport and exercise to those in need of persuasion to take part.

At this stage, it is useful to remind ourselves of definitions of sport, so that distinction from other aspects of physical activity can be clearly made. Notions of sport generally focus upon its competitive dimension and the presence of structure in the form of rules. Haywood *et al.* (1995: 42) outline the essential features of an activity in order for it to be deemed a sport:

- a symbolic test of physical or psycho-motor skills
- a competitive framework which requires codified rules
- continuity and tradition in sporting practices.

Bouchard and Shephard (1994: 79), from the USA perspective, link sport to wider concepts of activity: *'a form of physical activity that includes competition'*.

However, it is important to recall that some activities, which are considered by their participants and administrators as sports, do not sit comfortably within the American concept. 'New' games and co-operative sports have a significant role to play, and are often more welcoming to the reluctant or anxious participant. Cognisant of this, writers also acknowledge that the broadness of the term may also embrace recreation and exercise.

Exercise is something that can be gained as a consequence of participating in certain sports, or it can be practised outside of a sporting environment for its own sake. As with the above notion of sports, exercise is usually seen to be an essentially structured form of activity, undertaken with particular (fitness-related) objectives in mind:

> A form of leisure time physical activity ... with a specific external objective, such as the improvement of fitness, physical performance or health (in which the participant is advised to a) recommended mode, intensity, frequency or duration of such activity.
>
> (Bouchard and Shephard, 1994: 78)

It follows logically that physical activity is an over-arching generic concept, of which sport and exercise are two significant and meaningful forms. The idea of physical activity encapsulates the full range of major movements undertaken by a person, including those not subject to structure or form. Consequently, to paraphrase Bouchard and Shephard (1994: 77), physical activity comprises any body movement produced by skeletal muscles which results in energy expenditure above the resting state.

Clearly, this definition accommodates a wide range of actions not related to sport or formal exercise, but activity from which people can gain pleasure and fitness gains, e.g. gardening, walking, dancing or yoga. The sports development professional can promulgate the messages of the benefits of physical activity to further the cause of sport. This will be explored in detail later in the chapter; a summary of the benefits of physical activity, and sport in particular, identified in research, will help to set the scene for this discussion and provide a compelling discourse or rationale to motivate reluctant participants.

The benefits of physical activity

Recent governmental initiatives in the area of health have placed an increasing emphasis upon the positive aspects of physically active lifestyles. Policy shifts throughout the 1990s reflected the realisation that individual gains secured through greater activity were also shared by the wider society. Primary and preventative health care policies were encouraged for economic, political as well as medical reasons. Reduction in the incidence of coronary heart disease, stroke victims, and other illnesses would result in less strain placed upon pressurised health care budgets and growing waiting lists, whilst enabling individuals to play a more productive role in everyday life.

The benefits of participation in general physical activity are well documented, but it is useful to remember key health gains. Research (e.g. HEA, 1995) has indicated that participation in moderate level physical activity has a wide range of physical health benefits, including:

- reducing the risk of coronary heart disease by up to 50 per cent
- helping to control blood pressure
- helping to maintain strong muscles and healthy joints
- enhancing sleep quality and quantity
- controlling weight.

In each case, it can clearly be seen how the quality of a person's life can be positively affected. To this list can be added a series of less visible, but no less important, psychological and social benefits, such as stress reduction, increased opportunities for socialising, personal and community development.

As may be expected with such a variety of associated positive outcomes, nine out of ten adults believe that it is 'very' or 'fairly' important to exercise regularly (HEA, 1995). It may come as a surprise that in reality only four men out of ten and three women out of ten participate in enough physical activity to benefit their health (HEA, 1995). There is an obvious gap between what people know and what people do, or put more succinctly, between 'words' and 'deeds'. Britain's health statistics document the growing problem of coronary heart disease, and display one of the highest rates in Europe. This is despite the established preventive effect of physical activity and the general awareness of benefits gained.

The very real challenge for providers of physical activities is to develop existing awareness and to provide means for people to access activities which suit their needs and tastes. This is as true for sports development professionals as is it for fitness and leisure centre managers. The precise role of sport as a form of physical activity, with all of the attendant benefits, has not been as clearly defined as it may have been. The next section concentrates on sport as a force for health gain, and offers practical ideas as to how sports development professionals can exploit current research knowledge.

The health benefits of sport

For many non-participants, sport is less a source of health gain than an activity ripe with the potential for physical injury and social embarrassment. Those with responsibility for the provision and promotion of sporting opportunities need to be aware of common misconceptions regarding sport, and to be in a position to work towards overcoming them.

First, it is undoubtedly the case that numerous sports are intensely physical by nature, carrying inherent risks of injury. Many contact sports, ranging from rugby to martial arts, have a key role to play in the pantheon of opportunities, but have the capacity for physical harm. To participants, the extreme physicality of such sports is attractive; to the majority of the population, this is inhibiting. The association of sport with risk and physical harm is generalised to more 'gentle' sporting forms, with the result that participation does not occur.

Very many sports, though, provide players with the scope to obtain the full gamut of health benefits achieved through physical activity participation. This includes wider social and psychological improvements, as 'taking part' in sport is not restricted to merely playing the activity. Many volunteers, paid officials and administrators consider themselves to be more rounded, accomplished individuals as a consequence of their roles in sport.

Naturally, each person's current health status and their disposition towards given activities will be highly influential in decisions whether to take up any particular opportunity. The sports development professional, or other promoter of an activity, must identify the sections of the community to which the activity may be particularly suited or attractive. However, whatever the sport and the situation, the scope for health gains is vast.

Improvements to some or all of the five elements of fitness are intended or unintended outcomes of doing most sports. As has been stated, health gains do not have to be sought solely to improve athletic performance in a particular discipline. Physical fitness improvements can also enhance lost or diminished function, to those with any of the plethora of medical conditions affecting movement and daily living.

The components of fitness can each be advanced through participation in sport, without the need to risk injury. Consider endurance and strength, two dimensions with obvious and far-reaching application to everyday living.

Endurance

Sometimes referred to as stamina, this element of fitness is greatly diminished in a large proportion of the population. Current guidelines recommend that 30 minutes' 'moderate' level physical activity per day will contribute very profitably towards a person's cardio-vascular health and fitness. This can be gained by taking a daily brisk walk; equally, individuals taking part in accessible, organised sports activities, such as orienteering, will undergo noticeable changes in cardiac efficiency and muscular endurance. The British Orienteering Federation has acknowledged this in recent years, with a drive towards making the sport more inclusive.

Strength

Muscle mass can be increased without the need to embark upon intensive resistance training programmes. Sports such as cycling and swimming, which can readily be accessed by the majority of the population, feature a certain amount of resistance without significantly threatening to damage joints, and can result in a 'muscle toning' effect. Playing other non-contact sports, such as netball, may result in the participant being motivated to take up resistance training to meet the needs of the sport, but such additional training is not necessary to gain enjoyment and benefits.

Some benefits to be gained can include improvements in balance and co-ordination, and are of particular importance to older people in terms of accident prevention. There are currently over 200,000 fractures per year related to osteoporosis, a degenerative bone disease to which physical inactivity contributes (Chartered Society of Physiotherapy, 2000). Even taking part in a relatively 'gentle' sports activity, such as organised bowls will have a positive effect in this regard.

Recent research suggests that there are plenty of potential beneficiaries of the life-enhancing properties of sport:

- an estimated two-thirds of women and one-third of men would find it difficult to walk briskly (around 3 mph) up a slight slope for several minutes (Allied Dunbar National Fitness Survey, 1992)
- around a third of men and half the female population aged 65 to 74 do not have sufficient muscle strength or power to lift 50 per cent of their body weight, making everyday movements difficult, such as getting up out of a chair without using their arms (ADNFS, 1992)
- two-thirds of women aged 16–24 years do not participate in enough physical activity to benefit their health (Hansbro *et al.*, 1997)

This is an indication of findings from a number of British studies. The unequivocal message resonating throughout this work is that the UK, as a nation, is not physically active enough. Yet there is a general, if under-informed, awareness that physical activity is good for you. It is as if the individual acknowledges activity is good for others but not for oneself. There are always mitigating circumstances which excuse the majority of the UK population from routine physical exercise – tiredness, work, expense, lack of time, lack of facilities, family, life circumstances, not least alternative leisure opportunities.

The social and psychological gains to be found in sporting lifestyles should not be underestimated. Sport provides an ideal vehicle for individuals to express themselves in a variety of ways. Playing sport and affiliation to a club or team offer tremendous opportunities for improved self-esteem, socialising and community identity. However, sport can provide the means for social and psychological health gain in other ways.

Hundreds of thousands of people fulfil vital administrative and leadership roles at all levels of the sports development continuum, with no financial or other tangible reward. The estimated 1.5 million volunteers in UK sport (GB Sports Council, 1996) have a multitude of motivations for engagement with their chosen sport. Reasons for giving up free time to perform bureaucratic and coaching functions are often expressed as 'just doing my bit', 'helping with the kids', 'giving something back' or 'somebody's got to do it'. The volunteer acknowledges the importance of the role – the majority of sports opportunities are founded upon good will – and volunteers experience enhancement of self-esteem and community solidarity. Indeed, Bishop and Hoggett (1986) argue that the voluntary sector is where local democratic involvement is uniquely possible. Sports and leisure organisations can sometimes include those excluded elsewhere in the serious worlds of work, religion and politics. A person with perceived low status in society as a whole (e.g. unemployed, disabled, ethnic minorities, or the elderly) can achieve high standing and accomplish much of importance in a voluntary sports management setting. In other instances, people experiencing social isolation can tap into a vibrant network of friends by becoming involved in volunteering in sport.

To 'close the loop' in terms of the health benefits, many who may begin their involvement as volunteer helpers, administrators or leaders subsequently become active participants, and acquire the physical gains. Consider, for instance, the parent who, tired of spending three nights every week sitting and watching her daughter and son practising and competing in table tennis, decides to join in, and becomes an active club member as a result.

In summary, the case for the health benefits of sport is a compelling one, and researchers will doubtless continue to add to the growing body of evidence already in existence. The propensity for sports development and healthcare professionals to work together to encourage and enable sedentary and largely inactive people to take up sporting activity is great. The next section will examine how such initiatives can be realised.

Promoting the physical benefits of sport

> Recreationalists are often disparaged by social workers as being lightweights, and the social workers are often seen by recreationalists as talking the day away.
>
> (Etkin, 1993: 263)

From a position of suspicion several years ago, healthcare professionals have developed an appreciation of the advantages of working with partners outside the health service, often including local authority sports development officers. GPs, physiotherapists, occupational therapists, dietitians and others have become supportive of referral schemes, which involve patients being prescribed programmes of activity as remedial intervention for their medical conditions.

Such 'healthy alliances' have developed a variety of forms, as health practitioners have often exercised initial caution rather than enthusiastically creating direct pathways for patients into 'pure' sports settings. Most referral projects have centred on opportunities for structured, gentle exercise, e.g. gym-based programmes with instructors, walking groups, etc. However, as sports development officers have become more adept at forging relationships, and at communicating professionally with health practitioners, greater diversity of projects has ensued. Consequently, if the sports development officer can understand and articulate health benefits of sport, usually as an alternative or complementary therapy to structured exercise (which often has low appeal to many patients), new exciting opportunities can be generated.

Consider, for example, a physiotherapist working with patients with spinal injuries. Their rehabilitation may be aided by taking part in an activity supporting the development of wheelchair skills, whilst providing the all-round benefits of physical activity. The astute sports development officer may facilitate a link with a local wheelchair basketball club, which, with appropriate human and financial resources, may be able to provide the patients with an opportunity to learn the sport, and, where desired, progress from participation to performance level and beyond. A similar link with a health practitioner working with lower-limb amputees could also be cultivated.

There are many other examples of the value of sport as an instrument for medical rehabilitation, often (but by no means exclusively) where older patients are concerned. For instance, heart patients may access swimming through an organised club setting. Those recovering from stroke may be provided with a pathway into the local croquet club, where walking is combined with co-ordination skills.

Unfortunately, the importance of sport as a health promoter for young people needs to be restated. We say 'unfortunately' because of the sharp decline in the compulsory provision of physical education in schools. Only 33 per cent of young people in education now receive two hours or more PE and sport per week (Sport England, 2000). Moreover, the commitment to literacy and numeracy in the national curriculum by the present Labour government has resulted in further pressure on PE as on other subjects. The amount of teacher-led extra-curricular activities has deteriorated markedly, as the demands of the profession have become more onerous. Roberts (1996) is optimistic about the vitality of sports in schools as his review of national surveys detects pupils finding a diverse choice of indoor individualised sports rather than opting for the more traditional team sports, associated with school playing fields. Nevertheless, projections that increasing numbers of people will experience coronary heart disease when only aged in their twenties should not be treated lightly. It is to be hoped that this will not have to occur, alongside an ensuing media panic, to convince government to re-prioritise school PE. At the time of writing, the government voiced the aspiration that all pupils should 'spend two hours a week on physical activities within and outside the school day' (DCMS, 2000: 30).

Once again, the strategic importance of public sector sports development cannot be too strongly emphasised. Mutual trust and respect between Sports Development Officers and the teaching profession is generally assured, and the SDO must build upon this foundation to help schools open their doors to local voluntary sector sports providers. In most areas in the UK, a wide enough portfolio of sports clubs exists such that most young people can have their particular sporting interests served. Seduced by a plethora of competing sedentary leisure pursuits, and not least the attractive lifestyle choices about alcohol, tobacco, drugs and sex, the successful implementation of the complex task of establishing links from school to club is vital to the health of many youngsters and neighbourhood communities.

Sports development officers may also employ the tactic of disseminating information about the health benefits of sport to voluntary sector providers, for their use as a promotional tool for sport. Looking for activities of value to their children, parents may be persuaded by this form of marketing to encourage them to participate.

Using sport to promote physical activity

For those individuals and groups not disposed towards activity of any sort but with an 'armchair' interest in sport as a spectator, it is feasible to use sport as a device for the development of more active lifestyles. For example, the 'front line' in the war against physical inactivity, in many (especially northern) urban areas, is the network of social (or 'working mens') clubs. These are traditionally populated by men on low incomes, with high incidences of alcohol consumption, smoking and unhealthy eating; such clubs provide the key social focus in the leisure lives of their patrons. Conventional wisdom amongst health promoters sees clubs as a hard target, where significant resources can be deployed with little return in terms of behaviour modification. The recent Active For Life campaign (HEA) targeted middle-aged men amongst several other groups, and encouraged the establishment of 'Gut-Busters' schemes, where exercise interventions would be provided (HEA, 1998). However, the idea of participation in 'keep-fit'-style activity is anathema to many in this masculine working-class subculture, inviting the likelihood of peer ridicule. Aerobics classes, body toning and fat-free diets are not normally associated with male friendship networks.

A more suitable offering may be one allied to a common area of interest in this sector – competitive sport. The SDO may decide to try to develop an understanding of the interests of the target club members, before helping them to constitute a regular activity of their choosing. They may, for instance, be introduced to badminton at the local leisure centre, initially on an isolated basis, to avoid any issues of embarrassment. The players would be introduced to the rules and given basic coaching, as well as being shown how to organise fun competitive play. Further into the initiative, if desired, links would be forged with a local club, to sustain the activity beyond the initial flurry of interest.

Similarly, many inactive young people are accustomed to hero-worship of Premiership footballers and wear sporting merchandise, whilst being disinclined towards participation themselves. The shrewd SDO, in partnership with school PE staff and the local voluntary sector clubs, could attempt to induct these young people into the unique experiences provided by the physicality of sports, and not obtainable through computer games and sticker collections. Elements of competition provided by fun sports activities, when properly managed, can serve as significant motivators to young people's continued involvement. 'Community athletic teams . . . are excellent ways to get children who are not highly athletic into sports activities' (Rowland, 1990: 272).

Physical activity on the UK political agenda

Close links between 'exercise' promotion and sport were not developed until the early 1990s. The benefits of active living and the opportunities for a syndicate approach to health promotion were recognised in the Conservative government policies at the time. The Allied Dunbar National Fitness Survey, conducted around the turn of the decade and published in 1992, had highlighted the need for greater co-operation between agencies in the war against inactivity and ill health. Experts defined national 'standards' as to appropriate weekly levels of vigorous, moderate and low levels of physical activity. It became increasingly clear that the majority of people could articulate the health benefits of physical activity but were reluctant to embrace exercise regimes in their own everyday lives.

In 1992 the Conservative administration launched its major health policy statement – The Health of the Nation. Its strategy was to tackle the risk factors associated with five major disease groups. Coronary heart disease/stroke was identified as one of the five (the other four were cancers, mental health, accidents and HIV/AIDS). The status of physical activity within the initiative on coronary heart disease and stroke was not as high as may have been desired. Poor diet, smoking and other risk factors were given greater prominence. However, physical activity, individual lifestyle and preventative health were now on the New Right agenda for a variety of economic, political and ideological reasons.

Whilst only limited reference to physical activity was made in the 'Health of the Nation' White Paper, far-sighted sports development professionals, health promoters and medical practices throughout the UK were able to envisage a range of joint undertakings which could flourish from the Thatcherite endorsement of active living. For perhaps the first time, operational staff would have a political tool with which to persuade senior managers less sympathetic to the cause.

Lacking confidence in local authorities and the civil service, quangos flourished in the post-welfare era of Thatcherism. In 1993, as a more direct response to ADNFS, a Physical Activity Task force was created. This quango was made up of delegates from the HEA, the medical profession and higher education. Its remit was to develop a strategy for the wider promotion of physical activity, and to design a 'prescription' for health gain for the whole community through increased participation. After some expert debate, the traditional health prescription of 20 minutes' vigorous aerobic exercise three times a week was 'realistically' downgraded to a moderate level physical activity, five days of the week. Of great importance in the dissemination of this new message was that 'high impact' exercise was not mandatory and any everyday activity – including for example, gardening and walking – provided health gains and, most importantly, the concept of 'moderate' exercise was relative to the individual.

Although John Major claimed to be at one with Thatcherite policies for Europe, the economy and civil liberties, his decisive break with the 1980's New Right legacy came with the success of the National Lottery and his distinctive personal interest in sport. 'Sport: Raising The Game' highlighted that sport in schools enabled young people to

> 'appreciate the long-term benefits of regular exercise and (be) able to make informed decisions about adopting a healthy and active lifestyle in future years'.
>
> (Department of National Heritage, 1995).

The National Curriculum at Key Stage 4 encouraged PE teachers to develop health-related exercise and empower pupils to adopt active lifestyles on leaving schools and embarking on adult life.

'Active for Life' campaign

The Health of the Nation and the work of the Task Force initiated the HEA's 'Active for Life' campaign in 1995. 'Active for Life' heralded an overarching crusade both to elevate awareness and encourage the UK population to acquire the benefits of physical activity. The campaign took the form of comprehensive media promotion, allied to efforts to develop the HEA's level of contact with practitioners 'on the ground' to an unprecedented level. Over the three-year 'live' period of the project (April 1996–March 1999), it was intended to place physical activity high on the agenda of as many organisations as possible. This ranged from campaigning inwardly to maintain its governmental status to the launch of TV adverts, aimed directly at the general public. In between, practitioners at all levels of health care, in leisure management and in the voluntary sector were exhorted to embrace the ideals of physical activity participation and to work together to promote it to their customers.

Active for Life took a target group approach to physical activity. In each of its three year span, the bulk of its output was aimed at one particular segment of the population, with another group being selected for 'special targeted initiatives', where communication and access needs were of high importance. (For example, in 1997–98: the lead target group was young women aged 16–24, with 'special targeted initiatives' aimed at disabled people.) This approach may be criticised for politically correct tokenism, i.e. 'name-checking' as many special interest groups as possible in the three-year term. However, for those sport and health professionals who engaged with the project for the full three years, valuable information and contacts were nurtured with the prospect of sustained development in the years to come.

One of the most positive outcomes of this project was the way in which professionals and volunteers did indeed adopt the campaign as a 'brand' to publicise their physical activity-related offerings. Regular regional campaign briefings, staged by HEA staff, were valuable sources for information dissemination as well as an opportunity for people from different sectors to network.

Active for Life was by no means a sports-specific initiative; the organisers were at pains to build into their messages that the term 'physical activity' referred to something much wider. However, it did succeed in drawing the sports development profession to the attention of people with strategic power – to the so-called 'commissioners' of health care, i.e. those with the responsibility for purchasing services for their local populations. The internal market of health care provision, introduced by Thatcher in 1988, provided sports development professionals with diverse opportunities to focus on health aspects of sport when they became policy priorities for the Major administration.

The run-up to the 1997 General Election provided a timely reminder that quangos and their campaigns always operate within a political environment. For a six-week period in March and April 1997, the HEA felt unable to make any public pronouncements that could be construed as partisan campaigning. Active for Life was effectively put on ice in this period. Fortunately, no impediment from the incoming Labour regime was encountered, allowing the campaign to run its course.

Policy evaluated and renewed

The 'Health of the Nation' evaluation document, compiled for the Department of Health (Department of Health, 1998), made little reference to physical activity in its own right. Significantly, leisure managers were consulted as part of the appraisal process. This hopefully illustrates a recognition (at least on the part of the academic researchers conducting the evaluation) that the public sector leisure industry has a continuing role to play in the delivery of health-enhancing services.

Meanwhile, at the onset of the Labour administration, it became clear that new public health priorities would overwhelm the 'Health of the Nation' message. New Labour's health action plan *'Saving Lives: Our Healthier Nation'* heralded a shift away from New Right policy priorities, and offered a social reformist commitment to tackle health problems associated with social, economic and environmental inequalities. The paper made little reference to physical activity *per se*, and distanced itself from setting performance indicators, icons of the early 1990s health policy. The emphasis shifted away from specific risk factors liable to bring about the onset of disease to the broader determinants of health. A dominant aim of this political era was the eradication of social exclusion, or conversely, the promotion of social inclusion. Health was no longer seen as a private domain where individuals were free to make lifestyle choices, but rather as a collective issue where citizens had rights to health care, guaranteed by strong government action and funding.

Improvements in overall living standards were equated to better health. *Our Healthier Nation* talked of improving the health of everyone and in particular, economically disadvantaged and deprived populations. New targets were established for key areas highlighted in 'Health of the Nation' (with the exception of HIV/AIDS), and smoking was identified as the 'single biggest preventable cause of poor health' (Department of Health, 1999). Once again, little or no specific mention of physical activity was made in the governmental health agenda, although the potential for a positive contribution was evident.

The diminution of physical activity on the health agenda was offset against a more prominent role for sport elsewhere, not least in the establishment of the Department for Culture, Media and Sport in 1997. Government proclamations on sport in the late 1990s frequently centred upon the need to increase participation in sport amongst the whole population, often alluding to the health benefits. In addition, numerous local health strategies now recognise the value of physical activity (sometimes with specific mention of sport), whilst local government sports strategies generally refer at some stage to the healthy benefits of active participation.

Campaign overload?

In the wake of Active for Life, numerous other physical activity ventures were launched, each with relevance to the sports development profession. Perhaps the BBC's 'Fighting Fat, Fighting Fit' programme generated the greatest mass publicity. This received a high profile television launch in early 1999, and focused directly upon the general public; a series of television programmes were supported by an information pack, Internet site and roadshow during 1999.

A key implication for sports development professionals of all this promotional activity was the need to be able to respond to any increased consumer interest in physical activity. In addition, as with the Active for Life campaign, highly visible initiatives such as 'Fighting Fat, Fighting Fit' provide professionals with a 'brand' or message to develop in their own publicity material.

It can be argued that a multitude of such campaigns can lead to public confusion and exhaustion. Provided that consistent and realistic messages are put forward, such an elevation in promotional activity can only serve to increase general awareness of the benefits of active living. This presents the sports development professional with numerous local opportunities to increase participation.

Local initiatives in practice

A multitude of opportunities has been instigated for people to gain health benefits through sport. The range of provision is comprehensive, from strategic partnerships between senior managers in discrete organisations to voluntary level activity in small communities. The three case studies below constitute only a small sample of the work that has been undertaken, but serve to illustrate to sports development professionals that anything is possible when sufficient imagination and creativity are exercised.

Case Study 1: Vintage Sports

Provided by the Leisure Department of Wealden Council in East Sussex, this scheme had the aim of promoting 'physical activity within the Wealden area, targeting sheltered housing, older (people's) voluntary agencies and village halls through use of the CCPR Community Sports Leader's Award Scheme' (HEA, 1998). Such an explicit link between sport and health, particularly in relation to older people as the desired target group, is worthy of further examination.

The CSLA is potentially an excellent tool for the integration of sporting and health-related themes. In the context of Vintage Sports, it was used to provide a safe, fun experience for the older clients, whilst allowing the CSLA candidates themselves to develop their skills in contact with a new audience. Most CSLA courses utilise fellow candidates or groups of young people as the 'guinea pigs'. Consider that, as the scheme developed, older participants may have also expressed a wish to undertake the CSLA training, thereby accessing the wider mental and social health benefits of sport for themselves.

Case Study 2: Football on prescription

This programme highlights a number of important principles. Set up by the Borough of Crewe and Nantwich, the scheme was designed as a means for adults who had dropped out of regular participation in physical activity, and had perhaps adopted other negative health lifestyles, such as smoking, to become active once more. Football was deliberately chosen as the means to achieve behavioural changes because of its popularity and its accessibility. Football was likely to be less of a barrier to many people than another sporting activity of which they had little or no previous experience. The activity was provided in a safe and supervised environment, with the emphasis on fun, with appropriate support and counselling given to encourage ongoing participation.

Interestingly, the professional in charge of the scheme was Crewe and Nantwich's 'Health Development Officer'. This is an example of a growing trend towards people with a health specialism gaining employment in local authority leisure departments. The manager's understanding of the strong relationships between sport and wider health issues provides extra value in developing local sport and leisure services. This enhanced strategic aware-ness is also illuminated by the next case study.

Case Study 3: Middlesbrough strategy for sport

Middlesbrough Council has a sizeable and active sports development team, which has a history of close co-operation with the local health promotion team, as well as a wide range of providers of primary and secondary health care (GP practices, cardiac rehabilitation service, occupational therapy and so on). For instance, a successful partnership with the local community mental health trust has operated for a number of years. This 'Fitness for

Fun' activity programme, aimed at clients of mental health services, intersperses physical activity of a general nature with recreational sports such as lawn bowls. Information is always provided to participants to encourage them to take up activities away from the scheme.

In producing an overarching strategy for sport provision in the borough, the Council strove to recognise the status of the health benefits of sport in a formal way. The introductory section on the value of sports development featured a discussion on the health benefits of sports participation, and how these influenced the work of the sports development team. An entire chapter of the document was devoted to the portfolio of current and planned 'healthy alliances' in Middlesbrough. In so doing, this and the many similar documents send out a clear signal to the organisation's allies in the healthcare profession that their collaboration is valued at a strategic level. More tactically and pragmatically, a copy of the document can be sent to important people within the health authority, as a means of confirming or securing their support.

The production of sports strategy documents by local authorities has a strong political dimension. Usually, as is the case with Middlesbrough, such a document will be submitted to the appropriate Council committee(s) or commissions for the approval of the elected members. Having given a high profile to health aspects of sports provision, securing political approval will ensure some of potential barriers to inter-agency working are weakened.

Clearly, there are a great number of other, equally diverse and successful initiatives in place around the UK. Sports development and healthcare professionals alike need to be aware that this vast body of work already exists. Students intending to gain employment in these developing disciplines should engage with examples of good practice to assist in their efforts to become reflexive practitioners. Other tools to enable them to provide a high quality service are also in place, including a growing body of academic research work and associated theoretical material.

One example of this facilitates an understanding of how individuals are likely to respond to the stimuli provided by sports development promotional material, which, whilst assisting practitioners, also enables students and scholars alike to appraise and evaluate existing initiatives.

Transtheoretical model of behaviour change

Studying models of practice developed by academics can often present a bewildering and intimidating prospect. The transtheoretical model developed by Prochaska and Marcus (1994) is based on psychological studies of human behaviour, and can be of great relevance to those without a specialisation in this area. The model was developed from the work of Prochaska, DiClemente *et al.* when helping people to cease a common negative health behaviour – smoking. In studying a group of people attempting to quit smoking without professional intervention, they cultivated the notion that these individuals were at differing *stages of change*, and that identifying the stage a person occupied would enable suitable 'treatment' to be offered to future clients. They and others have since applied the notion of stages of change to the scrutiny of other health behaviours.

Physical activity is one such area of study. As opposed to the majority of health promoting interventions where people are encouraged to cease a negative behaviour (smoking, alcohol, drugs, etc.), the message of physical activity and sport focuses upon the adoption of a positive lifestyle choice. This is hopefully a 'friendlier' theme than simply regulating or overcoming undesirable physical addictions and dependencies.

The six stages of change

The researchers propose that six stages of change exist on a continuum: from people with no intent to change whatsoever to those who have successfully and permanently modified their behaviour. Prochaska, DiClemente *et al.* have linked the model to physical activity participation; it can be usefully applied specifically to the health dimensions of sport. The six stages have been labelled thus:

Precontemplation. The individual has no intention to change (i.e. take up sport) in the foreseeable future (for instance, usually the next six months). The person is defensive about their willingness and ability to change, and has evaluated that the benefits of sedentary behaviour outweigh the costs of becoming active.

Contemplation. There is a serious intent to change within the next six months. Change, however is often put off ('I'll come to the badminton club next week . . .'). Chronic or long-term contemplators 'substitute thinking for acting' (Prochaska and Marcus, 1994: 162). They have identified that the pros of sedentary existence are roughly equal to the cons of changing, so taking up sport seems like a good thing but is not an urgent priority.

Preparation. The individual intends to act within the next month. They may have a plan of action, and could have made small changes without attaining the desired level (e.g. may have attended an organised sports session sporadically). This person has evaluated that the pros of changing outweigh the cons of remaining sedentary, and change of some form is therefore likely.

Action. Significant changes have occurred in the last six months, and the desired criterion or level has been attained (e.g. attendance at the swimming club twice weekly). This phase has the greatest risk of relapse into less active behaviour. Note that, whatever criterion has been reached in terms of active participation, this must have been previously determined in one of the earlier stages.

Maintenance. This is the period from six months after the criterion for change was initially reached, until the point where the risk of returning to the old behaviour has been eliminated (e.g. the previously sedentary person is now an active and permanent member of the cycling club). This is a period of continued change – the smoking research suggests that five years of maintenance leads to the final termination phase.

Termination. There is no temptation to return to the old behaviour. The person has attained 100 per cent 'self-efficacy' (in other words, their participation in health-enhancing sport is completely self-managed). It is questionable – and currently no research exists to confirm one way or another – whether it is realistic for a person to progress from a sedentary lifestyle to termination; they may always remain at risk of relapse.

Along the continuum from precontemplation to maintenance, individuals are considered to experience a linear increase in self-efficacy, whilst temptation declines at a similar rate (see Figure 7.1).

Note that the *action* stage is where a 'precarious balance' between the two factors is seen to occur. For example, an individual, having joined a netball club and participated actively in sport for the first time since school, may be experiencing doubts despite gaining enjoyment from the activity, and will still require appropriate support from fellow club members, coaches, etc. to make the change more permanent.

The reader, particularly if involved in the delivery of sports services, may still require some convincing as to the usefulness of this theoretical model. Prochaska and Marcus forward a series of 'intervention issues', which link the stages of change to the provision of opportunities aimed at encouraging

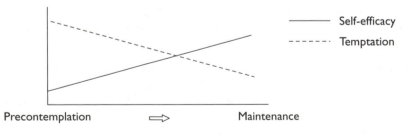

Figure 7.1 Changes in self-efficacy and temptation.

participation. Sports development professionals may choose to bear these in mind when designing programmes of health-enhancing sport:

The 5 Rs of intervention

Recruitment. Promoting opportunities requires great care and skill, in order to ensure that the right messages reach the right people. People in the precontemplation and contemplation phases have been observed to respond poorly to 'action-oriented' recruitment strategies, where too much emphasis is placed on the individual to access the activity on offer. Proactive recruitment techniques should be used when targeting sedentary people. A simple example is that of the sports development professional choosing to visit groups or individuals in person to promote programmes rather than relying upon advertising alone to generate a response.

Retention. In the smoking research, and in the experience of sports development professionals working with sedentary people, high drop-out rates are commonly experienced. The stage that a client has attained has been shown to be a predictor of the likelihood of dropout. Consequently, close attention should be afforded to individuals identified as precontemplators and contemplators, in terms of support and counselling, in order to identify and tackle risks of relapse as early as possible.

Resistance. Increased 'prodding' by the service provider can lead to increased resistance to the messages encouraging positive behaviour change. Participants should be counselled to target small, manageable changes to their lifestyles. For example, a person who has recently taken up swimming may choose to set goals related to the distance swum, or, equally, may focus on basic attendances at the club as a measurable target.

Relapse. Clearly, the risk of this is a major issue, predominantly for individuals at the action stage. The better prepared that a participant is in the earlier stages, the greater the chance of successful progression towards the maintenance phase. The researchers are, however, convinced that, regardless of the nature and quality of the intervention, 'the majority of people will relapse after any single attempt to overcome most chronic behaviour problems' (Prochaska and Marcus, 1994: 168). Sports development professionals should endeavour to 'recycle' relapsed participants, to enable subsequent attempts to undertake a sporting activity to 'stick'.

Recovery. The researchers view this as 'a process rather than an immediate outcome' (Prochaska and Marcus 1994: 162). In sports development terms, the 'recovery' taking place is one from a sedentary existence, and practising professionals will be all too aware of the pitfalls which can prevent this from being successfully accomplished. The research has demonstrated that individuals already in the preparation stage at the time of the intervention are more likely to 'recover'. As a consequence, those identified as precontemplators or contemplators may benefit from well-placed support and advice to enable them to progress, rather than being thrust into the potentially threatening environment of a sports activity from the outset.

A key principle to adhere to is appropriate 'treatment matching' to ensure that intervention by the sports development professional is in line with the individual's current stage of change. If time and resources permit, one useful strategy is to help clients to progress by one stage per month. This can present new obstacles to successful progression, as the sports development professional must articulate this relatively complex information in such a way that it has meaning to the client. 'Get Moving', a project led by Health Promotion Service Avon, utilises 'stage of change leaflets' to encourage increased participation in physical activity (HEA, 1998).

There is the implicit assumption that an individual's current stage of change is known, but, clearly, there must be some means of obtaining this information from the client. One such method is adopted in Project PACE (Physician-based Assessment and Counselling for Exercise), an American initiative designed to enable general practitioners to counsel patients into becoming more active (Patrick *et al.*, 1994). As part of an initial consultation, PACE utilises a short questionnaire. The patient is asked to indicate which of eleven statements most accurately reflects his or her current physical activity status (e.g. precontemplator – 'I do not exercise or walk regularly, and I do not intend to start in the near future'; contemplator – 'I am trying to start to exercise or walk'). This idea could readily be adapted by the sports development professional in order to contextualise a set of questions to the activity opportunities on offer.

Much of the foregoing, in terms of matching interventions to individuals' stages of change, etc., is already performed by sports development professionals, usually on a 'common-sense' basis. Utilising a deeper and systematic understanding of the change process, by means of a modified PACE questionnaire, can help provide an enhanced service.

Conclusion

The overriding message of this chapter is that sport has a vital role to play in health enhancement. An understanding of the health benefits of specific sports enables the sports development professional to negotiate partnerships with healthcare practitioners and to access a vast potential clientele. Sport can provide the impetus for sedentary people, often not disposed to structured exercise, to become active.

Recent governmental policy moves have opened the door a little wider for work in this area to progress, although greater explicit political endorsement is desired. Strategic recognition of the health-enhancing properties of sport is a useful bargaining tool within and outside of the host organisation.

Many highly innovative and successful initiatives already take advantage of the opportunities provided by the link between sport and better health. An appreciation of academic research material, such as the transtheoretical model of behaviour change, can assist with critical appraisal of initiatives, and can help practitioners to offer more relevant sports opportunities.

Note

1 See definition from the World Health Organisation, 1968.

References

Bishop, J. and Hoggett, P. (1986) *Organising Around Enthusiasms*, London: Comedia Press.
Bouchard, C. and Shephard, R. (1994) 'Physical activity, exercise and health: the model and key concepts,' in C. Bouchard, R. Shephard and T. Stephens (eds), *Physical Activity, Fitness and Health: International Proceedings and Consensus Statement*, Champaign, IL: Human Kinetics.
Bouchard, C., Shephard, R., Stephens, T., Sutton, J. and McPherson, B. (eds) (1990) *Exercise, Fitness and Health: A Consensus of Current Knowledge* Champaign, IL: Human Kinetics.
Chartered Society of Physiotherapy (2000) *Osteoporosis – The Facts*, posted at Website http://www.csp.org.uk
Department for Culture, Media and Sport (2000) *A Sporting Future For All*, London: DCMS.
Department of Health (1992) *The Health of the Nation*, London: The Stationery Office.
Department of Health (1998) *The Health of the Nation: A Policy Assessed*, London: The Stationery Office.
Department of Health (1999) *Saving Lives: Our Healthier Nation – Executive Summary*, posted at Website http://www.doh.gov.uk/ohn/execsum.htm
Department of National Heritage (1995) *Sport: Raising The Game*, London: The Stationery Office.
Etkin, S. (1993) 'Active living programmes for low socio-economic individuals,' in H. A. Quinney, L. Gauvin and A. Wall (eds), *Toward Active Living: Proceedings of the International Conference on Physical Activity, Fitness and Health*, Champaign, IL: Human Kinetics.
GB Sports Council (1996) *Valuing Volunteers*, London: GB Sports Council.
Geddes & Grosset (1997) *Dictionary of Quotations*, New Lanark: Geddes & Grosset.
Hansbro, J., Bridswood, A., Antony, M. and Hickman, M. (1997) *Health In England 1996: What People Know, What People Think, What People Do*, London: The Stationery Office.
Haywood, L., Kew, F., Bramham, P., Spink, J., Capenerhurst, J. and Henry, I. (1995) *Understanding Leisure*, Cheltenham: Stanley Thornes.
HEA (1995) *Health Update 5: Physical Activity*, London: HEA.
HEA (1998) *Physical Activity 'Swopshop'*, 6th edn, London: HEA.
Middlesbrough Council (1997) *Middlesbrough Strategy for Sport*.

Naidoo, J. and Wills, J. (2000) *Health Promotion: Foundations for Practice*, 2nd edn, London: Baillière Tindall.

Paish, W. (1998) *The Complete Manual of Sports Science*, London: A. & C. Black.

Patrick, K., Sallis, J., Long, B., Calfas, K., Wooten, W., Heath, G. and Pratt, M. (1994) 'A new tool for encouraging activity: project PACE', in *The Physician and Sportsmedicine*, 22 Nov.: 45–55, New York: McGraw-Hill.

Prochaska, J. and Marcus, B. (1994) 'The transtheoretical model: applications to exercise', in R. K. Dishman (ed.), *Advances in Exercise Adherence* (pp. 161–80), Champaign, IL: Human Kinetics.

Roberts, K. (1996) 'School children and sport', in *Sport, Education and Society* 1(1): 47–57, Oxford: Carfax Publishers.

Rowland, T. W. (1990) *Exercise and Children's Health*, Champaign, IL: Human Kinetics.

Sport England (2000) *Young People and Sport: National Survey 1999*, London: Sport England.

Chapter 8

Resources for sport

More people, more places, more medals – and more money?

David Jackson and Mark Nesti

Introduction

This chapter provides an overview of some of the major resourcing issues relating to the development of sport in recent times. A wider consideration of resources incorporates the hugely important 'people element' especially in relation to volunteering. From a more financial perspective, focus is directed at public sector involvement in sports development during a climate of greater economic accountability. Whilst individual local authorities and different regions of the country have faced their own specific challenges in terms of resource provision these have been largely overtaken by three major changes taking place at macro levels. The first of these, and in many ways the most radical and controversial, was the extension of Compulsory Competitive Tendering (CCT) to the management of sports facilities. Coming at the end of the 1980s, CCT represented the tool by which the then Conservative government hoped to force the market disciplines of the private sector upon those in public services in an effort to reduce waste, clarify roles and maximise income. Although painful for most providers of public services, the experience was even more of a shock to a sector where the service ethos was omnipotent and 'Sport for All?' was often translated into sport for free.

The fallout post-CCT was considerable and lessons are still being learned. However, the New Labour government in 1997 has been able to build on the positive aspects of CCT. Through its introduction of Best Value it hopes to provide a legislative framework within which a more sensitive balance can be struck between the need to provide a service for all against an overstretched public sector budget.

Finally, the National Lottery introduced in the last years of the Conservative government represents a policy initiative where cross-party support has been clearly evident. Thoughts that the New Labour administration would abandon the National Lottery were quickly dispelled and as the DCMS strategy *A Sporting Future for All* (DCMS, 2000) has emphasised, the success of sports development at all levels appears closely connected with the effective use of National Lottery capital and revenue monies.

The importance of human and financial resources in sport development can be measured by the £12 billion of consumer spending and the employment of 420,000 (*A Sporting Future for All*, DCMS, 2000). Interest in the economic impact of sport has been extended to consider the impact of sport on other areas of activity such as tourism, urban regeneration and the media. Work by Gratton (1999) has confirmed that major international events of a 'one-off' nature and major domestic spectator events such as the FA Cup Final generate the largest economic benefit for host cities. These financial attractions and high profile media coverage continue to highlight the resource implications associated with sport at the top level. This interest in elite sport has been identified by the government and Sport England through directing greater resources at the World Class programme and the UK Sports Institute.

As the country's most important sport development agency Sport England has recently stated that its aim is to lead the development of sport in England by influencing and serving the public, private and voluntary sectors. Under the banner of 'More People, More Places, More Medals', Sport England is aiming to facilitate the creation of what they claim will be the 'most comprehensive sport development system in the world' (Sport England Website). The intention is to encourage a sustainable system that can equally provide sporting opportunities for all and across all levels of achievement. In a sense, this arguably very ambitious goal, could be seen as one final attempt to resolve the conflict and contradiction apparent in the drive for 'Sport for All' and more recent interest in elite sport at performance and excellence levels. Whether this is achievable will ultimately depend upon the commitment of disparate partner organisations such as governing bodies, clubs and local authorities through whom Sport England channels its work. Whilst funding, facility provision and development are essential components of this, the role of those working within sports development has received a level of recognition not seen previously. Indeed, Sport England has emphasised that it 'is determined to improve *the entire* community in sports – as participants, spectators or volunteers'. This clearly echoes governmental philosophy and policy in terms of social inclusion and if genuinely achievable, will challenge those critical voices (e.g. McDonald, 1995) who have argued that 'Sport for All' has been abandoned both in practice and as a concept.

Participation

Sport England has claimed that current sport participation rates are high, although they have acknowledged that equality of opportunity has not been achieved. Whilst there are those for whom the term equity rather than equality more closely represents their goal, all agencies involved in sport development continue to strive to meet the needs of non-participant groups. (For a fuller discussion see Chapter 4.) For its part, Sport England intends to evaluate sports development initiatives through the introduction of measurable sports equity targets. In addition, it has indicated that it will focus government and lottery funding on priority groups and deprived communities. These measures, it is anticipated, will help shape sports development work at grass roots level within local authorities, clubs and governing bodies.

However, a cursory glance at the strategies and plans of most sports organisations, particularly those operating on the national stage, reveals that equality or equity policies and initiatives have received considerable attention. Whilst successes have been achieved there are equally many examples of failure. The reasons for this state of affairs are many and complex. Some researchers and writers (e.g. Hylton, 1998) have laid much of the blame for this at structural inequalities and weaknesses and inconsistencies in the policy process. However, many SDOs and deliverers of sport development programmes more prosaically have identified a lack of funding as the major obstacle to achieving equality of opportunity.

It could be argued that the very significant increase in funding provided by the lottery will not only assist agencies to meet the sporting needs of more people, but that of equal importance it will begin to highlight where the challenges and difficulties faced are not primarily about finance. The next five to ten years will provide much information about how realistic and achievable current targets are and bring a sharper edge to discussions around sporting opportunities, needs and individuals motivations. Although not addressing equality *per se*, research at Hull University by Clough and Sewell (1999) into the attraction of exercise and physical activity highlights the importance of recognising individual choice and differing motivations. Using a daily diary method their study revealed that positive mood was experienced by committed exercisers during sport and physical activity sessions and, more interestingly, that non-exercisers reported strong negative effect states during a physical activity programme. When both groups experienced non-exercise based sessions involving playing chess and a board game, the exercise group experienced strongly negative mood states, and the non-exercisers reported very high positive affect. This clear finding is remarkable arguably, not because it could not be reasonably predicted, but that few if any studies have reported the common-sense position which is that non-exercisers do not exercise or take part in sport (enough, if at all) because they prefer to do other activities they enjoy!

Sport England's call for 'More People' may intensify current academic debates between those advocates of a sociological perspective, where emphasis is on society and structures, and psychologists such as Chelladurai (1985) where the focus is more on individual motivations and intentions. Again, the renewed drive to finally attain authentic, genuine Sport for All, may well founder during what has been described as a post-modern era. Post-modernism has been linked to the apparent rise in individual freedoms, in Western culture at least, as seen in lifestyle choices and the rapid disintegration of society in the face of global materialism. In terms of sport development during the past two to three decades, a much professed respect for individual choice and motivations has been accompanied by increasing efforts to convince all groups in society to participate in sport. This tension between providing opportunities for all, whilst recognising that not all individuals will want to become involved is well understood by many at the sharp end of sports delivery. Interestingly whilst it has been generally accepted that financial cost usually represents the major barrier to greater participation, especially from the low participant groups, research by Coalter (1991) has suggested that this is not always the case. Recent studies (Coalter and Allison, 1996) have begun to include a greater focus on lifestyle and individual choice in terms of identifying reasons for low or non-participation. Nevertheless, Sport England's determination to involve the entire community in sport may turn out to be largely unattainable where individual people within groups and society itself exercise their choice to avoid sport. The sometimes missionary and even evangelical zeal of those agencies and organisations committed to sport must be understood against an increasingly value free culture, where talk of the value of sport is reminiscent of Victorian ideals of muscular Christianity, character building and moral development through sport (McIntosh, 1987). That policy documents such as *The Value of Sport* (1999a) have emerged from a Labour administration is difficult to analyse until closer examination reveals the strong Christian beliefs of the current Prime Minister and his cabinet's enthusiastic embracing of traditionally conservative concerns such as respect for the rule of law, sound public finance and self-sufficiency. However, policy statements and strategies cannot effect a change without the concerted efforts of those closest to the point of delivery. That apparently not everyone is convinced that solutions to increasing participation in society and in sport can be achieved by following the government's exhortations seems to have been overlooked. Sport England and its partner agencies in sport development may have been set a challenge which must remain forever unattainable, unless new powers are to be granted to allow authorities to coerce all people to take part in sport!

The focus of more people is in another sense much broader than 'Sport for All?'. Effort is to be targeted at increasing volunteers, spectators and participants. Whilst spectators are vital in terms of generating revenue either directly or indirectly through sponsorship opportunities and advertising, and help generate 'atmosphere' at events, the main concern is with volunteers and participants.

Volunteering and developing sport

The role of the volunteer in sport has recently received much greater attention and even scrutiny. There are several important reasons for this, however;

arguably the most significant relates to the special place occupied by volunteers in the formation and development of sport in the UK. Historically the state and the government left provision of most sport and physical recreation to the unpaid, dedicated and enthusiastic amateurs. It can be argued that sport in the community beyond that offered by schools or in a small number of professional sports, was designed, delivered and built up by a disparate group of people who often shared a common love of sport in general and of their sport in particular. Communities both large and small and from the very affluent to the much less so, worked to lay the foundations for what was probably the most extensive and diverse sporting provision in the world. That this was owned, shaped and developed at almost no cost to government was quite remarkable; that individuals, companies and local communities nourished and sustained these opportunities without any significant outside help seems difficult to believe in these more individualistic times.

During the rapid expansion in local authority funded sport provision during the 1970s and early 1980s the contribution of the voluntary sector remained important despite its more low key profile. Whilst local politicians invested huge sums of money in building and staffing flagship sport and leisure centres in their areas, the volunteer workforce continued to supply the coaches, administrators, treasurers and club secretaries without which most formal competitive sport provision would have disappeared. Increasingly, local authorities began to seek closer ties and develop partnerships with the voluntary sector, most notably clubs and community groups. Sports development workers, with the remit to take sport to the people through outreach working, and those required to help young performers to fulfil their sporting potential both worked ever more closely with the voluntary sector to achieve these aims together. During the late 1980s initiatives such as Champion Coaching were launched by the National Coaching Foundation and the Sports Council to help improve performance levels in children and develop the network of coaches in the UK. Although often led by local authorities and sports development staff, these projects relied heavily on partnership with the voluntary sector in the form of coaches, leaders, parents and clubs and governing bodies.

The value, in monetary terms, associated with the extensive use of the 1.5 million volunteers in English sport has been estimated at £15.04 billion (Kokolakakis, 1999). Although local authorities and governing bodies were enthusiastic recipients of this work, little was done on a more formal and planned basis to attract, retain or reward sports volunteers. Champion coaching arguably represented the first truly nation-wide initiative where volunteers were provided with vouchers to assist them to acquire further and more advanced coaching qualifications. These subsidies were offered to coaches in return for their work in helping to deliver quality youth sports programmes for those aspiring to improve their performance levels. The success of many of these programmes around the country led to a number of positive developments which did much to further strengthen existing links between clubs and coaches, governing bodies (i.e. the voluntary sector) and local authorities in particular. Facility managers and sports development officers played a significant role in facilitating these ties and sought additional opportunities to establish initiatives aimed at other levels of the sport development continuum, through closer co-operation with the voluntary sector.

Interestingly, according to Shibli *et al.* (1999), the 1990s has witnessed a growth in a new type to volunteer in sport. Initiatives such as Champion Coaching at a national level, and a number of similarly organised local schemes, helped contribute to raised expectations amongst some volunteers in terms of greater and more tangible recognition of their role. In common with other areas of voluntary work, distinctions between the volunteer and the hourly paid casual staff sports worker have become increasingly blurred. Many volunteers, especially those involved in coaching and coach education have become accustomed to receiving payment for their services, although often the rates offered amount to little more than expenses and are used to convey recognition for the work provided. Nevertheless, governing bodies of sport, local authorities, Sport England, and the National Coaching Foundation have continued to press for a greater recognition of the work of the voluntary sector and have recommended that coaching in particular should be rewarded financially where possible. This has led to an increased profile for coaches and coach education; however, some sports either because of traditions or lack of funding are reluctant to offer remuneration. For example, some Rugby Union Development Officers have pointed out that leaders and coaches working within their sport have no desire to be paid for a service which they are willing to offer to clubs and others in their free time. In contrast, many coaches in football development do expect some form of payment, and not least because of the significant number of schemes at all levels of the continuum, where participants are charged for taking part.

Beyond this, a greater recognition of the key role of the voluntary sector in sports development work has emerged as a result of a number of changes at a macro level. One such change has been the transition by many local authorities from service providers to that of enablers. The notion behind this shift in focus and policy was that local authorities needed to share their traditional role more fully with their local communities. The intention was to move from what Henry (1993) has called a paternalistic form of provision to a more equal and active partnership with the broader community. In this way, it was hoped that needs rather than merely demand would be more likely identified and addressed. In addition, the pressures during the 1990s on capital expenditure, a declining revenue base and an ever increasing set of expectations facing local authorities made the new enabling role a necessity rather than an option. More positively, local authorities' sports providers in particular were forced to re-assess the vital role played by the voluntary sector and begin to involve them more coherently in their planning and work across the sports development continuum.

At a national level the Sports Council responded to this new environment with more support for voluntary groups, including devising training and education initiatives such as the Running Sport programme. The aim of this programme according to Sport England is to improve the quality of sport management, sports development and the delivery of sporting experiences for everyone involved in sport in England. Recently re-designed to meet the needs of sports development professionals and school teachers, the workshops and home study materials were primarily aimed at the voluntary sector in the sports clubs and governing bodies. A further development along similar lines is the Sport England's Volunteer Investment Programme (VIP). This aims to increase recognition of the important roles of volunteers in sport, encourage good practice in recruitment and retention of volunteers, and to help volunteers develop their leadership and managerial skills as appropriate.

The major problem according to Shibli *et al.* (1999) is that with ever more expected of the voluntary sector in sport any substantial decline in numbers could be very harmful. Unfortunately, there are signs that this may be happening as people's leisure time declines and the numbers in full-time work continue to rise. Increasingly, it is not a matter of whether people possess the skills and the motivation to become involved in their local clubs or with sport development initiative but is more related to lack of time. The increase in those over fifty appears to be a welcome development because traditionally this group has been heavily involved as sport volunteers often as club administrators and advisers. However, recent data suggest that fewer seem able or prepared to devote themselves to these voluntary roles in sport and are being attracted by a myriad of competing leisure pursuits and interests.

The professionalisation of sports development

There have been periods of substantial growth in full-time paid employment within sports development during the past three decades. Those working in the public sector all have a varied role to play in developing sporting opportunities. The growth in the commercial and private sector has been more difficult to chart given that much of this has been within existing business. For example the increase in health, fitness and sport provision in the tourism and hospitality industry, or the emergence of broad-based leisure theme parks offering an expanding range of sporting opportunities, highlights just how difficult it is to identify precisely the scale of this part of the sports development industry. What is more clear is that the human resource involved in all of these forms of sports development is the key factor in improving (and conversely, undermining) sport participation. Haywood (1992) has accused the sport development and leisure industry of pursuing professional status to enhance its own status and preserve their own position of power and influence. Haywood has argued that this drive for professionalisation has been achieved at the expense of a more legitimate concern of serving the community.

Within local authority settings staff have experienced a number of important changes associated with the greater emphasis on accountability, planning and cost effectiveness which have arisen alongside the culture of CCT, performance indicators, planning and capital spending controls. Effective sports development workers have had to develop skills and qualities to work in partnership with a range of others within and outside sport. This has led arguably to greater concern with the training, education and qualifications of those working in the area. Governing bodies of sport, local authorities, national agencies and higher education initiatives currently provide a plethora of courses and training opportunities ranging from one-day seminars to post-graduate qualifications in Managing Sports Development (e.g. Leeds Metropolitan University). In terms of providing ongoing training and education for those at lower and more intermediate levels, the Certificate and Diploma courses in sports development offered at the Carnegie National Sports Development Centre LMU have been attended by over 500 individuals since their inception in 1992. Within this group at least 25–30 per cent of the course participants have come from sport facility backgrounds in comparison to 50–55 per cent in more community or sports specific SDO posts.

Although not everyone would agree, the drive towards professional status for those working in sports development is likely to further establish this area of work as something likely to raise standards of operation and improve service delivery. The newly formed National Association of Sports Development is an example of the continued movement towards professional status. It will be interesting to see what support this body receives from other key associations and agencies, such as ILAM and Sport England, and whether it will take an active role in establishing national codes of practice and validating qualifications and training. This level of activity will of course require generous resourcing, not the least of which is funding. From a broader consideration Sport England and their partners may be unable adequately to achieve their aims and objectives for Sport Development in the twenty-first century without a sizeable and expanding budget.

More money

If there is to be a realistic chance of Sport England's strategy achieving its objectives, the mission of More People, More Places, More Medals is

implicitly underpinned by another catchline of More Money. This expansive and optimistic attempt at building the best sports development
programme in the world was clearly unrealistic in the increasingly cash
starved environment of recent years; but salvation, in the form of the
National Lottery, has in recent times transformed both the theory and
the practice of how we view our sporting expectations. In order to consider
the true impact of the lottery as an important seachange in the environment, it is necessary to set a context that describes some of the major
influencing moments of the resourcing of sport in recent years.

In the period from the early 1970s there have been enormous changes
in the financial landscape in sport. In the commercial sector there has been
the impact of the media and sponsorship on professional football, golf and
many other mainstream sports. This has taken place on a national and
transnational scale and is another indicator of the impact of globalisation.

On a more parochial level the emergence of a health and fitness industry
based on private clubs has seen not only a shift in large-scale business away
from public sports centres to increasingly well-known brands such as David
Lloyd and Virgin, but a massive growth in total turnover based on increasing
awareness of the benefits of healthy lifestyles and improvements in national
prosperity. More detailed analysis of this phenomenon is contained in
Chapter 7.

In considering the ever-changing financial and sporting environment of
recent times, one of the key periods of change is centred on local government reorganisation in 1974. In the run-up to 1 April 1974 many small
authorities saw the opportunities for facility building on a comparatively
grand scale which was fuelled by a number of influences. First, councils
that were about to be absorbed into much larger bodies saw the opportunity to make popular political capital by spending on modern up-to-date
leisure facilities that had come into vogue. Although the cynical might
view this as political gesturing, there was clearly a huge and growing
demand in local communities and the ability to satisfy it.

This coincided with a period of relative prosperity in local government
which meant that budgetary provision on the increasingly important welfare
service that leisure was becoming was readily available in local government
coffers to meet these contemporary aspirations. The Sports Council also
supported capital investment in policy and financial terms with a modest
but often crucial budget that was used often to great effect as a pump
primer for projects. Consequently there was a massive input in resources in
capital terms over a comparatively short period of time and the corollary
of more expenditure on facilities was an increase in the revenue budgets
required to run these establishments of enjoyment. The nature of providing
these types of public services also meant that the majority of this ongoing
expenditure was spent on the essential element of staffing. Sport and leisure
is often described as a people business and this newly emerging profession

was providing job opportunities at all levels from cleaners and catering staff to managers and directors of burgeoning new leisure services departments in town halls across the country.

The emphasis during the 1970s and early 1980s was clearly about spending on facilities. The underpinning drivers of policy centred on the view that if good facilities were provided then local communities would take full advantage of them and develop their sporting involvement in a way that would satisfy a range of social, political, individual and sporting aspirations. This focus on community facilities inevitably resulted in a significant element of compromise in the funding and provision of specialist facilities. For example, whilst many large urban conurbations had ambitions for major swimming and athletics facilities, local authority budgets were concentrated on the lower levels of the continuum.

This strategy of bringing people to sport proved to have serious limitations and the subsequent attempts to change the emphasis and bring sport to the people during the mid-1980s was the beginning of 'sports development' as many understand it today. In local authorities across the country this was the first time that budgets were dedicated for direct community sporting intervention in this way. This meant that leisure departments began to expand their remit beyond the operational function of facility management into the realms of both generic and sport specific sports development. The resources for this expansion came partly from within local authority budgets but also as a result of government funding through the Sports Council. This was substantially initiated by the promotion of Action Sport in response to urban unrest in the early part of the decade, but there was also a clear determination on the part of many authorities to establish strong leadership in the development of sport. At the beginning of this process there was still a climate of relative affluence and making budgetary provision was not too problematic. But the growth of both facility building and what was in effect an exercise in sports marketing being delivered by a growing band of teams and lone officers, began to falter as the pressure exerted by central government started to take its toll on local government finances.

The subsequent introduction in the early 1990s of the Compulsory Competitive Tendering regime with its concentration on the management of sports facilities also had an impact on the resources provided for sport in the public sector. As the result of both serious managerial analysis and the fear of competition even more pressure was being focused on the true cost of providing sport. The potential for savings in expenditure and hoped-for growth in income produced a holy grail of a significant all-round improvement to the bottom line. Within CCT contracts being operated by supposedly freestanding Direct Service Organisations (DSOs) the reality often proved to be that out-turn figures for both income and expenditure did not always match up to the expectations of original estimates. This led to a deepening cycle of downward pressure that often resulted in the impoverishment of both the range and quality of sporting services. There is considerable anecdotal evidence that facility managers concentrated on revenue generation rather than quality sports development in order to try to balance the books in an increasingly straitened contractual environment. Five-a-side football and mass aerobics often became the order of the day to the detriment of high-level performance programmes designed to produce future champions or provide purposeful activity for local youth.

This whole scenario was exacerbated by a backdrop of negative external influences which affected the whole economy in the early and mid-1990s. A powerful mixture of high interest rates, general economic recession and the exertion of increasing financial stringency by central government made life increasingly uncomfortable for service departments. Both the client departments and their contracting arms were subject to the difficulties of trying to achieve the targets of business plans in the face of a public with the discretion not to spend a diminishing disposable income with them. All of this within the reality of a non-statutory (i.e. discretionary) service within local government. Further difficulties were encountered such as the rise of a range of competing leisure interests and the emergence of a very competitive, high quality health and fitness product from the commercial sector. The heat was really on.

It is of more than passing interest to register the arrival of the new entrepreneurial developments in private health, fitness and leisure clubs. It could be claimed that much of the groundwork in developing awareness and opportunities in personal fitness training was explored (often on a shoestring) by local authorities and that as soon as the commercial possibilities emerged, their lack of ability to compete on an equal footing led to a haemorrhaging of business in a paradoxically expanding market. In an environment during the Conservative years in government which seemed unrelentingly hostile to local government finance and which brought about much soul searching and entrepreneurialism in the public sector, the reality of life clearly came to show that any type of sport or leisure service that had a viable commercial future would quite naturally be supplied by private enterprise operating in a free market. There are few that would argue that this should not be so as the whole of the economies of the developed world revolve around a system of market economy and there is no reason why this should not apply to sport as much as to any other service. The inevitable conclusion from this, however, is that whilst private enterprise takes away and develops the best of the commercially viable ideas, the remaining services are by definition non-profit making and therefore in need of support if they are to continue to be provided. The necessary financial support for this to happen may come in the form of public subsidy, below-the-line resourcing through the voluntary sector, or perhaps via commercial sponsorship.

Faced with an array of real pressures the advances made in easier times in both facility and outreach sports development often went on hold or into retreat in the early 1990s. The opportunities for access to sport were under constraint from other elements of government policy, notably the Local Management of Schools and the National Curriculum which were outlined in the Education Reform Act (1988), planning policy in relation to the selling of school playing fields, and the teachers' disputes of the late 1980s. Against this background the Major government began to show interest in what was happening in sport and set out to provide policy guidance on how improvements could be achieved. *Sport – Raising the Game* (1995) was viewed by many working in sport in both public and voluntary sectors as a flawed attempt to raise the profile of sport on the political agenda and the achievements of national teams on the international stage after a series of uncomfortable defeats. Whilst there was much food for thought in the plans for raising the nation's sporting capabilities there was also the potential for at least some salvation with the promise of considerable resourcing from the soon-to-be established National Lottery. The emergence of sport as one of the lottery's five good causes and the subsequent election of a Labour government held the potential for real change in the outlook for sport, and the subsequent success of the lottery has proved to have had a major impact. Much of the future of the nation's plans for sport are inextricably linked to the gambling habits of the population, and this has now become a key matter of resourcing that requires some examination.

The National Lottery

The introduction of the Lotteries Act in 1993 and the implementation of the National Lottery in 1994 by the then Conservative government was viewed in a number of ways. To some it was a sparkling new initiative designed to capture the imagination of the country with the added potential of providing real benefit for a range of causes close to the nation's heart. To others it was succumbing to the forces of darkness and it would lead us into a socially undesirable dependence on gambling which would sap the poor and create unrealistic expectations of an escape from poverty. The reality of the situation that faced the government was that a number of lottery games were emerging in nearby European countries. The inability to prevent people in this country taking part was impossible even if it had been desirable and this would have led to any monetary benefit, other than prizes, going elsewhere. In setting out to embrace the inevitable the National Lottery has changed the complexion of the financial support for the sporting endeavours of the country. Though not perhaps in exactly the way he intended, the words of the former prime minister John Major do have a ring of a certain truth, 'The existence of the National Lottery has transformed forever the prospects for British sport' (*Sport – Raising the Game*, 1995).

Despite concerns about the selection of Camelot as the operator for this massive financial undertaking (a discussion beyond the scope of this book) the lottery has generated enormous interest and significant amounts of revenue both as prizes for individuals and funds for good causes. It has also made a sizeable contribution to tax revenue for the government as well as rapidly establishing itself as an integral part of national life. The breakdown of how each pound of lottery income was used is shown in Figure 8.1.

Interestingly there has been little debate about the fact that the government receives a windfall of 12 per cent of the total revenue generated, and it is clear that much more could have been made available for distribution to the original five good causes nominated at the inception of the lottery which were: Sport; the Arts; Charities; Heritage and the Millennium. Each of these received one-fifth of the designated 28 per cent of funds generated. The original estimates of what this would actually mean in financial terms was at the time a mouth-watering prospect for potential recipients of this new bounty and the reality actually far outstripped those figures (see Figure 8.2).

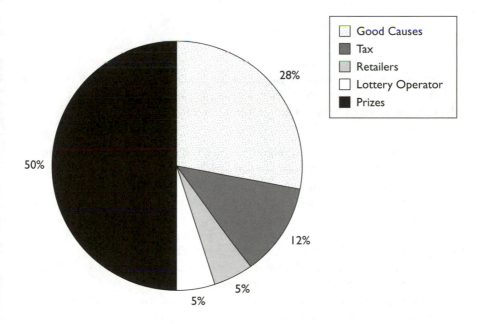

Figure 8.1 National Lottery distribution. How each National Lottery pound is spent.

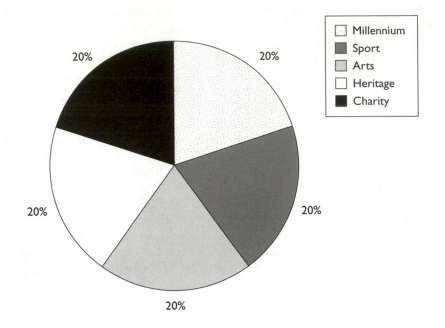

Figure 8.2 Each good cause receives 5.6p from each £1 ticket bought

Rules for the distribution of the proceeds from the lottery were delivered to the relevant bodies which in the case of sport was the Sports Council. Nevertheless, several important problems were encountered.

- None of the money designated for the Lottery Sports Fund was to be used for revenue purposes; the intention was to provide funding for a new wave of modern facilities and refurbish older ones. The breadth was expected to stretch from major international venues to changing rooms for local clubs.
- Partnership funding of a minimum of 35 per cent of the cost of the project was to be provided by the organisation applying.
- The Sports Council as distributing body was not allowed to solicit bids and had to remain neutral in the process.
- Funds provided by the lottery were intended to be new, additional resources with no reductions in existing budgets.
- Grants could not be made for commercial enterprises.

It soon became clear that as much as there was suddenly a new stream of previously unavailable money to tap in to, it was not necessarily reaching those sectors of the community who perhaps needed it most. Many organisations foundered on an inability to comply with the bureaucratic requirements of the process as well as finding their minimum 35 per cent capital funding. In addition, even if they could overcome these obstacles there was still the need to provide a realistic business plan that could robustly predict a sustainable income and expenditure stream for the project. Beyond these problems there were clearly issues around certain sectors of the community being disenfranchised from the whole process. How realistic was it, for example, to expect small community groups in impoverished inner-city or rural locations even to begin to develop the dream of lottery funded facilities?

> In the early days . . . a lot of the grants in London tended to go to suburban boroughs which reflected the fact that these places have lots of articulate wealthy people in the voluntary sector running sports clubs that already owned their own land and were able to make the most of the scheme.
>
> *The Guardian*, Downes (1996)

The role of local authorities in the early days of the lottery was also interesting in that there was a need to fulfil a multiplicity of roles. They were part of the consultation process for applications but soon saw that the attraction of lottery funding for sport and other projects in local communities was something for which they had a responsibility and desire to promote, co-ordinate and develop. There was also a clearly sharpening focus on the need to plan strategically to ensure maximum benefit.

The limitations of the distributive regulations of the Lottery Sports Fund were tackled in an incremental way by the Sports Council through the introduction of the Priority Areas Initiative and the Schools Community Sports Initiative scheme; but the real opportunity for change came with the election of the New Labour government in 1997. The Department of Culture, Media and Sport instigated a thorough review of the ways in which lottery funds were allocated and after extensive consultation and consideration of options the newly rebranded Sport England produced a strategy document in May 1999 entitled *Investing in Our Sporting Future* (1999b). The main thrust of this new plan was to split the estimated £200 million per year (projected over each of the following ten years) into a Community Projects Fund using three-quarters of the total, and a World Class Fund that would use the balance to support sporting endeavours on the national and international stage. The total amount available to sport had been reduced by falling revenues and the introduction of the New Opportunities Fund (NOF), but this amount was still beyond the original estimates made when the lottery had first begun. The Community Projects fund incorporates three elements to try to ensure a more thorough coverage of the population, these being Small Projects (Capital and revenue schemes up to £5,000), Revenue Awards for schemes over £5,000 and Capital Awards for larger-scale developments. It is anticipated that National Lottery funding will address the major shortfall in specialist sport facilities relative to other nations. There is considerable potential for the aspirations expressed in strategic plans for facility development to be substantially achieved. Figure 8.3 shows the overall strategy for the distribution of money from the Lottery Sports Fund.

There are significant differences between the new and the old lottery strategies, the most important of which are the active participation in the process by Sport England and the inclusion of support for a wide range of revenue activities that were previously excluded. There are clear links drawn between lottery funding targets and the application of Sport England's overarching strategy of More People, More Places, More Medals (1999c). The supporting Active Programmes form a fundamental element of the development of sporting opportunities particularly at participation levels and the objectives of the new lottery strategy are clearly devised to direct funding at those communities most in need in designated Sport Action Zones, the Priority Areas Initiative and the School Community Sports Initiative. The stamp of current national policies is clearly seen throughout the process in that sporting aspirations that are deemed supportable by the Lottery Sports Fund are significantly wedded to issues of social inclusion, community development and health and the other targets of Best Value services as defined by both government and Sport England.

The introduction of the New Opportunities Fund led to a subsequent change in the distribution ratios from October 1999, as shown in Figure 8.4. The share of the Sports Lottery Fund pound was reduced from 5.6 per cent to 4.66 per cent but this still represents an estimated lottery income of £200 million per annum on which the projections for the next ten years are made.

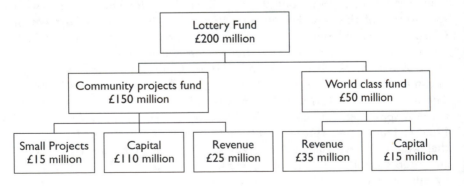

Figure 8.3 Lottery Sports Fund – distribution strategy.

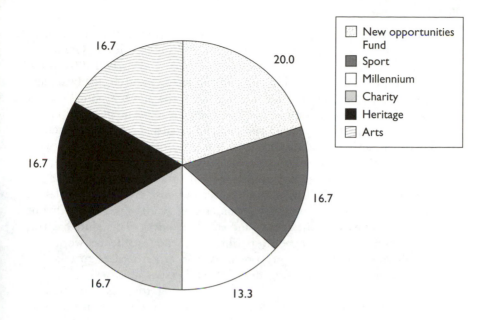

Figure 8.4 Sport, the arts, heritage and charity each receive 4.06p from each £1 ticket bought

The proactive role of Sport England allows for a strategically directed process to achieve maximum benefit from the largesse of lottery money. There is also an increasingly highlighted role for local authorities to play in attracting lottery funding into its geographical area and increasing evidence of the employment of lottery specialists to lever in funds from a range of partners. Without a co-ordinated strategy for sporting development in all sector provision there will inevitably be concern that lottery money may not reach where it may be needed most. This requires local authorities to work with the many partners in the sporting environment to ensure that the plans for provision are clearly defined and agreed as part of a comprehensive strategy (see Chapter 6). Similarly, national governing bodies are required to ensure they have well-developed strategies for their own sports at all levels if they are to receive funding to support their activities on the national and international stage. The World Class fund is itself split between revenue and capital schemes and aims to support a continually contentious and politically sensitive UK Sports Institute alongside a facilities and events programme and a range of support services targeted at producing future champions.

More medals

A major challenge facing governing bodies in the past has been a lack of adequate funding to support those at the very highest level. Grant aid awards from the Sports Council during the 1980s and early 1990s rarely satisfied the expectations of athletes or administrators and arguably undermined success on the international stage. Whilst the Sports Council (as has been discussed elsewhere) promoted the concept of performance and excellence amongst its partner agencies, political, financial and structural obstacles limited this to an aspiration rather than a reality for most. However, with the advent of the National Lottery in 1994 a dramatic increase in capital and subsequently (and most importantly) revenue was made available specifically to address this challenge. The role of national governing bodies in planning, managing and supporting this area of work was given a major lift with this influx of substantially increased resources. This shift has put governing bodies centre stage in performance and excellence work and reduced the need for increasingly pressurised local authorities to take the lead in this and other conflicting demands and responsibilities.

Alongside the prize of increased lottery funding there is the essential corollary of the responsibility to deliver. It will be interesting in the years ahead to chart how closely resources will follow success (see Table 8.1).

There is much optimism about the potential for success in developing sport at all levels of the continuum and for achieving the strategic objectives set out for sport by government, Sport England, local authorities, national governing bodies and all those with a stake in the sporting fortunes and future of the country. The significant input made by National Lottery funding has the potential for considerable achievement but success is far from guaranteed. The ability of other countries to apply similar principles more effectively has to be considered as far as international achievements are concerned and the emergence of complementary and supporting policies may play a role in determining the potential for success at other levels.

Sport England and the DCMS have emphasised that resources must be targeted to enable more medals to be won at major competitions. They hope that this will be achieved through the establishment of specialist sports colleges for talented young performers. In addition, substantial sums of lottery money have been allocated to a network of UK Sports Institute

Table 8.1 Sports Lottery Fund: distribution of funds to May 2000

Total amount requested	£3,347,668,479
Total project costs	£5,538,947,402
No. of projects funded	3,110
Total awarded	£995,215,738
Total project costs	£1,769,010,992

Ref: http://www.english.sports.gov.uk

centres around the country to provide access to high level coaching and sports science and medicine support. Working in partnership with national governing bodies, the Sports Councils have been instructed by the government to co-operate and ensure '. . . the development funds and lottery funds must work together with the aim of creating an efficient, transparent and accessible support system', *A Sporting Future for All* (DCMS, 2000: 16).

Future changes to the format of the National Lottery and a changing emphasis from government on the continuation of sport as a beneficiary of the nation's gambling habits may well have an impact on this significant area of resourcing for sport. It is perhaps well to reflect on the position of sports development in all its guises had the National Lottery never come about.

Case Study: Fairfax Metropolitan District Council

The National Lottery

The introduction of the National Lottery came as a source of some long-sought-after relief for FMDC. After year-on-year cuts in capital programmes and progressive deterioration of revenue budgets due to decreasing central government support and self-imposed stringency due to the real and perceived rigours of CCT, the politicians and senior officers of the Council saw an element of potential salvation arriving. Staff in the Leisure Services Department felt that they would be the front-runners in the race for this new bounty as the Good Causes espoused were aligned to their daily service provision. Quickly they drew up plans that met the criteria laid down and hopes were high that the longed-for refurbishment of the sports centres and the dreams of a new athletics facility may be at hand. After all, they had managed to deal with an enormous amount of essential ongoing maintenance to roofs, boilers and pool plant from their shrinking budgets, as well as managing some self-financing developments such as fitness training suites and aerobics studios. Now there were new opportunities for achieving some real progress in developing sporting opportunities for their local communities.

Although potentially massive amounts of money were coming on stream from the Lottery Sports Fund and much of the early advice had talked about the race for funding being a marathon not a sprint, a deflated air spread around the department as it soon became apparent that, for a variety of reasons, all that had been hoped for might not arrive.

Senior politicians became aware from a very early stage that the demands across the Council area for funds for sport would not be just coming forward from their own Leisure Services Department. The Education Department particularly, as well as Social Services also saw the opportunity for achieving long-held ambitions for all-weather pitches, refurbished tennis courts and new fitness suites. Not only did this mean competition within the council for which projects would be supported both in principle and with the necessary finance; it also meant that hard decisions about the political priorities of the Council had to be declared.

On top of this there was a mobilisation of the forces of voluntary sport who shared these dreams but who also required political support in terms of strategic approval, finance, planning permission and ranking ahead or at least alongside the Council's own bids.

The Council set about resolving these issues by setting up a Lottery Support Team that was to try to co-ordinate all bids so that an overview could be taken and informed decisions made as to which bids would be supported. There was also a realisation that certain sectors of the community were disenfranchised from the whole system of lottery application and a supporting, proactive role in developing projects amongst under-represented populations was required. That all this was happening at the same time as the New Labour government was introducing as yet undefined plans for a system of Best Value to replace the CCT regime made for a very complicated picture.

The realisation of the implications of both Best Value and the National Lottery was that clear, strategic plans for the development of sporting opportunities across the Council's area were no longer just desirable but essential. Sport was an integral component of Council services and therefore had to have a strategy in its own right that incorporated public, voluntary and private sector contributions and aspirations. Not only that, but under the banner of Best Value, the services provided by sport had to be clearly integrated into the overall Council strategies to meet the cross-cutting agenda relating to social exclusion, economic and community development and health.

Whilst all this big picture planning was exercising the minds of senior politicians and managers in the Town Hall, an array of lottery funded schemes in schools, sports centres and voluntary clubs were appearing on the ground making the dream of the lottery a reality for some, and holding out aspirations for others that their turn may yet come. However, the Council's own flagship scheme for a major new international multi-sports complex was foundering as there were insufficient funds for such large-scale projects and there were question marks about long-term viability and strategic fit with other facilities across the country.

Meanwhile in neighbouring Priestly MDC the early decision to go for a grandiose international standard athletics stadium as a priority ahead of a range of smaller community-based schemes had paid off and construction was under way before many others started to put their bids together.

Within a short space of time, seemingly infinite demands were being made on lottery funding and as much as there was a desire to see these dreams fulfilled, the reality soon became clear that there was simply not enough money to support all the worthwhile schemes that came forward.

References

Chelladurai, P. (1985) *Sports Management – Macro Perspectives*, Victoria: Sports Dynamics.

Clough, P. and Sewell, D. (1999) Paper presented at BASES Annual Conference, Leeds Metropolitan University, September, 1999.

Coalter, F. (1991) 'Sports participation: price or priorities?', *Leisure Studies*, 12: 171–82.

Coalter, F. and Allison, M. (1996) *Sport and Community Development*, Scottish Sports Council.

Department of Culture Media and Sport (2000) *A Sporting Future for All*, London: DCMS.

Department of National Heritage (1995) *Sport – Raising the Game*, London: DNH.

Downes, G. (1996) 'Poor hope of rich pickings', *The Guardian*, 13 September.

Gratton, C. (1999) 'The economic importance of major sports events'. Proceedings of European Association for Sport Management. EASM, Sport Management in the Next Millennium.

Haywood, L. (1992) *Leisure in the 1990s: Rolling Back the Welfare State*, (LSA Publications No. 46). Eastbourne: Leisure Studies Association.

Henry, I. (1993) *The Politics of Leisure Policy*, Loughborough University: Macmillan.

Hylton, K. (1998) 'Equal opportunities and the sport policy process', paper presented at 'Sport in the City' Conference, Sheffield: Hallam University.

Kokolakakis, T. (1999) 'Leisure volunteering: the economic significance of volunteering in the UK'. 7th Congress of the European Association for Sport Management. EASM, September 1999.

McDonald, I. (1995) *Sport for All – RIP?*, in S. Fleming, M. Talbot and A. Tomlinson (eds), *Policy and Politics in Sport, Recreation and Leisure* (LSA Publications. No. 55). Eastbourne: Leisure Studies Association.

McIntosh, P. (1987) *Sport in Society*, London: West London Press.

Shibli, S., Taylor, P., Nicholls, G., Gratton, C. and Kokolakakis, T. (1999) 'The characteristics of volunteers in UK sports clubs', *European Journal for Sports Management*, 6: 10–27.

Sport England (1999a) *Investing in Our Sporting Future*, London: Sport England. Available HTTP: http://www.english.sports.gov.uk

Sport England and the Local Government Association (1999b) *The Value of Sport. Best Value Through Sport*, London: Sport England. Available HTTP: http://www.english.sports.gov.uk

Sport England (1999c). *More People, More Places, More Medals*, Available HTTP: http://www.english.sports.gov.uk/whatwedo/htm

Chapter 9

Legal principles and issues

Managing disciplinaries in sport and recreation

Hazel J. Hartley

Introduction

'Vinnie Feels the Pinch'[1]

'IAAF Anger at Modahl Verdict'[2]

'Ice Queen Wars Bare Skating's Dirty Underside'[3]

'Norman Goes in Fudged Sacking'[4]

'Women Cleared to Stand for Top Rugby Administrative jobs'[5]

'Football Racists Face Trial by Video'[6]

'Vickery Ban Challenged by England'[7]

'Yates waits for RFU "biting" verdict'[8]

These are just some of the headlines in recent years, where sport and recreation participants may be facing disciplinary action following alleged breaches of codes or rules which can range from doping offences, violence, sexual discrimination, racism, as well as slander, fraud, eligibility to compete, a breach of sponsorship rules and the more general category of 'bringing the sport into disrepute'. In reviewing what is meant by a 'recognised sport' in relation to lawful exceptions from criminal liability, the Law Commission of England and Wales noted that governing bodies would be expected to have 'adequate disciplinary procedures', alongside other requirements laid down by recognising authorities, such as 'assuming responsibility for their members', and operating democratically within the relevant constitutions, rules, codes and charters (Law Commission, 1995; Wearmouth, 1995).

PART I

This chapter will briefly outline the principles of natural justice, which the law expects of governing bodies when writing and implementing their disciplinary codes of conduct, with reference to incidents and case law, where relevant. During this part of the chapter some of the broader issues will be reviewed, which create real challenges for governing bodies such as harmonisation of rules, and anti-doping rules of strict liability. Following this rather formal overview of what the law expects, Part II will explore a broader socio-legal approach on the issues of masculine subcultures, with a view to tracing their influence from the games field to the law courts. It will indicate some of the powerful group norms which are in conflict with societal norms and some of the formal rules of sports competition and codes of conduct.

> Sports related organisations have a responsibility to publish clear guidelines on what is considered to be ethical or unethical behaviour and ensure that consistent and appropriate incentives are applied.
> (European Code of Sports Ethics, 1992: Council of Europe, cited in Wearmouth, 1995: 31)

Disciplinary guidelines should be available and explained to all members through the rules and educational programmes. The rules should state clearly and precisely how to set out any allegations or charges.[9] Welch and Wearmouth (1994) suggest that information to members should include any costs incurred in submitting the complaint; procedures and penalties; any time limits on the submission of information; what happens at each stage and who has the power to deal with it; levels of privacy and confidentiality required at each stage and availability and grounds for appeal. In addition, consideration might be given to the inclusion of:

> policies and procedures relating to intimidation, breaches of confidentiality by or affecting someone involved in the process. If this is not addressed in the policy or guidelines it remains invisible and only the problem of the victims.
> (Welch and Wearmouth, 1994; Wearmouth, 1995: 32)

Rules, codes and laws: harmonisation or conflict?

> Of the many disputes prevalent in the industry at the moment many can be put down to the governing bodies' inability to uphold and enforce their own rules and regulations.
> (Parker, 1995: 3)

Sport development officers should encourage governing bodies in developing their disciplinary rules, and governing bodies in sport and recreation should be aware of, and cross-check, the range of rules at regional, national, international and Olympic level, which have jurisdiction over their sport.

In addition, there may be relevant local authority policies[10] or charters such as the Fair Play Charter or the Brighton Declaration on Women in Sport, and codes such as the National Association of Sports Coaches. In seeking to recognise and incorporate a wide range of rules and avoid conflict within them or between them and the civil and criminal laws of a particular nation-state, governing bodies face real challenges in this area of harmonisation (Felix, 1998; Houlihan, 1999).

> Harmonisation is an attempt to achieve broad agreement between different legal systems whether codified [put in the form of a statute] or common law variety so that, for example, the penalties meted out to individual competitors for infringements are treated in a similar fashion: as such it is the opposite of conflict.
>
> (Stinson, 1995: 180)

Greenburg and Gray (1994) clearly articulate the difficulties which faced the various skating governing bodies after a member of their national team, Nancy Kerrigan, was assaulted with an iron bar at a US skating competition a few months before the 1994 Winter Olympics. It was alleged that Tonya Harding, a potential Olympic Team member, had conspired to assault her rival, and hired her ex-husband's bodyguard to carry out the assault. The United States Figure Skating Association (USFSA) did not have enough time to follow though all the disciplinary processes, including the right to an appeal under the 1978 Amateur Sports Act, before the Olympic Team departed for the Winter Games. They could not anticipate the outcome of a criminal investigation, since it was still ongoing at that time. The relevant national and Olympic bodies faced problems related to the conflicts between rules, their jurisdiction; the context of the incident; the timescale of the hearings. Greenberg and Gray (1994: 17) summarised the issue:

> Can the United States Olympic Committee Administrative Board eliminate the arbitration appeal process as provided in the Amateur Sports Act of 1978 in order to make quick decisions at the Olympic Games?[11]

Shortly after returning from the Winter Games Tonya Harding faced a conviction and 200 hours of community service. There may also be a lack of harmonisation between the governing body rules and the laws of the nation-state. Gulland (1995); Nafziger (1995); Roberts (1995) and Viewig (1995) all deal with such conflicts in the area of doping in sport.[12] It appears that there are increasing problems of the conflict between governing body rules of doping and the principle of the 'restraint of trade'.[13] Stinson (1995: 182) believes that there is:

a grave danger that a major conflict could develop between the laws of a country which is sympathetic to restraint of trade arguments and the rules of sport, which may well be more severe.

In *Gasser* v. *Stinson*, 1988, the IAAF argued that 'the restraint of trade rules of English law should not be applied to the IAAF rules which are concerned to regulate the eligibility of athletes of many different nationalities to appear in athletic competition in many different parts of the world' (Felix, 1998: 248). The argument was rejected by J. Scott, since there was authority case law against it in *Grieg* v. *Insole*. He asked the question whether or not it is to be said that the IAAF should be beyond the reach of the law? (Felix, 1998: 248). Stinson (1995: 182) is also concerned that international harmonisation of penalties, both within individual sports and between different sports has become 'a matter of urgency'. Clubs, governing bodies and individual players should be aware of and check potential conflicts. In the area of doping control there appear to be differences in the tolerance and attitude of governing bodies or clubs towards athletes in different sports players, particularly in relation to cocaine and steroids.[14]

Had Paul Merson been a 400m runner he would still be banned today.
(Bitel, 1995: 8)

There is also an ongoing debate around the appropriateness of 'recreational' drugs, such as cocaine, being included in the banned list of performance enhancing substances (Welch, 1998a, 1998b). Questions have been raised about the rules of 'strict liability' in doping control regulations. Wise (1996) asks if the rules themselves are legal. They only require the presence of the substance as the baseline criterion and do not seem to allow for proof of fault or mitigation.[15] Making such rules goes against advice given by Devlin LJ in *Merchandise Transport* v *BTC* [1961] 3 All AER who said that tribunals should not 'make rules which prevent . . . examining each case on its merits' (Bitel, 1995: 7).

The rules of the British Athletics Federation, slavishly following IAAF rules have created a system of strict liability in which what should be the central question of effect on performance is irrelevant and there is no place for findings on culpability merely guilt.
(Bitel, 1995: 7)

Rules have been introduced in some governing bodies which include a rule on secondary liability of those supplying or administrating doping substances, whilst some countries, including those who may host Olympic and international events, include supplying 'or possession' within their criminal laws[16] (*IAAF Handbook* 1998–1999; *Sports Law Bulletin*, 1(5), September 1998, p. 13). Changes in English law in September 1996 brought steroids under the Misuse of Drugs Act 1971, criminalised trafficking and made

> possession with intent to supply and supply illegal and punishable with a two year jail sentence and possibly unlimited fine. Possession itself, for personal use remains lawful
>
> (Lowther, 1998: 53)

Ros Robagliati, a snowboarding competitor in the US Olympic team, was found guilty of doping when marijuana was found in his sample at the 1998 Winter Olympics in Japan. He was reinstated after a vote of 13 to 12 on the Appeal Panel, but could also have been subject to the criminal laws of Japan, the host nation.[17] There is also a lack of consistency in the penalties meted out by governing bodies, if at all, for violence on the field. Governing bodies and clubs often have a vested interest in getting the disciplined player back in the club or national side as soon as possible. In relation to punching and earbiting in rugby union, there have been questions raised about the consistency of punishments by governing bodies.[18] Bitel (1995) is critical of the tendency of governing bodies to be more concerned about the sanctity of rules, as the end and not a means to an end, failing to evaluate them critically in a broader context of fairness. Participants and clubs in sport and recreation, who are more involved in the development and rationale of rules, at grass roots level, are more likely to be committed to them and enforce them. From the point of view of the individual athlete Bitel (1995: 9) any discussion on disciplinary procedures should warn governing bodies:

> (a) do not use your rules to pursue untenable aims, (b) involve sports participants at all stages in the discussion and drafting of disciplinary rules, and (c) try to remember that rules can be changed.

Natural justice? Principles into practice in disciplinary processes

Governing bodies in sport and recreation are expected to conduct their disciplinary processes according to the rules of 'natural justice', which, broadly speaking, means a duty to be fair, reasonable and impartial. There is much debate in legal circles as to whether a governing body of sport or recreation is or should be subject to judicial review of their disciplinary practices. Are all their disciplinary disputes private, contractual and located in administrative law? Or should they be regarded as within a public body (whose power is derived from a statutory framework) (Bond, 1993; Beloff and Kerr, 1995). Welch and Wearmouth (1994) suggest that the principles of natural justice can be translated into practical guidelines, under general themes of rights and duties relating to the following themes:

- correct procedure
- evidence
- fair and reasonable
- impartial and thorough
- conclusions.

In following correct procedure governing bodies should be aware that a person has the right to be given notice of the charge and a reasonable chance of answering it; be clear which rule or code has allegedly been breached; be given an opportunity to state their case and notice of a disciplinary hearing where relevant.[19] In *Keighley RFC and Anor.* v. *Cunningham* (1960) Mr Holmes, a rugby player, was:

> sent off during a cup tie on 13 February 1960. On the following day, 14 February, the referee submitted his report to the appropriate disciplinary committee in accordance with the rules. On 15 February the committee met to hear the case and suspended the player. Neither the club nor the player had been notified that the case was going to be heard.

Mr Justice Dankwerts held that:

> On the grounds of natural justice it was the duty of a body like this to hear the player and it should be the onus of the committee to notify him that the case would be heard on a certain day.
>
> (Grayson, 1994: 298)

A person accused of a breach of rules or codes has the right to be assisted or represented by someone of their choice at any hearing. Wearmouth (1995: 33) suggests that:

> the role of this person should be clarified; they should not be someone who will play a part in the decisions in the case and will be subject to the rules of the association relating to the handling of disciplinaries and appeals.

In the early 1970s a decision by a governing body to refuse legal representation was refused by the tribunal and upheld by the courts.[20] However, Grayson (1994: 305) advises that 'in case of difficulty or complexity, consider carefully any request for legal representation'.

It is useful to have someone to advise and or speak on behalf of the accused or complainant. They can monitor procedure, clarify points, speak on behalf of that person, during a traumatic and disorientating process.[21]

(Wearmouth, 1995: 33)

In conducting the hearing the procedure should be explained to all parties in advance of the hearing and standardised for all cases; the complainant or governing body normally present their case first and may identify questions which they wish to be answered[22]; the meeting should have an accurate record made by someone in a recognised official capacity, who is not part of the decision-making process; the panel members should not give advice or ask leading questions. They should merely seek information, clarification and explanation on relevant matters and avoid making any judgmental comments during the hearing (Welch and Wearmouth, 1994).

Matters of evidence often create problems for both governing bodies and accused persons or complainants. A person charged has the right to be given access to the evidence, respond to the evidence, know the names of persons giving evidence and for the evidence to be presented systematically and thoroughly (Welch and Wearmouth, 1994). The evidence presented ranges from written oral and increasingly, video evidence, although there are reasons for viewing the introduction of video evidence with some caution.[23] In 1993 John Fashanu was disciplined by the FA for an incident in which his elbow shattered the cheekbone of Gary Mabutt. It highlighted the difficulties of a referee making a decision, in the game, not to send players off – then when confronted with slow-motion, then frame by frame video pictures of the incidents, feeling under pressure to alter his /her view of the incident. In McIllvaney's opinion, the referee's 'original opinion appears to have been eroded by repeated viewing of video evidence' (McIllvaney, 1993: 3).

In an unusual case in rugby league in 1990, Andy Currier was sent off, allegedly, for a high tackle. However, a video recording revealed that it was 'nothing of the sort, more of a shoulder charge in fact. The opponent on the receiving end didn't think Currier should have been sent off and gave evidence at the hearing. More importantly, the referee who sent him off, admitted he had made an error' (Corrigan, 1990). However, in a High Court hearing, when Currier appealed against a two-year suspension from his professional work, the judge rejected his appeal, commenting on the need for the integrity of the sports contest and the fair and proper proceedings of the governing body (Corrigan, 1990; Wearmouth, 1995: 34).

In 1988 Mark Bosnich, a soccer player, was given a yellow card for wasting time during Aston Villa's UEFA cup quarter final match against Athletico-Madrid. The referee was unaware that Bosnich was being pelted with objects and thought he was just standing there wasting time. Video evidence supported Bosnich's explanation, yet, because the referee did not include that in his match report Bosnich was unable to include it in his appeal (Holt, 1998). Following an alleged violent incident on the field, a rugby player's legal representative was not allowed to discuss or challenge the videotape evidence during the disciplinary hearing. It was discussed in private by the panel (Rose and Albertini, 1997; Felix, 1998).

The third practical guideline relates to the duty to be fair and reasonable (Welch and Wearmouth, 1994) under which a disciplinary panel is expected to conduct the affairs of the sport 'fairly and reasonably, in line with the constitution and rules of the association' (Wearmouth, 1995: 34). A panel must act on good faith, deal with cases consistently and fairly, by standardised procedures making their decision on evidence relevant to the case, disregarding extraneous considerations (Wearmouth, 1995: 34). The fourth practical guideline covers the duty to be impartial and thorough. Parties to any disciplinary hearing should be notified of the panel membership, well in advance of the hearing, to allow opportunities for any challenge on the grounds of impartiality.

In the case of *Revie* v. *the F.A.* [1979] the protests of the England team manager, regarding the 'constitution of the disciplinary tribunal, imposing a ten year ban, because of members' adverse attitudes personally expressed to him by tribunal members' were upheld by the court and described to him as 'contrary to natural justice because of the likelihood of bias which is among tribunal members' (Grayson, 1994: 308). This was despite the fact that Mr Justice Cantley called Don Revie 'greedy, deceitful and selfish' and that it was 'reasonable for the FA to be satisfied that his conduct brought the sport into disrepute' (Bitel, 1995: 7). It is not necessary to prove actual bias, only the likelihood of bias and conduct indicative of such apparent bias need not be restricted to the formal hearing itself.[24]

At the end of a disciplinary hearing, the person charged with a disciplinary offence, or a complainant, has no right of access to the deliberations or discussions of the panel. The punishment should fit the case and the panel can take into account previous good conduct. Views and practices vary among lawyers and governing bodies on the wisdom of giving reasons for a judgement. Some panels choose to make a standardised statement on whether or not the case was proven on the standard of proof required by the rules.[25] Others articulate further reasons for the decision (Wearmouth, 1995). Whatever the policy of the governing body, the approach to this matter should be a consistent one across the various disciplinary panels of that body. There should be a right of appeal if there is new evidence which would have had a major impact on the findings, not available to the original hearing, or evidence of unfairness or bias or procedural impropriety in the procedures themselves (Welch and Wearmouth, 1994; Wearmouth, 1995). These grounds could be used to mount a legal challenge in the form of a private writ, served against the governing body in the High Court.[26]

PART II

Managing disciplinary matters in the real world: from the games field to the law courts. During this part of the chapter possible influences of masculine subcultures on official responses to violence in some contact games will be explored drawing on socio-legal sources.

Moments of madness or a normal game?

In disciplinary, civil and criminal contexts, players, past and present, as well as their representatives, often use the excuses of 'rash moments of madness' or 'part of the normal game' in relation to punching on the rugby field. A rugby player is up in front of a disciplinary committee for punching another player during a match. His representative tells the committee:

> It was a rash moment of madness from a person, a gentleman, of a normally impeccable character.

A month later, the same player, facing another disciplinary hearing, again, for punching during a game. His representative tells the committee:

> It was a rash moment of madness from a person, a gentleman, of impeccable character . . . he just lost it.

The chairperson of the disciplinary committee responds: 'What, again? It is about time we restricted that excuse to once per player. (The number of times we hear that one . . . maybe we should forget disciplinary concerns, or Offences Against the Person Act and just apply the Mental Health Act!?).' A month later, the same player is facing the committee again (he has been punching). His representative has learnt something from the previous occasion. He tells the committee:

> Punching is part of the normal game, this very physical game of rugby. It is the rule rather than the exception; players come to expect it. We have expert witnesses, players who will explain this as common practice.

Should the disciplinary committee and indeed, a court of law, accept such explanations on behalf of an accused player? When Jonathan Callard received a serious facial injury, as a result of being raked in a rugby union match in 1993, he said, 'I won't stand by and let so-called officials put this down to rugby being a hard game . . . or just a normal game of rugby (Cleary, *Rugby World*, 1995). In June 1997, during the British Lions rugby tour of South Africa, Weir, one of the Lions players, was considering civil

action against Bosman [the lock on the opposing team], following an incident where Bosman, allegedly, deliberately targeted Weir's knee with his
boot and viciously stamped on it, causing serious ligament injuries. Weir
refused to accept that this conduct, is part of the normal risks of the game.
He said, 'If it had happened in a tackle or some other contact situation, it
would not have been quite so bad . . . it is one of the risks you take as a
rugby player', Taylor (1997) *The Mail on Sunday*, 15.6.97.

> I know that, if I end up on the floor, even if it is well away from the
> ball, someone is going to come along and boot me. Being a fly-half,
> you get used to it, especially if you kick goals as well. People always
> seem to be out to get you, but that's all part of the normal game.
>   (Rob Andrew in Stewart and Silver, 1993)

Attempting to define and understand terms like 'normal' game voluntary consent, is very important and relevant for players, coaches, officials,
expert witnesses, sport managers, educators and lawyers. In various contexts,
including disciplinary hearings, civil and criminal cases, arising out of sports
events, expert witnesses are often asked, 'In your opinion is "X" conduct
part of the normal game?' What kind of task is this? Is it simply a matter
of observing, reporting and reinforcing empirical observations regarding
what *is* common? Or, is it a question of what ought to be accepted and
justified by all those involved in sport, with reference to recognition criteria
and a broader moral or values-based framework? These are matters for those
involved at all levels in sport and recreation development; for players, officials, coaches, educators, policy makers, taking personal responsibility for
justifying, as opposed to just explaining, conduct by reference to common
practice.

Criminal liability, civil liability, consent, and a normal game

Criminal liability can arise out of a player's conduct, if it can be proven
beyond reasonable doubt, that the relevant offence took place; that the
player had been guilty of intentional or reckless conduct, causing serious bod-
ily harm, outside the 'normal game', to which reasonable people would be
expected to consent, where there is no lawful justification or excuse. A normal game is thought to contain only the inherent risks which we should
accept, as part of playing that sport. Voluntary consent *volenti,* a complete
defence to negligence, has three elements, all of which must be proved, on
the balance of probabilities – a lower standard of proof than a criminal case.
First, such consent must be voluntary and made by sane, rational people who
are able to make such a choice. Second, the players must be fully informed
of the risks of the activity. Third, players are only expected to consent to

the *inherent* risks of the game (Nygaard and Boone, 1985; Wearmouth, 1988).Those risks are difficult to define. Hartley (1997:20) suggests:

> those risks which are left, when everyone involved in the sport contest has taken reasonable care to avoid reasonably foreseeable harm; to remove these risks would take away from that sport/recreation activity, the agreed physical challenges, which are valued and justified as good things for individuals and society.

Defining the boundaries of a 'normal' game: are rules a guide?

Is it useful to use the rules as a boundary of a normal game? First, which rules are those: the technical rules or the code of conduct rules? (the latter being much broader than the former). Second, as Fraleigh (1984) suggests, there are regulative rules, based upon health and welfare principles, which impose a penalty for proscribed conduct (high tackles or dropping the scrum). Such conduct is expected and catered for by such rules. Is a boundary of technical rules too narrow for a normal game? In legal contexts, attempts to define a normal game with reasonable risks have included 'the general expectations of players' (LCCP, 1995), 'risks which are associated with the activity' (Collins, 1987) 'such an integral part of the game that a player cannot possibly avoid it' (Gardiner, 1994); 'or so frequent as to be viewed as normal . . . authorised by other players or an ordinary happening' (R v. Green 1969 cited Horrow, 1980; Young, 1993).

Learning from 'over there' – North American experiences, on the field

Gardiner (1994) suggests that rather than using rules as a boundary, a more useful guide might be the 'working cultures' or group norms of the players at a particular level. The appeal of such a guide is understandable, but this approach raises questions around the following reservations or concerns. An account of a 'normal' game, based only, empirically, upon what players commonly do and expect, without being exposed to external moral scrutiny, rights and duties (Nicholson, 1987), or even Sport England recognition criteria, has its drawbacks. It has the potential to weaken the ability of a sport to retain its strong public policy position. This section will attempt to illustrate some of those concerns with reference to the power and influence of masculine subcultures in some sports and their capacity to normalise deviant behaviour, by drawing upon the work of Horrow (1980), Messner (1990), Coakley and Hughes (1991), Young (1993), and Frey (1994).

The culture of a society or group is captured by its traditions, beliefs, values expectations, unwritten codes and language, which are indicators of its normative system. Beal and Crosset (1991: 74) see the subculture of sport as a means for illuminating the back regions of sport and:

> to illuminate the normative system by which groups demonstrate the ways in which they differ from such things as language, values, religion, diet and style of life, from the larger social world of which they are a part.

They identify rugby as having a distinctly masculine subculture in which they tend to form 'their own rules' and 'deviate from the normal game'. Messner (1990) argues that players' tolerance to extreme conditions and injuries emerge as a 'process of masculinisation that brings central meaning to the lives of many athletes'. For Young (1993: 374) sport becomes viewed as:

> for the expression and reproduction of hegemonic masculinity where violence and its results, including injury, are legitimised and make sense.

Deviation, in the form of violence and drug taking, for example, becomes normal in the masculine sport subculture. A common situation can develop where:

> there is a violation of normative expectations surrounding the organi-sation and this behaviour has peer and elite support, conditions that facilitate group rule-breaking and the adoption of goals inconsistent with societal values.
>
> (Ermann and Lundmann, 1978, cited Frey, 1994: 110)

> It is still common for sports organisations to be seen as existing outside the regulatory and moral frameworks which operate in other spheres of institutional life.
>
> (Brackenridge, 1994: 288)

In critically evaluating practices and attitudes in sport and recreation, all those involved need to judge their conduct, not just against the subcultural norms of that sport, but against wider notions of moral and public policy. It is assumed that this will happen when a sport is empowered with regulatory or supervisory roles and largely left to operate, independently, as a 'lawful' sport. Frey (1994: 110) in his research into organisational deviance of college athletic departments found that the athletic subculture viewed 'the use of performance-enhancing drugs, excessive violence and under the table payments, as 'normative cheating' strategies that are necessary to meet the goals of winning'. The structural arrangements, the sub-unit autonomy, the gap between resources and expectations and the lack of university financial back-up for athletic programme deficits, were all seen to contribute to the

university permitting deviance, which helps the institution's athletic programme to maintain the competitive edge (Frey, 1994: 113).

Young (1993) explores the nature and influence of powerful sport subcultures upon players, coaches, officials and the law courts. He argues that the
health and safety of professional sports workers is repeatedly compromised,
as they are expected to face intolerable working conditions, severe and unreasonable punishments and dish out and accept violence on a regular basis.

> Failure to conform, especially for mid-career athletes, could result in
> unemployment . . . player to player violence, continues to be ratio-
> nalised by many athletes and coaches.
>
> (Young, 1993: 376)

Messner (1990:303) and Young (1993) argue that socialisation into
masculinity in some sport subcultures required 'routinely giving and
accepting injury, where self-esteem and power derived from doing violence
to the bodies of co-workers'. Coakley and Hughes (1991) surveyed the attitudes of over five hundred elite athletes/players in the USA. They found
that players accepted, uncritically, the often extreme expectations of coaches
and others, reinforced by peer group norms. These influences were seen to
be so powerful and all-embracing that, rather than viewing drug-taking,
violence as deviant behaviour, going against the expectations of coaches:

> many forms of deviance in sport are not caused by disregard or rejec-
> tion of social values, or norms, instead, they are caused by an unqualified
> acceptance of unquestioned commitment to a value system.
>
> (Coakley and Hughes, 1991)

This is partly based upon expectations that athletes automatically (a) make
sacrifices for the game (b) strive for distinction, (c) accept risks and play
through pain even when injured and (d) refuse to accept the normal human
limits in pursuit of possibilities in sport (Coakley and Hughes, 1991).

> When you learn to ignore other people's pain you lose your capacity
> for empathy. When you learn to ignore your own pain as well, you
> lose your understanding of what it is to cause pain and it becomes of
> value to cause pain.
> (Michael Messner, interviewed in *On the Line*, Bad Sports, May 1994)

Coakley and Hughes (1991) reported examples of players having to work
under extreme and dangerous training and competition conditions, face
suicide drills in the forms of extreme punishments from their peers, as a
result of making a mistake on the field. Young (1993) suggests that such
practices and attitudes are institutionalised, rather than just individual

exceptions. Players who are steeped in such norms and traditions often go on to become coaches, officials, sports writers, committee members, or expert witnesses in disciplinary, civil and criminal cases. In these roles they may find it difficult to step back from this subculture and bring some impartial, external, moral scrutiny to bear on matters of misconduct. Is there a danger that they will continue to attempt to rationalise unacceptable practices as part of the normal game, dictated only by common practice and group norms? In Canadian ice-hockey, if a player is not prepared to *fight* on the ice, using sticks and fists, then he is likely to end up on the bench, with the word going round that he was unemployable because he wouldn't 'mix it'. Participants, sports development workers, coaches and governing bodies, have a public duty to challenge such trends and the broader, common practices within Coakley and Hughes (1991) 'sport ethic'.

From the games field to the law courts: the influence of sport subcultures

It would be reasonable to assume that the law courts will bring some kind of external scrutiny to such conduct. However, it seems that sports participants and officials, who rationalise unacceptable practices as part of the 'normal game' in their own sports communities, take such messages to the courts when they appear as expert witnesses, and, often, remain unchallenged. In Canada, fist-fighting in ice hockey was viewed by the courts as 'normal' as long as 'the force did not exceed that level authorised by the players' Young (1993). In the case of *R* v. *Green* 1969, the defendant retaliated to being hit by the gloved hand of another player:

> by chopping his opponent on the head with his stick. The victim sustained serious concussion, massive brain haemorrhaging and has never really recovered 100% ... Green used the self-defence argument and was acquitted with the following judicial assessment:

> No hockey player enters onto the ice without consenting to and without the knowledge that he is going to be hit in one of many ways, while he is on the ice. We can come to the conclusion that this is an ordinary happening in a hockey game and that players really think nothing of it.
> (R v. Green [1969] cited Young, 1993: 386)

The author views with serious concern, the apparent acceptance, by those in authority, in sport and the law courts, of the 'physical skill' of punching and stick-fighting, with the associated extreme risks, as part of the normal game, based *only* upon the criterion that players commonly do it and accept it, i.e. on merely an empirical observation without any moral justification. This is, in the writer's opinion, a neglect of the welfare duties of those at all levels in sport and the law.

From stick-fighting in ice hockey . . . to punching in rugby union, over here

It is easy to dismiss such research and sporting examples from the other side of the Atlantic as, peculiar to North American professional sport contexts. This chapter would warn against taking such an attitude and suggests that there might be some very disturbing similarities between the trends and concerns observed by Young (1993), 'over there' and the challenges facing some sports 'over here'. The next section of this paper will outline what appears to be attempts to rationalise punching as part of the 'normal', hard game of rugby union. The favourable position in public policy, enjoyed by rugby union, rests partly on its traditionally perceived value as one of the middle-class 'manly diversions'; developing character, muscular Christianity, leaders of the future (Mangan and Walvin, 1987; Nauright and Chandler, 1996). It is, along with boxing often viewed favourably in relation to recognition criteria, in contrast to 'imported' sport cultures, such as some of the martial arts (Gardiner, 1996, 1998). It is seen as a subcultural arena of masculine identity and socialisation, displaying remarkable similarities to the trends of institutionalised attitudes towards violence raised earlier by Coakley and Hughes, 1991 and Young, 1993. Concerns regarding violent acts of individuals and teams, the responses of the regulating authorities, and resistance to legal intervention draws attention and comment from the media and academics on a regular basis (see Salmon, 1990; Jones, 1992; Butler, 1993; Hubbard, 1993; Cleary, 1995; Nauright and Chandler, 1996; Harris, 1997).

What kind of explanations are given and accepted for questionable conduct on the games field? Are players or expert witnesses challenged, who routinely base their 'defence' or opinions upon a misguided notion of a 'normal' game being dictated only by common practice or group norms? In particular, are there comparisons to be made between stick-fighting in Canadian ice-hockey and punching in rugby union over here?

In the criminal case of *R* v. *Billingshurst* [1978] in Newport Crown Court, a rugby union player was charged with assault, following an incident on the field, where the defendant punched another player and broke his jaw in three places. An expert witness for the defence informed the judge that punching was the rule rather than the exception, implying that it was part of the normal game. The judge was not terribly impressed and the player was convicted of the charge. In 1985, during a televised rugby match in Wales, the referee, George Crawford, walked off the pitch, refusing to referee, after warning the players that he would do this if they did not stop punching. In his opinion, they were not playing the 'recognised physical skills' of the game. In making this protest, he abandoned all hopes of an international career in refereeing, and yet he was fulfilling his welfare duties to both the players and the sport. Later in 1992, he said:

I took my action as a protest against violence in the game. I said that someone would be killed if severe action was not taken against all players who commit acts of foul play and expressed concern that many of my refereeing colleagues see fit to [merely] caution people for a punch on the rugby field. There seems to be a reluctance to send people off for punching (unlike soccer).

> (George Crawford, interviewed for *On the Line*,
> BBC 2 Sport in the Dock, 1992)

However, in the same programme, Dudley Woods, the then general secretary of the Rugby Football Union (RFC), commented:

In the heat of the moment, things of this instance would *inevitably occur*. I don't think you would achieve anything, quite honestly, by instantly a punch was thrown, a player was sent off the field, except perhaps *a lack of commitment*. (Emphasis added).

Is Woods implying blamelessness through inevitability? What kind of commitment . . . the Coakley and Hughes (1991) version? Surely there is a difference between committing a hard tackle – between being committed to the recognised physical skills of this exciting and dynamic sport, and . . . *punching people?* Such violence has often been explained (as opposed to being justified), by such comments as:

It's just a bit of fisty-cuffs . . . the lads will settle down soon!

> (Sports commentator)

You have to show them, early in the game, that you will not be intimidated . . . you have to get your retaliation in first.

> (A common rugby excuse)

Where hormones flow aggression will follow.

> (Butler, 1993)

When complaining, bitterly, about the conduct of the All-Blacks rugby team (whom he described as *boot boys*), who injured Philip De Glanville, an English player during a serious raking/stamping incident, Butler (1993:2), a former player, who went on to be a sports writer, observed:

The ruck in question did not appear to be heinous at the time; there was no roar of disgust from behind the goal, no flurry of retaliatory punches, which normally provide a sequel to excess and a warning of scandal.

Butler (1993) appears to be indicating, without critical comment, that punching was not only a 'normal part of the game', but was an 'acceptable means' for players to communicate to their peers that the preceding incident was 'off the scale'. It is also common for both academic commentators (Gardiner and Felix, 1995) and players alike, to point out that, of course we are not as bad as we used to be, sometimes reminiscing with affection, about times gone by:

> The amount of shoe going in these days, is but a fraction of the good old days, and even then we were called 'namby pamby' by the previous generation, for whom the ball really was an impediment to an afternoon of sport.

He reported that in the dark days, when he was a player, there were group norms and expectations, illustrated by such unwritten rules like *Only first men boot, last men tiptoe* (Butler, 1993). There may well have been considerable improvements since their playing days, and these are to be applauded. However, one can only take the argument *but we're more civilised than we used to be*, so far. Surely, it is a matter of evaluating whether or not the conduct on the field in the 1990s ought to be considered acceptable, to society as a whole, at this time? Furthermore, what is interesting about all these responses to and 'explanations' of incidents, is that they display a disturbing similarity to trends in North America, with players, commentators and officials appearing to rationalise, normalise and implicitly encourage misconduct such as punching. This bears all the hallmarks of Young's (1993) concerns regarding the difficulties which some members of the sport community may face, of removing themselves from such powerful, coercive sport subculture, in order to bring some external moral responsibility and scrutiny to bear on such matters. Can governing bodies and policy makers in sport and recreation afford to leave things as they are, if such trends are visible in their activities? They not only have serious legal implications, but have the capacity to drive people out of the sport and ruin experiences in it, for both participants and spectators.

The 'Killing fields'

Were lessons learnt from George Crawford's protest in 1985? In March 1993, Seamus Lavelle was 'felled by a punch while playing rugby [union]. He suffered severe swelling of the brain and was placed on a life support machine. He died two days later', Cleary (1995). In July 1994, Hardy, the Centaurs hooker, stood in the dock at the Old Bailey, charged with manslaughter. During the early days of the criminal investigation, the police took some time to establish that it was indeed, Hardy who threw the punch which led to Lavelle's death, because, *so many players were punching*. The court, in *R. v. Hardy* July [1994] (unreported) heard evidence, from Hardy, regarding the ill-tempered match where he 'saw one of his side, punched and kicked by three Hendon forwards'. He said:

> I told them to leave it out and play rugby. But one of their players came towards me looking menacing. I thought he was going to hit me

> . . . as he [Hardy] squared up he was hit from behind by two punches from Lavelle, and this caused the hooker [Hardy] to 'lash out blindly'.
> (Hardy in evidence, July 1994, the Old Bailey)

When it was suggested in court that he was not acting in self-defence Mr Hardy replied, 'No sir. I hit out because I was going to be hit some more . . . whether or not you call that self-defence, I don't know', Cleary (1995). In the same article, George Crawford commented, 'It gives me no pleasure to report that I was right.' As players become stronger and fitter, they may be faster and more powerful, but their brains do not improve their capacity to deal with blows to the head delivered by punching. In my opinion, such risks ought not to be accepted or encouraged as part of the normal game of rugby.

Scottish governing bodies and the courts have a reputation for taking a hard line on violence on the games field, based mainly on the policy issue of the risk of player violence inciting public order problems. Recently, there was a glimmer of hope that things might be improving on the issue of sport communities and the courts challenging efforts to normalise punching. *The Scotsman*, 14 February 1997, reported that in the case of Jason Fayers, a Scottish rugby player, fined £1,500 for a violent assault, the defendant's solicitor stated that 'Fayers had reacted to persistent fouling in the same way as many players when he threw the punch' (Duff, 1997: 30). Four former Scottish players had written letters in evidence (on behalf of the defendant), which 'basically, said that punching is part and parcel of the game' (Duff, 1997: 30). The Procurator Fiscal is reported as saying that such letters 'reveal a certain amount of cynicism concerning the laws of rugby and the laws of the land. It is rather worrying that it seems acceptable to carry out this sort of attack' (Duff, 1997: 29). Fayers admitted the offence and the judge later commented:

> The views expressed in the letters . . . that punching is normal and appears to them to be acceptable conduct by players playing rugby, is at stark variance with the views of the SRU because that body regarded the punch to be so outrageous that they have imposed a 4 year, world-wide ban on Mr Fayers. I am not prepared, given that ruling, to take into account the views [expressed in mitigation]. This was a deliberate and unprovoked assault.
> (Duff, 1997: 30)

The SRU pointed out, 'We do not want people in rugby who consider it [punching] is part and parcel of the game', Duff (1997: 30). In recent years players have been disciplined for conduct such as eye-gouging and ear-biting (Kitson, 1998). There is a danger that such activities might push conduct like punching even further into the 'normalised zone' of expectations.

Summary

This chapter has conducted a formal examination of the legal principles of natural justice and the challenges they present to the management of sport and recreation disciplinaries. Part I dealt with the range of rules, codes and laws and the problems of harmonisation, with some reference to consistency in anti-doping rules. Natural justice was translated into five practical principles which were supported by relevant case law and incidents from sport and recreation. Part II moved from the formal to the contextual, drawing on socio-legal literature, dealing in the broader context of masculine sport subcultures and their possible influence on the expectations of players/officials, and accounts of the 'normal' game, which they bring to disciplinary processes and court cases. In particular, the trends in stick-fighting in North American ice hockey were compared with the normalisation of punching in rugby union in England. It has provided a socio-legal lens, for both students and practitioners to reflect on and evaluate the challenges of managing sport disciplinaries. It is relevant to those who study and develop policy in disciplinary processes at the level of administration, education, coaching and officiating. In addition, it encourages participants to reflect on justification of their actions beyond the level of common practice.

Notes

1 Vinnie Jones, of Wimbledon FC, was fined £20,000 and banned for six weeks for his part in *Soccer's Hard Men* (Vision Video, 1992) in which he discussed ways of committing unlawful conduct on the field of soccer. © *The Observer*, 1993.

2 International UK athlete, Diane Modahl, was tested positive for the presence of a steroid, testosterone, in a urine sample taken at an athletics match in Lisbon in June 1994. She was forced to return home from the Commonwealth Games in Victoria, Canada, just before defending her 800m title and was banned from competing for four years. The ban was upheld after a British Athletics Federation Hearing in December 1994. Diane Modahl won her appeal at the Independent Appeal Tribunal in July 1995, when it was shown that incorrect storage of the urine sample probably led to bacterial degradation, resulting in a testosterone ratio of 43:1, without the steroid ever having passed through the athlete's body (see Grayson, 1995; Reid, 1995). © *The Guardian*, 27/7/95.

3 Tonya Harding was allegedly involved in a conspiracy to assault another US skater, Nancy Kerrigan, with an iron bar, during a skating competition in the USA a few months before the Winter Olympics in 1994. The governing bodies

in national and Olympic Skating were unable to complete disciplinary processes, including time for an appeal, in parallel to an ongoing criminal investigation, before the USA team including these two skaters left for the Winter Olympics. On her return to the USA, after the Olympics, Tonya Harding faced a conviction and was ordered to serve 200 hours community service (see Greenberg and Gray, 1994; Wearmouth, 1995). © *The Times*, 16 January 1994.

4 Andy Norman, a BAF promoter and agent, was dismissed by the BAF three months after the suicide of Cliff Temple (athletics correspondent for the *Sunday Times* and former athletics coach). See Rodda, (1994). © *The Guardian*, 9/4/94.

5 A woman dentist from Cornwall successfully challenged the Rugby Football Union, regarding their policy of refusing to allow women to stand for the National Executive Committee of the RFU. © *The Guardian*, 29/3/95.

6 'Players who make racist remarks could be the subject of trial by television' reported Ivan Speck (1998) *Daily Mail*, 25/2/98: 75, following an incident involving Ian Wright and Peter Schmeicel and an announcement of new anti-racist policies by David Mellor MP and the Football Task Force. © *Daily Mail*.

7 Rugby union player, Phil Vickery, appealed against his 30-day ban for a punch which struck the thigh of flanker, Colin Charvis, during an international rugby union match between England and Wales in February 1998 (see Cleary, 1998; Squires, 1998). © *The Guardian*.

8 Kevin Yates, a Bath rugby union player, was banned for six months in 1998, after being found guilty of biting the ear of another player in an inter-club rugby union match. Initial investigations faced difficulties in identifying which of the three possible suspects actually committed the act (see Cleary, 1998, in the *Daily Telegraph*, 4/2/98; Kitson, 1998 in *The Guardian*, 11/2/98: 23). © *Daily Mail*.

9 Some governing bodies ask for a specific description of the grievance, with dates and times and any other witnesses; which section of the code or rules or policy is allegedly being breached; what is the effect on the member's participation in that sport or recreation activity?

10 Local authorities who employ people involved in sport and recreation in both a professional and voluntary capacity, may have policies covering health and safety, equal opportunities, grievances and disciplinary processes, etc.

11 In other words, 'Can Tonya Harding leave the United States and arrive at the Olympics and lose her rights for appeal as provided by federal law in order to allow the United States Olympic Committee to make timely decisions during Olympic competitions?' (Greenberg and Gray, 1994: 17).

12 These authors give an overview of the cases of Butch Reynolds, Randy Barnes and Katrina Krabbe.

13 For example, some rules may result in athletes being banned from competition, and thus their professional earnings, for four years (whilst other national governing bodies only ban for two years), both of which may be in conflict with the 'restraint of trade' principle.

14 Paul Merson, a professional soccer player, facing problems of drug dependency, was treated leniently and supported through his rehabilitation by the FA and his club; Ed Giddings, a county cricket player, was summarily dismissed from one club, although they say his contract was deemed to have terminated automatically as a result of the cancellation of his registration with the TSSB (Welch, 1998b: 383), after being found guilty of taking cocaine, but then faced a list of clubs who were prepared to employ him immediately; Phil Tuffnell, the Middlesex and England spinner, was fined £1,000 and given an 18-month suspended ban in October 1997 when he failed to provide a urine sample after being given written notification by the Sports Council (*Sport Law Bulletin*, January 1998: 3). Peter Korda, an international tennis player, brought a case

against the ITF Ltd on the grounds of lack of knowledge, by the player, of taking or being administered the prohibited substance (see *Drugs and Doping R* v. *ITF Ltd*, 1999, *The Independent*, 21 April, Court of Appeal (Clarke LJ, Auld LJ, Morritt LJ) and the court decided that a full and binding decision of the Anti-doping Appeals Committee (ADAC) of the ITF, under the terms of the Tennis Anti-Doping programme (TADP), could not yet be subject to reference to the Court of Arbitration of Sport (CAS) and allowed the appeal by the ITF. 'Roger Stanislav was clearly regarded by Leyton Orient as being guilty of gross misconduct once he had been found guilty by the FA of having been tested positive for cocaine' Welch (1998: 383). Lawrence Dallaglio, the former England rugby union captain, fell victim to a 'honeytrap' by a female journalist, of a tabloid newspaper, in 1999 where he allegedly admitted, on tape, taking cocaine in his younger days and/or on a British Lions tour of South Africa. This led to a heavy fine and a suspension recently. Track and field athletes usually receive harsh bans for prohibited drugs.

15 See IAF Handbook 1998–1999: 82, Rule 55 Doping, where it states 'the offence of doping takes place when either:

> (i) the prohibited substance is found to be present within an athlete's body tissue or fluids; or (ii) an athlete uses or takes advantage of a prohibited technique; or (iii) an athlete admits having used or taken advantage of a prohibited substance or technique.

16 Greece is one of the few countries whose Criminal Code currently includes provision for athletes who use drugs – law 1646 of 1986 Article 8(1), with a prison sentence of one year (see *Sports Law Bulletin*, 1(5), September 1998, p. 13). Japan also includes possession in their Criminal Code. In 1996, in English law, the trafficking and intent to supply steroids were brought under the control of the Misuse of Drugs Act 1971, although personal use remains lawful (Lowther, 1998: 53).

17 See Nichols 1998, 'Medal Goes up in Smoke', *The Guardian*, 12/2/98, and Wilson, 1998, 'Boarding Bratpack who Shame the Games', *Daily Mail*, 13/2/98. There was much comment in the press regarding the culture clash between the snowboarding sub-culture and the appearance of a more conventional culture of the Olympic fraternity.

18 See Cleary, 1998, 'England Enraged by Ban on Vickery', the *Daily Telegraph*, 23/2/98; and Squires, 1998, 'Vickery Ban Challenged by England', *Yorkshire Post*, 24/2/98, p. 19; see Jackson, 1998, 'I wish I'd been that lucky – Le Roux criticises verdict over double standards', *Daily Mail*, 11/2/98, p. 77; Gallagher, 1998, 'Yates-A fair verdict?', the *Daily Telegraph*, 12/4/98, p. 52. In 1990 Frederico Mendez of Argentina was suspended for only four weeks after he punched an England player (Paul Ackford), with such force that he broke his nose and knocked out four of his teeth (*The Times*, 15/11/90). In a Five Nations rugby union tour, the English hooker, Brian Moore, was gouged in the eye; a French prop who stamped on Martin Bayfield's head was subsequently sent off, but no formal charges were made against him (*Sunday Times*, 8/2/92).

19 Often the parties concerned may be spread over the globe and if it is not practical to hold a meeting, other forms of stating a case (such as written), need to be considered. In *Currie* v. *Barton* (1988) CA, *The Times*, 12/2/88, it was held that 'refusal of a personal hearing but receipt of a written explanation of the plaintiff's side of the story by a county tennis player who had been banned for three years after a dispute with his non-playing captain, was found not to be in breach of natural justice' (Grayson, 1994: 306; Wearmouth, 1995: 33).

20 See *Enderby Town* v. *The F.A. {1971}*.
21 In *Jones* v. *WRU 1997* the player whose conduct was called into question had a legal representative, partly because the player had a speech impediment (see Rose and Albertini, 1997).
22 If the panel has a series of questions, after reading any written submissions they should be identified, checked, approved by the panel chair, in advance of the hearing.
23 See Gardiner and Felix (1994) 'Elliot *v.* Saunders – Drama in Court 14', *Sport and Law Journal*, 2(3): 1–3 in which the authors observed the preference of the Judge for written and verbal evidence.
24 In a case arising out of a leisure/recreation disaster, the sinking of the *Marchioness* pleasure (disco) boat on the River Thames on 20 August 1989, resulting in the loss of 51 lives, the Coroner for Inner West London, Dr Paul Knapman, was removed as Coroner in the judicial review case in 1993, partly due to his apparent bias. Mrs Lockwood-Croft, a bereaved mother, had told the press about the removal of the hands of 27 victims, when the Coroner informed her of this nearly three years after the disaster. During a meeting with the two journalists who wrote an article on the matter in March 1992, Dr Knapman called Mrs Lockwood-Croft 'unhinged' and also referred to the mental state of other members of the *Marchioness* Action Group (see *R* v. *Coroner Inner West London ex parte Delagglio and another* CA [1993] 10 June, Simon-Brown LJ; Bingham LJ, MR; Farquharson J).
25 The standard of proof for disciplinary hearings could be a criminal standard of proof, 'beyond reasonable doubt' or equivalent to a civil standard, to be proven 'on the balance of probabilities'. A disciplinary code should state clearly which standard must be reached.
26 However, see the debate in Bond, 1993; Parpworth, 1994 on judicial reviews of governing bodies of sport and recreation.

References

BBC 2 *Bad Sports* On the Line 26 January 1994.
Beal, B., Crosset, T. (1991) 'The use of sub-culture and sub-world ethnographic works on sport: a discussion of definitional distinctions', *Sociology of Sport Journal*, 8: 307–25.
Beloff, M. J., Kerr, T. (1995) 'Judicial control of sporting bodies: the Commonwealth jurisprudence', *Sport and Law Journal*, 3(1): 5–9.
Bitel, N. (1995) 'Disciplinary procedures from the point of view of the individual', *Sport and Law Journal*, 3(3): 7–8.
Bond, C. (1993) 'Sporting bodies and judicial review', *Sport and Law Journal*, 1(1): 7–9.
Brackenridge, C. (1994) 'Fair play or fair game? Child sexual abuse in sport organisations', *International Review for Sociology of Sport*, 29(3): 287–97.
Butler, E. (1993) 'Climb down boot boys', *The Observer*, 7/11/93.
Cleary, M. (1995) 'The killing fields', *Rugby World*, January.
Cleary, M. (1998) 'Yates waits for RFU "biting" verdict', *Daily Telegraph*, 4/2/98, p. 8.
Coakley, J. and Hughes, R. (1991) 'Positive deviance among athletes: the implications of overconformity to the sport ethic', *Sociology of Sport Journal*, 8: 307–25.
Collins, V. (1987) 'Are you covered? The courts and sporting litigation', paper presented at the APPEL Conference Safety Frameworks in Physical Education, London 5/2/87.

Corrigan, P. (1990) 'The Ref's always right – Right?' *The Observer* 1990.

Duff, A. (1997) 'A Scottish update: a brief synopsis of newsworthy matters concerning football, rugby and others from October 1996 to date', *Sport and Law Journal*, 5(1): 25–30.

Felix, A. (1998) 'Legal regulation of governing bodies', *Sport Law*, 199–249, London: Cavendish Publishing.

Fraleigh, W. (1984) *Right Actions in Sport Ethics for Contestants*, Champaign: Illinois, Human Kinetics.

Frey, J. (1994) 'Deviance of organisational sub-units: the case of college athletic departments', *Journal of Sport and Social Issues*, 18(2): 110–22.

Gardiner, S. (1994) 'The law and the sportsfield', *Criminal Law Review*, 513.

Gardiner, S. (1996) 'Sport: a need for a legal definition', *Sport and the Law*, 4(2): 31–7.

Gardiner, S. (1998) 'Sport and the role of the state in Britain', Chapter 2, *Sports Law*, London: Cavendish Publishing.

Gardiner, S. and Felix, A. (1994) 'Elliot v. Saunders – drama in Court 14', *Sport and Law Journal*, 2(3): 1–3.

Gardiner, S. and Felix, A. (1995) 'Juridification of the football field: strategies for giving law the elbow', *Marquette Sports Law Journal*, Marquette Law School, Milawaukee.

Grayson, E. (1994) 'Fair play and reason in court', *Sport and the Law*, 2nd edn, London: Butterworth, p. 298.

Grayson, E. (1995) 'Drugs in sport – Chains of Custody', *Solicitor's Journal*, 20 January: 44, 46.

Grayson, E. (2000) 'Fair play and reason in court', *Sport and the Law*, 3rd edn, London: Butterworth, p. 405.

Greenberg, M. and Gray, J. (1994) 'The legal aspects of the Tonya Harding figure skating controversy', *Sport and Law Journal*, 2(2): 16–17.

Gulland, E. (1995) 'The Reynolds Case and the integrity of international dispute resolution', IAF Symposium on Sport and the Law, Monte Carlo, 1991, updated 1995.

Harris, N. (1997) 'Punch gets Johnson a video trial', *The Observer* 23/11/97, p. 7.

Hartley, H. J. (1997) 'Moments of madness or a normal game?' A Socio-Legal, Philosophical Response to the LCCP 1995 Consent and the Criminal Law second paper, submitted to Law Commission December 1996.

Hartley, H. J. (1998) 'Hard Men – Soft on Sport?' *Sport and Law Journal*, 6(3): 37–59.

Holt, O. (1998) 'UEFA ignores Bosnich's pleas', *The Times* 1/5/98, p. 36.

Horrow, R. (1980) *Sports Violence? The Interaction Between Private Law-making and the Criminal Law*, Arlington, VA: Carlington Press.

Houlihan, B. (1999) *Dying to Win: Doping in Sport and the Development of Anti-Doping Policy*, Council of Europe.

Hubbard, A. (1993) 'Up and under the carpet', *The Observer* 7/11/93.

Jones, S. (1992) 'When a code of silence is a code for violence', *Sunday Times* 2/2/92.

Kitson, R. (1998) 'Hard evidence that lacked video teeth', *The Guardian* 11/2/98, p. 23.

LCCP (1995) *Law Commission Consultation Paper No. 139, Consent and the Criminal Law*, December 1995, London: HMSO.

Lowther, J. (1998) 'A fine body of law? The new status of anabolic steroids', *Sport and Law Journal*, 6(3): 53–8.

McIllvaney, H. (1993) 'Rough justice put football in the dock', *Sunday Times*, 20/12/93, p. 3.

Mangan, J. A. and Walvin, J. (1987) *Manliness and Morality: Middle class masculinity in Britain and America 1800–1940*, Manchester University Press.

Messner, M. (1990) 'When bodies are weapons: masculinity, violence and sport', *International Review for the Sociology of Sport*, 25: 203–21.

Nafziger, J. (1995) 'International sports law as a process of resolving disputes', IAF Symposium on Sport and the Law, Monte Carlo, January 1991, updated 1995, pp. 20–31.

Nauright, J. and Chandler, T. (1996) *Making Men: Rugby and Masculine Identity*, Newbury Park: Frank Cass.

Nicholson, R. (1987) 'Drugs in sport: a re-appraisal', *Institute of Medical Ethics Bulletin*, August 1987.

Nygaard, G. and Boone, D. (1985) *A Coaches' Guide to Sport Law*, Champaign, IL. Human Kinetics.

Parker, R. (1995) 'Disciplinary proceedings from the governing body point of view', *Sport and Law Journal*, 3(3): 3–6.

Reid, R. (1995) 'The Modahl case', *Sport and Law Journal*, 3(2): 6–8.

Roberts, G. R. (1995) 'Harmonisation of laws as they relate to sport', IAF Symposium in Sport, Monte Carlo, January 1991, updated 1995, 87.

Rodda, J. (1994) 'Norman goes in fudged sacking', *The Guardian* 9/4/94, p. 1.

Rose, N., Albertini, L. (1997) 'Jones and the Welsh Rugby Union: new law for a new era', *Sport and Law Journal*, 5(1): 20.

Salmon, J. (1990) 'No place for cowards who kick and stamp on defenceless rivals', *Daily Telegraph* 2/1/90.

Speck, I. (1998) 'Football racists to face trial by video', *Daily Mail* 25/2/98, p. 75.

Squires, N. (1998) 'Vickery ban challenged by England', *Yorkshire Post* 24/2/98, p. 19.

Stewart, D. and Silver, J. (1993) 'Rugby – catastrophic injuries, claims and insurance', *Sport and Law Journal*, 2(1): 15–17.

Stinson, R. (1995) 'Harmonisation of laws as they relate to sport', IAF Symposium: Sport and the Law, Monte Carlo, January 1991, updated 1995.

Taylor, J. (1997) 'A man like this should never be allowed to play again', *Mail on Sunday* 8/6/97.

Viewig, K. (1995) 'Judicial review of sports related cases in Germany', IAF Symposium on Sport and the Law, Monte Carlo, January 1991, updated 1995, p. 87.

Wearmouth, H. J. (1988) *Volenti non fit injuria* in Sport and Physical Education, Legal Liability and Physical Education Conference Proceedings, Leeds Polytechnic, England.

Wearmouth, H. J. (1995) 'No winners on the greasy pole?' Ethical and legal aspect of evaluating disciplinary processes in sport, *Sport and Law Journal*, 3(3): 29–35.

Welch, M. (1997) 'Violence against women by professional football players: a gender analysis of hypermasculinity, positional status, narcissism and entitlement', *Journal of Sport and Social Issues*, 21(4): 392–411.

Welch, M. and Wearmouth, H. J. (1994) *Getting it Right: A Guide to Sports Ethics, Disciplinaries and Appeals*, London: The Sports Council.

Welch, R. (1998a) 'A puff and a snort: recreational drugs and discipline in professional sport', paper presented at British Socio-Legal Studies Annual Conference 16 April 1998, Manchester Metropolitan University, School of Law.

Welch, R. (1998b) 'Termination of contracts of employment in sport', *Sports Law*, London: Cavendish Publishing, pp. 381–409.

Wise, A. (1996) 'Strict liability: drug rules of sports governing bodies – are they legal?' *Sport and Law Journal*, 4(3): 70–82.

Young, K. (1993) 'Violence, risk and culpability in male sports culture', *Sociology of Sports Journal*, 10: 373–96.

Chapter 10

Working in sports development

Mark Nesti

Introduction

Opportunities to work in sports development continue to expand in the UK. A number of important structural, legal and funding changes (e.g. the National Lottery) both within the sports industry and in broader society have increased demand for volunteers and paid professionals in sport. Those who are currently part of this existing workforce face an ever more volatile and dynamic environment. Managing change is no longer an option but a necessity; development must be real and progressive and aim at least to meet individual needs as well as demand.

It has been argued that one of the benefits of the post-modern era is that choice is sovereign, whether at a personal, community, national or supra-national level. Not to offer authentic choices and quality provision is to face extinction. However valid or accurate this assessment may be, it is undoubtedly true that for sports development to continue to achieve its aims the key factor is the motivation, resilience and inventiveness of those working in the area. Several well-known commentators on organisations such as Charles Handy and Tom Peters have argued that persons (unfortu-nately increasingly referred to as human resources) are the most important element in any successful business. However, where the concern is with sport and its development the significance of the skills and qualities possessed by persons working in the field is magnified. Some of the reasons for this are considered in the opening section of this chapter. A brief historical overview of the nature of work in sports development is provided. This reveals that especially after the advent of outreach work and the appoint-ment of sports development officers, a greater importance has been placed on the interpersonal skills and personal qualities of staff. In addition, this change has been highlighted by the increasing recognition that to be effec-tive, development work must be proactive, interventionist and, 'involve a challenge of challenging tradition' (Eady, 1993: 16). This clarification of the role of sports development and further explication of how its practice should proceed has been developed by the Sports Council and several other interested agencies. A closer examination of this material strongly suggests that only recently has there been serious formal consideration of the person specification and consequent education and training needs of those working in sports development. This chapter includes a brief overview of the possible career paths facing individuals working in sports development. Several themes emerge from this analysis of work patterns and responsibilities, arguably the most important being that personal skills and qualities are increasingly important for staff at all levels whether in facility or outreach work settings.

The second section more closely interrogates the link between the value of sport and the technical skills, knowledge and psychological qualities possessed by successful sports development workers. Comparisons are made with career development and athlete transition. Career theory (e.g. Schlosberg, 1981) is used to investigate the relationship between sports development practice and other related areas of work. In particular, attention is drawn to the extensive and at times unique set of psychological aptitudes which are possessed by effective sports development persons. The importance of these in terms of facilitating career development and career transition is examined, and finally suggestions are made concerning future work options for SDO's and others involved in sports development.

Working in sports development

It remains a difficult, and some would argue impossible task, to identify the exact point at which it is legitimate to talk about the beginning of sports development work. For example, Torkildsen (1999) appears to suggest that this took place with the opening of the first dedicated local authority sports centres at the start of the 1970s. Others have challenged this, claiming that the appointment in the 1950s of paid full-time professional national coaches such as Winterbottom at the FA and Dyson in Athletics signified the real commencement of this work. However, most would agree that the Action Sport initiative, launched in 1981 in the aftermath of the inner city riots which afflicted several of the largest cities in the UK, represented the clearest example of outreach focused sports development work. The notion of outreach is based on the premise that, where the people are not using a service, the service must be taken to the people. In its most radical and orthodox form (as seen in Action Sport) this meant in practice that sports development workers devised programmes and created opportunities with and alongside the local community. Inevitably this power shift resulted in a greater use of non-specialist local community recreation facilities and was driven more by a European rather than an Anglo-Saxon definition of sport, which included broad-based leisure and recreation activities as well as more traditional competitive sports.

Although Action Sport can be confident that it represented an important juncture in sport and recreation provision through its focus on the primacy of outreach work, a common if at times rather narrow view contends that real sports development only began with the appointment of SDOs by governing bodies and local authorities in the mid-1980s. Indeed, as has been discussed, there is some justification for this view when individual Action Sport programmes are considered. Action Sport was criticised for operating with such flexibility that non-active pursuits with little or no connection to sport and physical recreation were supported and even encouraged. Disagreement as to the value and appropriateness of Action Sport raged within and between local authorities and the Sports Council, with one side accusing the other of being overly prescriptive and narrow in their view of sport development whilst opponents tended to dismiss Action Sport as social work rather than sport development.

The outcome of this recent history is that according to Lowe (1995) by 1995 there were at least 342,000 people working in UK sport. This includes SDO's, community recreation officers, and others for whom sports development and outreach work is a key element of their role, and facility based staff, coaches and PE teachers who may be closely involved in developing sporting opportunities. In addition to this group, those working in health promotion, health and fitness within private clubs and hotel chains and even in the media, can at least on occasion be considered as a vital part of the sports development movement.

The above makes it quite clear that sports development is the concern of a much broader group than SDOs. The suggestion is that whilst there remains much (healthy) disagreement about definitions of sport and recreation, the concept of development is much more widely accepted and understood. The skills and personal qualities required to operate successfully in such a demanding area appear to be very similar, whether the work is facility based, more community focused, concerned with developing participation and performance in traditional sports, or providing broader physical recreation opportunities. Eady's (1993) account of the rationale behind this type of work and his attempt to discuss what this should mean in practice arguably represents the most coherent attempt at explaining what sports development constitutes.

The meaning of sports development

Eady (1993) places the accent on development, and in agreement with McDonald (1995), claims that development is always about initiating change. This view proposes that development must involve a movement from the old to the new and implies that this is progressive. In other words, sports development is about creating new and better ways of doing things in sport. However, there are those for whom the term development has been applied to a much more static and ambiguous state of affairs, where focus is on sustainability and support.

This is not merely an academic argument about terminology. Language conveys meaning and ultimately influences and shapes action on the ground. The financial resource implications, roles of staff, recruitment policy of organisations, and programme design, will be substantially different as a result of which view of development is adopted. In addition, the skill demands, competencies, knowledge base and personal qualities of those working in sport may also be different depending upon the interpretation given to the concept of development.

One way to view this work may be to consider the focus placed on development across different roles. Rather than accept the convential interpretation that facility based jobs are less concerned with development than typical outreach SDO posts, a more valid approach could be to examine how the organisation and the person understand and pursue their work. A closer analysis may reveal, rather unexpectedly that a particular governing body SDO and their employer may be more interested in servicing the needs of existing local clubs. They may be engaged in this rather than seeking to expand their range of initiatives and promoting the development of the game outside of the established clubs and with non-traditional participant groups. Conversely, a particular leisure centre and its staff may be actively engaged in trying to develop motivation and skills in junior players and seniors with the hope that new clubs will emerge in the future. Increasingly, according to Torkildsen (1999) a sizeable and disparate group of organisations and sport providers are claiming that their major role is in developing opportunities for participation and performance.

During the 1980s to the mid-1990s organisation involvement and role responsibilities for sports development could be represented along a continuum from minor to major commitment to proactive development (see Figure 10.1). Those involved in facility based work were subject to several constraining factors most notably CCT and central government capital spending controls, which heightened concern over income generation and cost effectiveness, arguably impacting negatively on development work. During this same period important legislative changes within education such as LMS, and the ERA placed increasing demands on schools PE and sport staff to work more proactively with local clubs and groups to improve

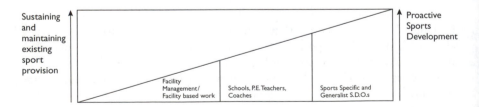

Figure 10.1 The traditional view of organisational practice.

school – community sport links. Finally, the period witnessed a sustained increase in the appointment of SDOs within governing bodies of sport, and local authorities. These posts often differed in terms of focus. However, whether sport specific, or of a more generalist nature, the rationale for each was clearly based on a strong commitment to proactive sports development.

A different approach taken to the question in the above model is to focus on the post holder, the person working within sport development rather than the organisational culture within which development may be promoted. From this perspective the motivation, skills and personal qualities of the individual are considered of great importance in determining the commitment to proactive sports development. It could even be the case that an individual's desire to operate in a genuinely proactive role may not fit comfortably within their organisation's practices or culture. This situation might lead to tension between the postholders goals and those of their employers, especially where short-term financial targets are not being fully achieved. Such conflict does have the potential to be productive and creative where organisations and staff are prepared to constantly review their aims and practices. In terms of the model outlined previously, it may be more important to identify people (volunteers and paid staff alike) by their active commitment to proactive sports development. For example, person X (Figure 10.2) is strongly supportive of the need to operate in a proactive way and translates this into practice where possible despite working in an organisation with little emphasis on sport development. Person Y (Figure 10.2) in contrast is employed in a role where their major task is to be involved in proactive sports development. However, in spite of this, their motivation, skills and personal qualities are not commensurate with the task facing them. Individuals experiencing this will often use a number of regressive strategies (R) to bring their role closer to their own position. For example, an SDO might devote a disproportionate amount of their time to supporting current administrative structures in local clubs and sports organisations and

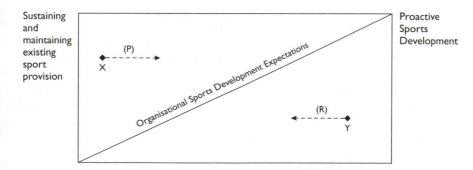

Figure 10.2 Personal choice framework.

by coaching on established sessions in schools and clubs. They will often avoid taking the lead role in difficult target based work with low participant groups or maybe avoid upsetting the status quo as would likely occur were they to push for a new strategic approach to sports development in their area.

Progressive (P) strategies used by person X are harder to accomplish given that most organisations seek self-preservation and, according to Abrams *et al.* (1996), sport organisations are no different. The creative and courageous employee may attempt to promote new initiatives (i.e. proactive work aimed at new development) where financial and quantitative targets are less easy to achieve, at least in the short term. In this way sport and leisure centres, clubs, schools and others involved in developing sport opportunities can be improved by staff with the appropriate skills and motivations, even where the organisational environment may be more ambivalent towards development.

The joint ILAM / Sports Council (1995) study into the roles of those working in sports development has provided empirical support to suggest that many SDOs are engaged in tasks which fulfil Eady's (1993) description of sports development and are also involved in several functions which arguably fall beyond. However, the ever-increasing demand for accountability, planning and focused approaches has undoubtedly impacted upon the practice of sports development work. Current government political philosophy, arguably based on a mix of social democratic values and bureaucratic managerialism, has reinforced a prevailing culture, where increasingly, unorthodox approaches are questioned and conservative pragmatism is championed. Interestingly, at a macro level the rhetoric of recent virulent attacks on conservatism and unfettered market liberalism may be in part more to do with the Freudian concept of projection. Put simply, projection suggests that the less distance between groups or individuals, the more likely they are to describe their own most negative features as belonging to the other. In this way, they can at least feel different even though real difference in practice is often difficult to discern.

Proactive sports development work requires creativity, innovation, is often unpopular with certain powerful groups, and it may even be misunderstood (by the media, for example). To persist and succeed within this type of work has always made special demands upon those people entering the area. This has been the case throughout the period that the term sports development has been commonplace. However, there are signs that many of those involved in the sports industry are much less likely to agree with Eady's (1993) claim that sports development is about challenging tradition. Indeed, so concerned are professionals in the area that the National Association of Sports Development has warned that SDOs in far too many cases, could be more accurately described as Activity Maintenance Officers. The clear and hard-hitting message contained in this centres around the degree to which sports development people are active in genuine development. This group has observed that due to a myriad of external changes and different personal perspectives, sports development workers are less inclined to utilise critical thinking and conceive of original and innovatory solutions. According to Fromm (1994) this is yet another indication of what he calls 'the fear of freedom'; a condition that results in conformity of ideas and the suffocation of alternative views (as seen for example, in political correctness). In building on this theme, Fromm (1994) echoes the thoughts of existential psychologists such as May and Schneider (1995) in claiming that the overriding desire to conform and to avoid original thought, occurs paradoxically when a shared universal system of values breaks down and a vacuum is left in its place. Social theorists have referred to this as post-modernism, that is where religious, spiritual and finally scientific concepts of the world and values have been rejected in favour of unbridled relativism.

That real achievements and a faithful adherence to the basic principles of the sports Development concept can still be seen given these very considerable obstacles, is a testimony to the psychological skills and qualities of many facility staff, SDOs, and other individuals. Whilst much of the interest has been in the technical skills and knowledge possessed by effective sports development staff, it may be that these are significantly less important than personal psychological qualities. Although discussing professional practice in sport psychology Corlett (1996) has criticised the materialist tendency which elevates skills over self-knowledge. This view has been further supported by Nesti (2000) in discussing career transition with elite athletes. These and other writers have emphasised that the personality of the therapist, teacher, coach or sports development person is an extremely important component in effecting a change. Key elements suggested include the qualities of empathy, courage in the face of anxiety and integrity – these of course can not be fully attained by any individual person; nevertheless according to these psychologists, they will be clearly present in those successfully involved in developing others' potentialities.

It can be hypothesised that the psychological qualities associated with effective sports developers will be particularly helpful in a range of tasks and occupational areas. These qualities may be found in anyone in the sport industry, from managers of traditional leisure centres to volunteer outreach community recreation workers. It is argued that this enhances the effectiveness of sports development work, and provides the person with attributes that are much sought after in a number of apparently unrelated areas of work.

Career development and transition

One of the most frequently witnessed events during periods of rapid change is the rebirth and re-emergence of former ideas. Whilst CCT has evolved into Best Value and as such represents a genuinely different approach towards economic and management issues in sport, recent discussions have focused on values and sport. Sport England's (1999) attempt (with government support) to redirect attention at values through its national strategy document, *The Value of Sport – Best Value through Sport*, has been noted in Chapter 3. However, a closer examination of the key policy issues reveals that arguably very traditional and conservative values have been identified as the most important benefits of sport. It is possible to argue that the Value of Sport strategy merely restates a long-established view that sport is beneficial for health, and fitness, physically and psychologically, and that it can bring communities closer together. In addition, government involvement is further advanced by stressing the economic argument for sport. However, beyond this level of critical analysis, an important element remains that at central government and within the Sports Councils at least, values are publicly being discussed.

In terms of articulating more fully the meaning that these values have for sports development work, Sport England has provided a guideline to assist this process. Nevertheless, values through sport, values and sport, and more prosaically, the value of sport, are centre stage. For those involved in sports development the question of values, judgements and decision-making has always accompanied their work. Indeed, it may be argued that to fulfil Eady's (1993) proactive and interventionist role properly requires the focusing of practice and actions in some directions and not others. In other words, sports development workers operating proactively are making choices and by definition value statements, albeit that these are often with and alongside the communities and individuals that they are trying to support. This ability to wrestle with values and make judgements should not (as is often the case) be mistaken for judgementalism. The person involved in developing sport is daily challenged to convert values into practical action, and at a deeper and more individual level, to reflect upon their own values and how these shape their work.

Before looking at how this personal and professional milieu involving values – action – reflection is key to understanding sports development roles and career transition, a final word on the question of discussing values and therefore making judgements on right action, seems apposite. The question of values presents a particularly thorny problem during an era that has been referred to as post-modern. Uncertainty, relativism and individual choice have been identified as the key features of post-modernism (Bech, 1992). In terms of values, the post-modernist would claim that these are relative and transient – in simple terms, that there is no single truth and that values constantly change across time and circumstances. Unfortunately, this perspective implies that what is considered good or bad is not based on universal moral and ethical principles, but on how something is understood and viewed at a particular time and place. In terms of sports development, this could mean for example that targeted work for people with disabilities could eventually be abandoned if societal values change towards disability. This logically could occur in a post-modern era where the concept of a universal truth identifying all human life as of equal value does not exist. Interestingly, there is much anecdotal evidence that sports development workers do not practise as post-modernists, although many would reject the idea that universal truths exist. This lack of consistency occurs in many other occupational settings, especially those where the focus of work is on helping people.

There are now newly developed paradigms, such as existential-phenomenological psychology and 'Fourth Way' or transcendental psychology which focus on identifying universals of human experience. These approaches would claim that common values do exist although their forms and presentation may vary across cultures and time.

Occupational groups for whom values are an important factor in their daily practice include, psychotherapists, counsellors, medical professionals, educators and human resource managers. Sports development workers could be included in this group; indeed according to the government and Sport England their major role is to promote opportunities because of the positive values associated with participation in sport. To achieve this, sport development workers need to become active advocates for sport. Skills associated with networking, use of information technology, time management, decision-making and critical thinking have been identified as of key importance for sports development officers (ILAM, 1995). Beyond this, little has been emphasised in the past, although there are signs that a greater recognition of desirable personal qualities is taking place (Torkildsen, 1999).

Given the demands of the work and the political, economic and social environment within which sports development tends to operate, genuine successes can only be achieved by those persons who develop appropriate psychological qualities and apply these to the tasks they undertake.

Personal psychological qualities and sports development

According to Nesti (1999) persons are unique, sovereign and free as well as determined and unfree. This account draws upon the earlier work of existentialists (e.g. Kierkegaard, Tillich, Aquinas) in refuting the idea that persons are completely determined by their genes and early experiences (e.g. Freud) or completely free to become anything they wish (Sartre). The sports development person, following this view, is able through their own will and efforts to influence change in their own ways of working and in those with whom they are working. Examining this further suggests that as existential psychology has made clear, the quality of the relationship is fundamental to any likelihood of success. Spinelli (1994) has identified that the specific personal qualities which must be possessed by those engaged in developmental or educative work with others, are those of presence, authenticity and commitment.

In terms of sports development work, commitment refers to the capacity to offer sustained and constant support to those with whom one is working. This requires clear and strong motivation, and may arguably only be achievable where the sports development person has retained a high level of intrinsic motivation towards their role and work.

Authenticity refers to the need to meet the other as a person and not a collection of cognitive processes and environmental histories. In sports development terms, the quality of authenticity would enable the sports development worker to avoid falling into the trap of stereotyping people and working to preconceived agendas. The much discussed concept of partnership working (see Chapter 6) is arguably impossible in practice without authenticity as a central element of the relationship. Trust, integrity and mutual confidence again flows from this quality.

Finally, presence involves an approach where there is an attempt to remain present to the persons with whom one is working by avoiding imposing their own thoughts and feelings on them (Spinelli, 1994). The most important part of this quality is the avoidance of imposition. The sports development officer, for example, may believe in the value of sport as a vehicle to allow for the development of excellence; however, this must never be imposed on the other although it can of course be discussed passionately and persuasively.

Such personal psychological qualities are central to effective and valuable sports development work. Although not always valued by the sports development organisation, they are essential for the sports development person.

These qualities are attractive and much sought after, both within and beyond the world of sports development. The final section of this chapter examines the career transition possibilities for sports development people wishing to progress into other different yet related areas of work.

Career structures in sport development

Effective sports development persons not infrequently face difficult choices in terms of career progression and work transition. Opportunities within governing bodies of sport, local authorities and the private sector may have increased significantly during the past two decades. However, pay and conditions have, in general, remained far behind other comparable areas of work. A further difficulty relates to the small number of senior posts in the industry in relation to the very sizeable cadre of well-qualified and increasingly experienced sports development workers operating more closely to the point of delivery. This issue has been noted recently, but, as yet, there is no sign of a strategy or plan of action to meet this challenge. Indeed it may be that the trend towards the increasing use of fixed-term contracts, project based work, and organisational downsizing will continue (Potter, 1993). A high profile example of this is the Sports Council since its restructuring into Sport England and UK Sport. In 1990 the nine English regions of the Sports Council and HQ in London employed over 650 staff; Sport England now totals around 300 staff.

The pressure upon the career structure in sports development looks set to continue, not least because of the higher expectations of new and recent entrants into this area of work. ILAM reported that in 1995 over 40 per cent of sports development officers were graduates and the Sports Council (1991) and professional bodies such as SPRITO have noted a sustained increase in the level of academic and professional qualifications of facility based staff. The expansion of degree and other courses in Higher Education is a welcome development although this too will impact on what is becoming a very competitive job market. Fortunately employment opportunities continue to expand. For those entering sports development work, however, at higher levels the situation is much less positive. Indeed, it could be argued that clear and progressive career pathways do not exist in sports development work outside of those working within schools and education. Sports development officers in particular may face additional obstacles where they have little or no experience of working in facility based work. Most senior posts in local authority settings require knowledge and experience of both facility management and outreach sports development work.

Whilst current structural limitations, economic conditions and employment practices appear to militate against the establishment of a comprehensive career pathway, those working in sports development are nevertheless in a very strong position to move into a range of employment situations beyond sport.

Conceptual models of career transition

According to Ogilvie and Taylor (1993), an individual's career transition is influenced by social, financial, occupational and emotional factors. Recent empirical studies in sport have investigated the emotional difficulties faced by sports performers when facing career transitions or retirement from high level competition (e.g. Lavallee et al., 1997). Two major issues have been identified as of key importance to how athletes deal with transition. The first centres on identity related concerns, and the second focuses on the use of coping strategies. Sports development persons seeking to move into other areas of work could be viewed in terms of these two factors. It has been reported by Chamaldis (1995) in his study of Greek and French athletes that those with strong athletic self-identity struggle more with career transition experiences than athletes who see themselves occupying a number of important social identities alongside their athletic one. Many in sports development, most usually SDOs and those working in more transient or multi-dimensional roles, may possess a more fluid and 'open' work identity. Many SDOs may perceive themselves as individuals who work in an industry where the most important tool for effecting lasting change in often difficult circumstances is their own selves. It may even be more accurate to highlight that the self itself, that is the core identity of a person, is the key to success in this demanding area of work. In recognising this truth, SDOs may be more likely to explore other career, training or education options.

In a sports development milieu the use of appropriate coping strategies is a vital skill. Without an adequate knowledge of these strategies and an understanding of how and when they need to be used, it is difficult for a person to operate successfully in the often exposed, volatile and stressful world of sports development. According to Torkildsen (1999) people in sports development are frequently expected to work long and irregular hours and to adapt to constantly changing work environments and tasks. Successfully dealing with this situation requires emotional resilience, and often a skilled use of emotion focused coping strategies. For example, many in the sports industry manage to maintain an extensive social network beyond their work, and are often active participants in a wide range of sport and recreational pursuits. The extensive involvement of sports development workers as coaches, club administrators and participants testifies to their use of activity beyond their work to fulfil emotional needs.

Again, sports development workers are likely to be highly proficient in devising what Lazarus and Folkman (1984) have called problem-focused coping strategies. Examples of these include developing a new personal and career focus, gaining further training and qualifications and devising new ways of working. Research with sport performers has reported that having a new focus is the most beneficial coping strategy affecting adjustment to career change and transition (Ogilvie and Taylor, 1993).

The creation of a new personal vision and the courage necessary to convert this into reality demands much of the individual. According to Schlosberg (1981), successfully facing the anxiety inherent in conceiving new roles and enacting these despite the difficulties which arise, depends largely on the presence of strong social support. However, for many in sports development work, little formal social support is evident. In addition, partly due to the perception often prevalent in schools, local authorities and the media that working in sport is fun, stress free and relatively easy, there is a general lack of empathy and understanding towards this work. This in itself may heighten feelings of stress, frustration and anxiety and can lead to the rather paradoxical situation where a major source of stress in sports development is that others are unable or unwilling to accept that this work can be as demanding and challenging as any other! Sports development work nevertheless is often very personally demanding, especially where individuals or organisations are attempting to follow Eady's (1993) call for innovation, creativity and active leadership.

This daily confrontation with stress and anxiety, however, has potential to both improve performance in the job and develop the capacities of the person. According to May (1977) the proposition that stress and anxiety can be either negative or positive has increasingly been overlooked in Western culture. However, Selye (1956), emphasised that stress can be experienced positively in certain situations, which he referred to as Eustress. Many in sports development experience both distress and Eustress in their occupational roles and responsibilities. Indeed, it seems likely that the dynamic, ever-changing and challenging world of sports development provides a highly stressful environment which is attractive to many already working in the area, and those seeking to enter into this type of work. As Csikzentmihalyi (1992) has forcefully pointed out, boredom, lack of sufficient stimulation and insufficient personal challenge, is generally associated with the strongest experience of negative stress. This does not mean though that individuals in sport development do not sometimes face an excess of stressors which in turn may lead them to feelings of negative stress (i.e. distress). In addition to the potential benefits arising from successfully dealing with a range of stressors, May and Schneider (1995) have highlighted that anxiety itself can bring out the best in people. Following existential-phenomenological psychology, they have distinguished between normal anxiety and neurotic anxiety. The former represents anxiety experienced as a byproduct of individual growth and facing the challenges of everyday life, both large and small; the latter is the result of an individual's attempts to escape from normal anxiety by avoiding the challenges of everyday life, through avoidance behaviour and by conforming to values arrived at by others, or through use of other similar psychological strategies. In terms of the positive value of normal anxiety Kierkegaard (1844) claimed over 150 years ago that contrary to modern understandings, the greater the self the greater the anxiety! He advocated that the growth of a person or, as he terms it, a self, occurs by facing up to and moving through normal anxiety. In this way the person is better prepared to face the experience of anxiety again, and as this process is repeated through life, individuals teach themselves faith and courage, and will be able to face their freedom and life, rather than devoting energies to evading anxiety experiences. This is particularly important because as Kierkegaard has argued, making choices, taking decisions and at a deeper level, being creative always involves the experience of anxiety. That innovation, creativity and decision making are fundamental to much sports development practices (Eady, 1993) demonstrates that this area of work can be highly effective in providing individuals with the opportunity to grow as a person.

Related work areas

The personal, psychological qualities possessed by many sports development workers, such as creativity, empathy, commitment, presence and authenticity, are highly valued in a number of other work settings. Notably these qualities are vital for the educator, therapist or counsellor. Increasingly, sports development officers and others are moving into teaching, lecturing and other educational roles at different stages of their working lives. As was discussed previously, an important reason for this is the poorly defined career structure at the higher levels in sports development, and the relatively poorer pay and conditions, although employers have challenged this by claiming that 75 per cent of graduates entering the area had unrealistic salary expectations (Leisure Opportunities, Jan., 2000). A more positive aspect associated with this is that often schools, universities and other educational establishments are keen to recruit staff with previous 'hands on' experience of the sports industry. This 'insider knowledge' it is anticipated, can bring a number of benefits, in terms of improvements in curriculum content and delivery, and further opportunities to develop partnerships with the local community. These improved links have the potential to benefit educational organisations in terms of new facility provision, provision of innovative projects, staff awareness and training, as well as in other important, albeit less tangible factors, such as public relations and an increased spirit of optimism.

Other obvious areas where the skills and psychological qualities of many in sports development would be an advantage are in sales, public relations, human resource management, advertising and recruitment consultancy. Recent developments in marketing, such as the concept of relationship marketing, connect surprisingly well with sports development practice. Relationship marketing argues that goods, events and services are most effectively marketed where the focus is on the relationship between the seller or provider and the customer. This view exhorts the service provider to make a major shift away from short-term gain and demand-led approaches. Instead, the central concern is that of building a genuine relationship with the customer; this in turn requires transparency, integrity, authenticity and commitment (i.e. long-term involvement). These variables are familiar to most in sports development work and arguably represent the key psychological qualities possessed by the most effective sports development workers. Whitrod-Brown and Nesti (1999) in assessing the value of relationship marketing in sport and leisure management, have suggested that Buber's (1994) profound concept of I–thou provides a fuller explanation of how relationships are formed and sustained. Buber contends that all genuine and authentic relationships are dialectical in that they progress in ever ascending spirals involving movement from what he calls the I–it mode of being to the I–thou. In simple terms I–it describes where the relationship is one of use, for example where the facility manager solely views a customer as a unit of revenue and the customer only thinks of the manager (and sport facility) as an opportunity to participate in an activity. In contrast, when in the I–thou mode, the relationship itself is centre stage. The aim is to remain in the I–thou mode for as long as possible, because it is in this form of relation that needs are most likely to be identified and met. The service provider also benefits by developing loyalty and a more personal, long-term commitment from the customer, which of course is often a vital goal of organisations, including those involved in sports development work.

Finally Goleman (1999) has identified that emotional intelligence is the most important factor in successful leaders and managers. According to his research, emotional intelligence is more strongly related to career success and performing well in organisations than the more familiar construct of IQ. Goleman has identified the five basic competencies of emotional intelligence as self-awareness, intrinsic motivation, self-regulation, empathy and social skills. This final psychological quality is more fully explained as the capacity to lead, persuade and negotiate, all of which are central to the work of those in sports development.

Recent tests with a sample of UK headteachers have revealed that those who lead the most successful schools possess the highest emotional intelligence scores. Interestingly, these findings have been partly explained in relation to the importance of flexibility of leadership style in an ever-changing environment. Those with poorly developed emotional intelligence may rely on a more coercive and controlling style which, according to Goleman, is likely to be strongly counter-productive in today's dynamic climate.

Goleman has argued that emotional intelligence is largely an innate ability; nevertheless he contends that those who go on properly designed and constructed courses find that in terms of productivity there can be increases of anything between 15 per cent and 25 per cent, as people start to build up and improve upon their own emotional deficiencies. Sports development work provides opportunities for the reflexive practitioner to enhance and improve their use of the capacities of emotional intelligence. As has been argued, the effective sports development person will need high levels of self (intrinsic) motivation, be able to demonstrate genuine empathy, and possess good social skills. If Goleman's assessment is correct, those wishing to survive and thrive in work environments way beyond what they have encountered in sports development, will find themselves much in demand. This is most likely, initially, in areas where emotional intelligence is clearly central to successful work. These work environments will usually be those where people, ideas and services are most important, rather than in jobs involving manipulation of materials and machines. The increases in service sector employment from 46 per cent of the workforce in 1996 to an estimated 49 per cent by 2006 represent an attractive trend for sports development workers seeking transition into different careers (source DFEE, 1997/98).

Summary

The increasingly diverse roles and responsibilities in sports development have placed a broad range of demands upon those working in the area. Most work at the start of the twenty-first century is characterised by constant change and the growth in pressures derived from an increasingly global, market-led consumer society. Contrary to the view of many, work in sports development has been subject to these same forces, and the effective worker needs to possess the appropriate level of skills and personal characteristics to do their job. Nevertheless, the special and unique role of sports development which requires that it is proactive and interventionist (Eady, 1993) arguably places a greater focus on the person doing the job. In one way, this locates the sport development worker closer to the counsellor, psychotherapist or educator, according to those psychologists (e.g. Fromm, 1994; Nesti, 1999), who argue that the personality is the most important feature of those successful in changing the understanding and practice of others. In more specific terms, it is the qualities of empathy, presence, commitment, vision and creativity, often in the face of considerable anxiety, that are so essential. Whilst there are signs that an increasing proportion of those involved in outreach development roles do not possess these psychological qualities, many others attempt to develop their own potentialities in these areas as they move through their work in sports development.

The empirical evidence from career transition research in sport has contributed to a better understanding of the difficulties involved in confronting role changes. A convincing body of literature now exists to support career transition theories which emphasise the central role played by coping strategies in this process. It may be hypothesised that the nature of sports development work provides a rich milieu within which emotion focused coping strategies are learned and refined. In such an evolving and at times precarious area of employment it seems reasonable to speculate that many sports development persons possess a strong sense of self and a variety of important psychological qualities or intelligences (Goleman, 1999). Somewhat paradoxically, this strong core self may often accompany a much weaker sense of self-identity in relation to work role. The newness of several of the roles in this type of work, low status and relatively poor pay and conditions has helped to undermine confidence in this area of work. In addition, for many in local authority settings, governing bodies of sport and even in quangos established by Royal Charter, job security and permanence of roles and tasks is considerably less secure and fixed than in other comparable sectors.

To be effective and continue to operate in, at times, such arduous circumstances, requires commitment, creativity, resilience and not a little courage! These and other qualities of the person are increasingly attractive to a broad range of organisations. This can include those involved in education to more commercially pressurised activities, where what is commonly referred to as 'people skills' are valued highly.

In conclusion, sports development work may be at the start of a period of sustained growth and could even progress towards full recognition as a profession, at least for those operating at higher and more strategic levels. However, apart from this, the diversity of the tasks and the skills and psychological qualities needed to succeed in this stressful and people centred area of work, make it an ideal platform to launch into an ever-increasing menu of jobs and careers.

Case study of career development in sports development

Upon leaving school at 16, worked at local Community Leisure Centre, gaining experience as pool lifeguard and eventually being promoted to supervisor. Major development tasks included working with centre staff and local clubs to develop gymnastics club at Performance and Excellence level, and initiating a 'learn to swim' programme with local health promotion unit aimed at high risk health groups. Returns to education to study part-time for qualifications in sports coaching and sport management at the local Further Education college. Gains high level coaching experience and pursues advanced coaching awards and attends National Coaching Foundation courses as part of own personal development. Applies for and is successfully appointed as Deputy Manager at Dual Use Sports Centre. Works closely with school head and head of PE and local authority to secure funding for development of facilities to include national level artificial pitch and netball Centre of Excellence. This involves negotiation and leadership skills as well as psychological qualities such as vision, creativity and resilience.

After three years' experience in this post, successfully appointed to new role as Health and Sport Community Development Officer. This outreach role requires partnership working with a vast and disparate range of agencies and organisations including Health Authorities, Sports Councils, schools and commercial sponsors. This post places particular demands on the person not least because of the isolation involved and because not infrequently the development officer is required to lead an initiative which is initially viewed negatively by the local community and involves working closely with other professionals at a much more senior level.

Towards completion of the first three-year phase of the Health and Sport project moves into a newly created Regional role for a well-established Governing Body of Sport. This post is aimed at providing and leading a strategic approach to sports development in an effort to integrate club development from grass roots to excellence with existing and planned facility provision. It requires a thorough knowledge of facility based issues and of participation and performance programmes at all levels of the sports development continuum.

Case study of career transition in sports development

Appointed as an Action Sport worker in London after successfully completing a degree in Sport and Exercise Science. Moved out of the region to take up a post as Fitness supervisor in a major local authority leisure facility. Promoted to assistant manager of the facility and closely involved in preparing for CCT. Given major role within the local authority to write CCT contract specifications relating to community sports development and performance and excellence work. Moves into newly created post with health authority as Health Promotion Officer with special responsibility for developing partnerships and initiatives with those agencies involved in health, fitness and physical recreation. This post requires in-depth knowledge of health and fitness policy and practice, and due to the innovatory and radical agenda, it requires considerable communication skills and demands an extensive set of personal psychological qualities. Much of the work involves being proactive and 'selling' the concept of 'health through physical fitness and sport' to the media, educational authorities and other sectors of the health industry. Specifically this requires vision on the part of the post-holder, drive and courage in the face of numerous frustrations and set-backs, and an empathetic understanding of those individuals and organisations who are reluctant to become involved.

Health Promotion Officer supported by employer to pursue an MBA part-time at a local university. This is seen primarily as personal development. It is also anticipated that this post-graduate qualification will develop levels of critical thinking and management knowledge. Finally, the individual is appointed as a lecturer at a Higher Education institution to lead and develop a new vocationally based degree in physical activity, exercise and health. In addition to this role, the post requires that new consultancy opportunities are sought with both the sports development and health sectors.

References

Abrams, J., Long, J., Talbot, M. and Welch, M. (1996) *Organisational Change in National Governing Bodies of Sport*, Leeds Metropolitan University.

Bech, U. (1992) *The Risk Society*, London: Polity Press.

Buber, M. (1994) *I and Thou*, Edinburgh, T. & T. Clark.

Chamaldis, P. (1995) 'Career transitions of male champions', in R. Van Fraechem-Raway and Y. Vanend Auweele (eds), *Proceedings of the 9th European Congress of Sport Psychology*, pp. 841–48), Brussels: FEPSAC.

Corlett, J. (1996) 'Sophistry, Socrates and sport psychology', *The Sport Psychologist*, 10: 84–94.

Csikszentmihalyi, M. (1992) *Flow: The Psychology of Happiness*. London: Rider Publications.

Eady, J. (1993) *Practical Sports Development*, London: Hodder & Stoughton.

Fromm, E. (1994) *The Art of Listening*, London: Constable.

Goleman, D. (1999) *Working with Emotional Intelligence*, London: Bloomsbury.

ILAM/Sports Council (1995) *Research into Sports Development*, London: Sports Council.

Kierkegaard, S. (1844/1980) *The Concept of Anxiety*, Princeton, NJ: Princeton University Press.

Lavallee, D., Grove, J. R. and Gordon, S. (1997) 'The causes of career termination from sport and their relationship to post retirement adjustment among elite amateur athletes in Australia', *The Australian Psychologist*, 32: 131–5.

Lazarus, R. S. and Folkman, S. (1984) *Stress, Appraisal and Coping*, New York: Springer.

Leisure Opportunities (January 2000) *Qualified to a Degree*, by R. Kerfoot (ed.), (p. 6).

Lowe, M. (1995) 'An investigation into employment levels within the leisure industry', in S. Fleming, M. Talbot and A. Tomlinson (eds), *Policy and Politics in Sport, Physical Education and Leisure* (pp. 285–97), Brighton: LSA.

McDonald, I. (1995) 'Sport for All – RIP?', in S. Fleming, M. Talbot and A. Tomlinson (eds), *Physical Education Policy and Politics in Sport and Leisure*, (LSA Publication No. 55). Eastbourne: Leisure Studies Association.

May, R. (1977) *The Meaning of Anxiety*, New York: Ronald Press.

May, R. and Schneider. K. J. (1995) *The Psychology of Existence: an integrative clinical perspective*, New York: McGraw-Hill.

Nesti, M. (1999) 'An existential psychology approach to counselling athletes', in D. Lavallee and P. Wyelleman (eds), *Career Transitions in Sport: International Perspectives*, Morgantown, WV: Fitness Information Technology.

Ogilvie, B. C. and Taylor, J. (1993) 'Career termination issues among elite athletes', in R. N. Singer, M. Murphy and K. L. Tennant (eds), *Handbook of Research on Sport Psychology*, pp. 761–75), New York: Macmillan.

Potter, J. (1993) *JP Guide to Jobs and Qualifications in Sport and Recreation*, Reading: ILAM.

Schlosberg, N. K. (1981) 'A model for analysing human adaptation to transition', *The Counselling Psychologist*, 9: 2–18.

Selye, H. (1956) *The Stress of Life*, New York: McGraw-Hill.

Spinelli, M. (1994) *Demystifying Therapy*, London: Constable.

Sport England (1999) *The Value of Sport*, Sport England, London. Sports Council Annual Report (1990–91), Sports Council.

Torkildsen, G. (1999). *Leisure and Recreation Management*, E & FN Spon.

Whitrod-Brown, H. and Nesti, M. (1999) 'The psychology of relationship marketing and public leisure provision in the UK – serving the person or meeting customer needs?' paper presented at ESAM Conference, Sport Management in the next millennium, Thessaloniki, Greece.

Index

Page numbers in **bold** refer to figures.